The

HCAHPS

Handbook

2

Tactics to Improve Quality
and the Patient Experience

By
Lyn Ketelsen, RN, MBA
Karen Cook, RN
Bekki Kennedy

Published by:
Fire Starter Publishing
913 Gulf Breeze Parkway, Suite 6
Gulf Breeze, FL 32561
Phone: 850-934-1099
Fax: 850-934-1384
www.firestarterpublishing.com

ISBN: 978-1-6221800-9-7

Library of Congress Control Number: 2014948934

Printed in the United States of America

This book is dedicated to Cam Underhill and Beth Keane. Both were true fire starters in each and every way.

Cam spent her life, which was ended way too early due to breast cancer, creating what this book is all about: a way to take better care of patients and their families. Cam also understood that to deliver excellent care, it is vital that healthcare providers have the right environment in which to work. This means making sure people have the right development, tools, and techniques so they can provide the care they are committed to.

Beth also dedicated her life not only to the improvement of healthcare itself but also to the betterment of all of us as human beings. She knew that passion and compassion were essential to our ability to deliver excellent care to our patients and families. For over 10 years, Beth traveled across the nation sharing her humor as well as the skills needed to make each of us better leaders, colleagues, and caregivers.

Cam and Beth, we will never forget you. Your flames burn in each of us in the form of an unselfish dedication to others.

Table of Contents

A Word from the Coauthors I

Introduction V

    Chapter 1: HCAHPS Counts: Why It's Your 1
        Key to Pay-for-Performance Success

    Chapter 2: The Survey: Basics Everyone. 33
        Needs to Know

    Chapter 3: The Fundamentals: What You Must 49
        Know and Do to Improve Your
        HCAHPS Results

SECTION ONE: NURSE COMMUNICATION

    Introduction 89

    Chapter 4: Courtesy and Respect (A Goal for. 95
        Nurses and *All* Staff Members)

    Chapter 5: Careful Listening. 109

    Chapter 6: Understandable Explanations 121

SECTION TWO: DOCTOR COMMUNICATION

    Introduction 131

    Chapter 7: Doctor Courtesy and Respect 139

    Chapter 8: Careful Listening by Doctors. 151

    Chapter 9: Doctor Explanation of Care 165

SECTION THREE: RESPONSIVENESS OF STAFF

    Introduction. 177

    Chapter 10: Bathroom Assistance 187

    Chapter 11: Call Button Response 197

SECTION FOUR: PAIN MANAGEMENT

    Introduction. 211

    Chapter 12: Control of Pain/Helpfulness of Staff . . 221

SECTION FIVE: COMMUNICATION ABOUT MEDICATIONS
Introduction 235
Chapter 13: Explanation Regarding 245
Medications and Side Effects

SECTION SIX: DISCHARGE INFORMATION
Introduction 261
Chapter 14: Staff Discussion of 271
Post-Discharge Help
Chapter 15: Written Symptom/Health 285
Problem Information

SECTION SEVEN: THE HOSPITAL ENVIRONMENT
(CLEAN & QUIET)
Introduction 295
Chapter 16: Room and Bathroom Cleanliness 301
Chapter 17: Nighttime Quietness 321

SECTION EIGHT: CARE TRANSITION
Introduction 333
Chapter 18: Recognizing Patient Preferences 339
for Care Continuum
Chapter 19: Helping Patients Understand 349
Post-Discharge Responsibility
Chapter 20: Purpose of Medications 363

SECTION NINE: OVERALL RATING OF HOSPITAL
AND WILLINGNESS TO RECOMMEND
Introduction 375
Chapter 21: Global Rating/Willingness 381
to Recommend
Chapter 22: The Importance of Validation: 395
A Closing Thought

Acknowledgments 401
Endnotes 405
Additional Resources 417
About the Authors 427

A Word from
the Coauthors

L ook at the cover of *The HCAHPS Handbook* and
you'll see it's coauthored by Lyn Ketelsen, Karen
Cook, and Bekki Kennedy. While it is true that the three
of us put the book together (along with an army of con-
tributors, editors, and other helpful souls), many others
deserve to share the credit.

We want to make it clear that we are only the distill-
ers and reporters of the content in this book. The hard
work—the real work—was done by two groups who have
our eternal gratitude: a) the Studer Group® coaches and
experts who discovered, harvested, and shared the tactics laid out in this book, and b) the organizations we've
worked with that provided the fertile field for the tactics
to take root and grow.

The men and women collectively known as Studer
Group have spent years doing intensive research in our
national Learning Lab of 850-plus healthcare organizations. They are masters at discovering what the people

inside these organizations are doing right—and taking that message to others in the field.

The knowledge our coaches refine and share has evolved over time. The tactics they've harvested and refined are a true work in progress and the result of many years of institutional memory. The tactics in this book will continue to evolve as health reform and other changes in the external environment place ever-increasing demands on healthcare organizations.

What's more, they'll be modified in a way that moves results in other healthcare settings. Studer Group will ultimately present them in a series of books based on the popular formula we've established with *The HCAHPS Handbook*. In fact, as we write this message, a group of coaches is putting the finishing touches on a book of tactics aimed at moving results measured by the CG CAHPS survey. Ultimately, we want to create a robust line of books that zero in on the patient experience in all parts of the continuum of care, from the Emergency Department to the inpatient arena to outpatient physician practices to long-term care facilities.

We believe the organizations we coach are comprised of many of the finest healthcare professionals in the world. It is their dedication, their passion for helping others, and their generosity of spirit that made this book possible. Every day, they work tirelessly to provide better and better care to the patients they serve.

To both these groups—the coaches and the leaders they coach—we offer our sincerest thanks. This relationship is a symbiotic one. Both parties are enriched by the work of the other—and the real beneficiaries are the patients. May we continue to care for them for many years to come.

Lyn, Karen, Bekki

INTRODUCTION

Welcome to the revised and updated 2014 edition of *The HCAHPS Handbook*. We are pleased to say that since Studer Group® published the first edition of this book, it has become an authoritative resource for healthcare organizations seeking to maximize clinical quality, patient experience of care, and reimbursement.

A lot has changed since the 2010 edition rolled off the presses. Five new questions have been added to the Hospital Consumer Assessment of Healthcare Providers and Systems survey, and, of course, value-based purchasing itself has continued to evolve. In the interest of helping our readers continue hardwiring excellence inside their respective organizations, we felt the need to expand and modify the advice provided in this book.

You will find that we've added a new section regarding the new Care Transition composite. What's more, we've made critical changes to many of the tactics you've already seen. That's because we've spent the past three years tweaking these actions and behaviors and studying the results.

Organizations coached by Studer Group are outperforming peers by an average of 23 percentile points across HCAHPS measures. They are also outpacing them in improvements at a speed nearly three times faster than the nation. And they performed better than the nation in all Core Measures.

These organizations perform well because they get leaders and staff aligned and hold them accountable for executing on their goals. We help them do this by installing our Evidence-Based Leadership^{SM} (EBL) framework, designed to reduce variances in leadership skills and processes and help organizations achieve predictable, positive outcomes. The goal is to create a culture of engagement that, in turn, creates the consistency that results in this kind of high performance.

We've been closely studying the Hospital Consumer Assessment of Healthcare Providers and Systems since the very beginning—in fact, even before HCAHPS became the official name. We knew that HCAHPS was going to be far more than the "patient satisfaction surveys" that were being used and would take on ever-greater importance as transparency was expanded and health reform got underway.

Studer Group has never been a "patient satisfaction" company. We've always been focused on executing through delivery of quality, patient-centered care—hence our understanding that HCAHPS is a metric that represents the patient's experience and quality of care.

This book does *not* contain an exhaustive list of every tactic Studer Group teaches. Instead, it zeroes in on each HCAHPS question and describes the most impactful tactics proven to make "always" responses more likely—consistently across your organization and over time.

When you get into the composites, you'll find that there are typically several tactics included for each question. We recommend that you pick one tactic and get it to the point to where it's always performed. This allows you to know how aggressive you need to be in implementing the other tactics—or whether you need to use the other tactics at all.

Our research shows that one of the reasons execution fails is because organizations try to implement too much behavioral change at once. Our job at Studer Group is to help you accomplish the greatest results in the most efficient way possible. This is why we zero in on the most specific tactics that will create the most impact for the right reason: to improve patient care.

While *The HCAHPS Handbook* is focused on improving patient care outcomes as measured by HCAHPS, it is our hope that you will keep in mind the *why* behind these efforts. We encourage leaders and staff members alike to realize that the results are meaningful—that they really do translate to better, more consistent quality care, which in turn translates to better patient outcomes. HCAHPS results are just another way to measure how often we do something that is important to patients—in other words, how often we demonstrate a culture of "always" and provide the very best care.

We know that creating this kind of culture is hard. Many things in healthcare are hard—supply chain management, creating new clinical programs, physician recruiting—but there is probably nothing harder than getting to always. It means we need every single person to get it right every single time. That would be difficult in any industry.

Yet consider this truth: The more difficult something is, generally, the more worthwhile it is. That's especially true in healthcare. We know that there is no other industry that has such a profound impact on people's lives. And while there is no easy way to create a culture of always, we're helping remove the guesswork by providing our partners with evidence-based tactics that are proven to work.

We hope you find this book helpful—and that it's the first step on a pathway that leads to higher HCAHPS results, better patient outcomes, and a more successful and fiscally sound organization.

CHAPTER ONE:

HCAHPS COUNTS: WHY IT'S YOUR KEY TO PAY-FOR-PERFORMANCE SUCCESS

W hether you are a new leader in healthcare and this is your first exposure, or you are a tenured, experienced leader and just need a refresher and reminder, this section will outline some of the basics of HCAHPS that every leader needs to know.

HCAHPS stands for "Hospital Consumer Assessment of Healthcare Providers and Systems." The operative words are "Consumer Assessment." That is because the survey was designed by and for consumers to assess their healthcare organizations so they could make informed decisions about where to go for their care. Essentially, it's the first national, standardized, publicly reported survey of patients' perspectives of hospital care. It was developed by the Centers for Medicare & Medicaid Services (CMS) together with the Agency for Healthcare Research and Quality (AHRQ), another agency in the Department of Health and Human Services.

In May 2005, the National Quality Forum endorsed HCAHPS. Then, in December 2005, the federal Office of Management and Budget gave its final approval for the survey to be implemented nationally.

In 2006, voluntary collection of HCAHPS data began, and the first public reporting occurred in March 2008. The results were posted on the Hospital Compare website: www.hospitalcompare.hhs.gov.

According to CMS, the survey was shaped by three overarching goals:

1. To produce comparable data on patients' perspectives of care so that consumers can make objective and meaningful comparisons among hospitals

2. To create incentives for hospitals to improve their quality of care

3. To enhance public accountability in healthcare by increasing the transparency of the quality of hospital care

Source: "HCAHPS: Patients' Perspectives of Care Survey."
http://www.cms.gov/Medicare/Quality-Initiatives-Patient-Assessment-Instruments/HospitalQualityInits/HospitalHCAHPS.html

HCAHPS is part of a broader value-based purchasing initiative that ties reimbursement to quality outcomes. Related programs include Home Health Care Consumer Assessment of Healthcare Providers and Systems (HH CAHPS), Clinician and Group Consumer Assessment of Healthcare Providers and Systems

(CG CAHPS), and Emergency Department Consumer Assessment of Healthcare Providers and Systems (ED CAHPS, alternately referred to as Emergency Department Patient Experiences with Care, or EDPECS).

These are the surveys currently in the process of execution, but make no mistake: No service line will be exempt. If you receive reimbursement from Medicare, there will be a CAHPS version of a survey coming your way.

Before we get into the details of HCAHPS, let's first look at it in a broader context:

The Changing Face of Value-Based Purchasing

When the Patient Protection and Affordable Care Act was signed into law (March 2010), patient-centered care—quality care—moved from being a legislative and reimbursement issue to being front and center nationwide. The program creates a new urgency for hardwiring high performance. The value-based purchasing (VBP) initiative that began in FY 2013 focuses on HCAHPS and Core Measures results.

VBP transitioned providers from HCAHPS pay-for-reporting to pay-for-performance, and the amount of reimbursement tied to the survey is scheduled to double by 2017. It's clearly about how well your organization demonstrates that it has hardwired quality.

Value-Based Purchasing Roadmap
CMS quality-based payment initiatives will put more than 11% of payment at risk

2010	2011	2012	2013	2014	2015	2016	2017	2018
Reporting Hospital Quality Data for Annual Payment Update								2% of APU
		Value-Based Purchasing						2%
		1%	1.25%	1.5%	1.75%	2%		
		Readmissions						3%
		1%	2%	3%	3%	3%		
					Hospital-Acquired Conditions			1%
					Meaningful Use			5%
				1%	2%	3%	4%	5%

Figure 1.1

The previous schedule demonstrates the go-forward plan for how CMS will impact up to 11 percent of reimbursements by the year 2018. On the next page you will see the breakout for the VBP reimbursement and how the 2 percent affected by this will be calculated.

For FY2015, CMS added an "efficiency" domain—Medicare Spending Per Beneficiary (MSPB)—weighted at 20 percent of the value-based performance (VBP) reimbursement formula for hospitals. They increased it to 25 percent for FY2016 (the current performance period). (The MSPB measure assesses Medicare Part A and Part B payments for services provided to a Medicare beneficiary during a spending-per-beneficiary episode that spans from three days prior to an inpatient hospital admission through 30 days after discharge.)

Value-Based Purchasing FY 2016

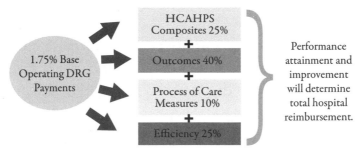

Figure 1.2

By measuring cost of care this way, CMS hopes to increase the transparency of care for consumers and recognize hospitals that are providing high-quality care at a lower cost to Medicare. It's just one more indicator that it's not enough for healthcare organizations to sustain performance. We must improve performance year after year to stay ahead of the curve.

The point is clear: Pay-for-quality is here to stay, and the requirements will only get more and more stringent. What's more, third-party payers are already following the lead of CMS and will almost certainly do so to a greater degree in the future. If ever there was a time to hardwire a culture of excellent patient care—to ensure your organization is consistently meeting its mission, protecting its bottom line, and enhancing its reputation—that time has clearly arrived.

The good news: If you've hardwired Studer Group's Evidence-Based Leadership^{SM} framework and tools, you will be well positioned in the future operating environment.

Understanding the Basics of HCAHPS

HCAHPS provides consumers with information that is helpful in choosing a hospital and standardizes questions for public comparisons.

Hospitals must submit a minimum of 300 surveys of eligible patients (18 years or older discharged from general acute care hospitals after an overnight stay) for each reporting period. Along with Core Measures and other quality metrics, the patients' perception of their experience results can be viewed at www.hospitalcompare.hhs.gov.

Original HCAHPS Survey

The original survey questions measure frequency (rather than satisfaction) on six composites (or categories) of questions and two additional questions. The scale is *never, sometimes, usually,* or *always* with regard to:

- Nurse Communication
- Doctor Communication
- Responsiveness of Staff
- Pain Management
- Communication about Medications
- Discharge Information—yes or no

In the first iteration of HCAHPS there was one more composite and two additional questions whose answers are in other formats:

- Hospital Environment, which includes separate measures for:

    ○ Cleanliness of Hospital

    ○ Quietness at Night of Hospital

- Willingness to Recommend (one question)— definitely no to definitely yes *(Note: While this question is asked, it does not "count" toward determining reimbursement.)*

- Overall Hospital Rating (one question)—0 to 10 rating scale

New HCAHPS Composite & Questions

Effective with July 1, 2012, eligible discharges, CMS gave hospitals the opportunity to add five voluntary questions to the existing survey. Beginning in January 2013, the new questions became mandatory for all HCAHPS users. (The composites in the original survey remained as they were.)

Three of the new questions, thoroughly covered in Section 8, make up a new composite: Care Transition Measure.

For these three questions, results will be reported on a 0-100 basis using a scale of *strongly agree, agree, disagree,* and *strongly disagree* or *don't know / don't remember / not applicable* to make the calculations.

Two more questions were also added to the HCAHPS survey:

During this hospital stay, were you admitted to this hospital through the Emergency Room?—yes or no

Until June 2010, this information was collected from hospitals as an administrative code and was used as a patient-mix adjustment variable for HCAHPS scores. CMS presented evidence that this variable is meaningful to its payment calculation and thus added it back in.

In general, how would you rate your overall mental or emotional health?—poor to excellent

This question was added due to requests from hospitals and researchers. Recent studies suggest that up to 20 percent of hospitalized patients suffer from severe depression. When other mental illnesses are considered, the incidence approaches 50 percent. Research has shown that there was *significant decline in HCAHPS scores in patients identified in standardized mental illness assessment questionnaires in the pre- and post-operative ambulatory setting as severely depressed.* Patient responses to this question will be factored into CMS reimbursement calculations.

One More Upcoming Change: The CMS Star System

To make it easier for consumers to compare and rate hospitals, CMS is in the process of incorporating a Star Rating System into its "Compare" websites. This system is currently in place for both Nursing Home Compare and Physician Compare. In April 2015, the Five-Star Quality System will go into effect for Hospital Compare and HCAHPS measures.

According to a CMS.gov blog post by Dr. Patrick Conway, CMS deputy administrator for innovation & quality and chief medical officer, "The star ratings empower consumers with information to make more informed healthcare decisions, encourage providers to strive for higher levels of quality, and drive overall health system improvement."[1]

Calculating HCAHPS Results

The percentage of patients who give their hospital a rating overall of 9 or 10 (on a scale from 0 to 10) are reported as the top-box result, as well as the percent of patients who report yes and definitely yes, they would be willing to recommend the hospital.

The "top box"—or most frequently reported *best* result in each composite—is reported for each hospital. In other words, if 75 percent of your surveyed patients reported that their nurses "always" communicated well, 20 percent said they "sometimes" communicated well, and 5 percent said they "never" communicated well, 75 percent is reported in response to that question. It is important to note that there is no "partial credit" for any results except *always*. There is no partial credit for "almost" (like patient satisfaction vendors provide).

HCAHPS "Top Box" Percentiles

Public Reporting for 3rd Quarter 2012 to 2nd Quarter 2013

HCAHPS "Top Box" Percentiles Public Reporting

Percentile Rank	Always quiet at night	Doctors always communicated well	Nurses always communicated well	Pain was always well controlled	Patients always received help as soon as they wanted	Patients who gave a rating of 9 or 10	Room was always clean	Staff always explained about medicines before giving to patients	Yes, patients were given information about what to do during their recovery	Yes, patients would definitely recommend	Hospital-environment (clean and quiet)
5th	45	73	70	62	54	55	61	54	78	55	55.5
10th	48	75	72	64	57	59	64	57	80	59	57.5
20th	52	78	75	67	60	64	67	59	82	63	60.5
25th	54	78	76	68	61	65	68	60	83	65	62
30th	55	79	76	68	63	66	69	61	84	66	62.5
40th	58	80	78	69	64	69	71	62	85	69	64.5
50th	60	81	79	70	66	70	73	63	86	71	66.5
60th	63	82	80	72	69	72	74	65	87	74	68
70th	66	84	81	73	71	75	76	66	88	76	70.5
75th	67	85	82	74	72	76	78	67	88	77	71.5
80th	69	86	83	74	74	77	79	68	89	79	73
90th	74	88	85	77	79	81	83	72	90	83	77
95th	79	91	88	80	84	85	87	76	91	86	81.1

Figure 1.3

Organizations can use the table in Figure 1.3 for goal setting and benchmarking. It allows you to compare top box performance and understand, based on your current result, where you stand in relation to others by composite. For example, if your current Nurse Communication result is 80 percent top box, then you are in the 60th percentile of hospitals nationwide.

This table represents the performance of the nation at the time of printing this book (public reporting period for 3rd Quarter 2012 to 2nd Quarter 2013), and that does change over time. Still, it will give you some perspective or point of reference. As updates become available, you can access them at www.studergroup.com.

Interestingly, we have seen improvement in performance across the entire database since HCAHPS reporting became available. This trend indicates that the healthcare industry is responding to patient experience metrics and making improvements.

HCAHPS Answer Descriptions

HCAHPS Answer Description	National Avg. 1Q07-4Q07	National Avg. 3Q12-2Q13	Nat. Avg. Increase 2007-2Q13
Doctors always communicated well	79	82	3
Yes, would definitely recommend	68	71	3
Pain was always controlled	67	71	4
Room was always clean	68	73	5
Nurses always communicated well	73	79	6
Yes, patients were given info about what to do during recovery	79	85	6
Staff always explained about medicines before giving them to patients	58	64	6
Patients who gave a rating of 9 or 10	63	70	7
Patients always received help as soon as they wanted	60	67	7
Always quiet at night	54	61	7

Figure 1.4

While the national improvement reflected here is encouraging, it also presents a challenge. With each performance period, the bar is raised. If your organization's performance remains the same, it means you are falling behind. Keep striving to improve your patients' experience—and then strive to improve it even more.

Important Things to Consider:

1. There is a clear connection between quality and the patient and family experience. HCAHPS has elevated our industry's attention to delivering patient-centered care. Historically, some have considered patient satisfaction "soft" or a "nice to have." Never has this been *less* true than it is today. The patient's perception of his or her care is a tangible reflection of your delivery of quality care.

A little later in this chapter you will see evidence of the connection between experience and quality. When we at Studer Group compare hospitals that patients rated in the top quartile for the HCAHPS responsiveness question, we found they experienced the lowest number of pressure ulcers (and they were highest in hospitals rated poorly for responsiveness). This also holds true for infections and manifestations of poor glycemic control.

This is just one of the reasons that Studer Group's Evidence-Based Leadership framework is so successful. It drives a continuous focus on quality and creates the consistency that, in turn, leads to the HCAHPS response *always*—meaning that every interaction occurs with every patient on every shift!

2. It may seem that nurses are the heart and soul of HCAHPS success—but don't ignore the impact of other staff members. Nurse Communication is highly correlated with patients' overall hospital rating. And it's true that if your HCAHPS overall ratings are low, you should review your organization's performance on this composite. However, it's also true that patients tend to perceive everyone they come in contact with as either "a doctor" or "a nurse"—even if they're really from an ancillary or support department. They just don't make the distinction.

Delivering safe, high-quality care requires an all-hands-on-deck approach; ancillary and support department leaders and staff must be engaged in the process and focused on the impact of patient experience and HCAHPS results. Whether it is achieved by participation in a strategy called No-Pass Zone (described in the Responsiveness chapter) or by assisting with conducting an environmental assessment of the patient's room (described in the Hourly Rounding® fundamentals), there are no shortage of ways all people can work together to achieve the important outcome.

That is why goal alignment is so important to success of HCAHPS. When ancillary partners carry goals for areas they own or share goals with nursing, it creates true synergy. Everyone works toward the same outcomes.

3. A consistent culture of excellence is vital. Patients expect a basic level of service and quality when entering your hospital. Your organization can sustain excellence at exceeding patient expectations only if you have an engaged, satisfied, and high-performing team of physicians, caregivers, and support staff.

Ask yourself: Do you consistently retain high performers and show no tolerance for low performers? Do employees believe leaders "walk the talk" with respect to mission, vision, and values? Do you identify and address any barriers to culture change and quality of work life for employees to improve your HCAHPS patient perception of care?

The HCAHPS frequency scale demands that you demonstrate zero tolerance for employees who are rude or otherwise violate your organization's behavior standards. The days of tolerating a staff member with good clinical skills who is otherwise abrupt or even rude with patients are over.

Rethinking HCAHPS: Your Compass for Navigating an Uncertain Future

The healthcare futurists don't paint a very pretty picture for our industry. They talk about declining reimbursements, escalating costs, capacity constraints with provider and staff shortages, and decreasing health status of an aging population. It's enough to make your head spin. At the same time, the accountability for achieving better outcomes with fewer resources and reducing costs in an environment of increasing transparency challenge healthcare leaders to be on top of their game.

Still, as we travel the country, we find that many of the best leaders are not defeated by this but rather are talking about the opportunity to truly meet the needs of those we serve. Yes, there is uncertainty around the way we will get paid and how much we will get paid. There is also uncertainty in the processes and systems we will use to deliver the care. Yet there is no uncertainty that there will always be patients to care for. And care for them we will.

At the most basic level, those patients have been pretty consistent over time in what they desire from healthcare. *Treat me as a person, manage my pain, listen to me, explain what you are doing and why, be responsive when I need you, tell me about the medications you give and if there are risks, tell me what to do when I get home, include my family, and keep the environment clean and quiet.*

The needs, which not coincidentally mirror the issues highlighted in the HCAHPS survey, are what any of us would want. The challenge is meeting them so well and so frequently that the patients say it was done 100 percent of the time.

HCAHPS Results and Clinical Outcomes Are Two Sides of the Same Coin

The *New England Journal of Medicine* found that quality of care was significantly better in hospitals that performed better on HCAHPS. The data also shows that the patient's experience is linked to great clinical care, reduced medical error, and advanced performance outcomes.

At Studer Group® our findings directly tie to those of the *New England Journal of Medicine.* As we worked with our partners to improve clinical outcomes, we observed their corresponding HCAHPS results went up, too. We now know many of these clinical outcomes were tied to the same metrics as future health reform reimbursement.

As you'll recall, organizations coached by Studer Group outperform the nation on HCAHPS, outpace it in improvements, and also beat the national average in every core measure. Let's look at some examples of the kind of results we are referencing.

Figure 1.5 shows that as patients' perception of care increases, rates of poor glycemic control decrease. The data shows hospital rate per 1,000 of Manifestations of Poor Glycemic Control by their percentile ranking for "Responsiveness."

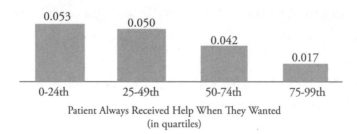

Figure 1.5

Figure 1.6 shows that as quality of care increases, the risk of infection decreases. The data shows hospital rate per 1,000 of Vascular Catheter-Associated Infection by their percentile ranking for "Responsiveness."

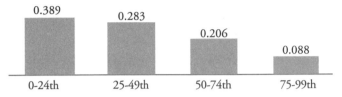

Patient Always Received Help When They Wanted
(in quartiles)

Figure 1.6

Figure 1.7 shows that as patients' perception of care increases, rates of Pressure Ulcers Stages III and IV decrease. The data shows hospital rate per 1,000 of Pressure Ulcers Stages III and IV by their percentile ranking for "Responsiveness."

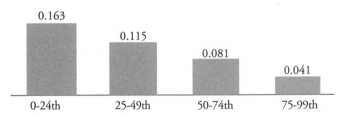

Patient Always Received Help When They Wanted
(in quartiles)

Figure 1.7

Figure 1.8 shows that hospitals with better HCAHPS Patient Experience of Care results have fewer never events. The data shows that as HCAHPS results increase, the frequency of hospital-acquired conditions decreases by Responsiveness of hospital staff.

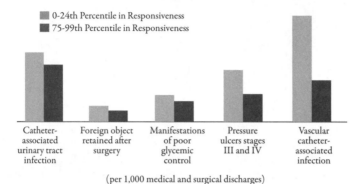

Figure 1.8

Figure 1.9 shows that hospitals with better HCAHPS Patient Experience of Care results have few never events. The data shows that as HCAHPS results increase, re-admission rates by hospital ranking in Communication about Medicines decrease.

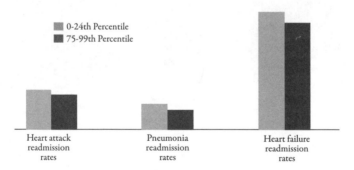

Figure 1.9

Figure 1.10 shows that hospitals with better HCAHPS Patient Experience of Care results have shorter ED wait times. The data shows the relationship between OP-20 door to diagnostic eval by medical professional (Door to Doc) and HCAHPS Rate Hospital a 9 or 10.

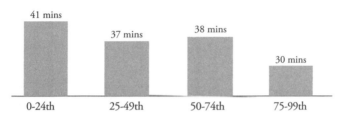

Hospital Score in "Rate Hospital a 9 or 10"
(Percentile)

Figure 1.10

Figure 1.11 shows that hospitals with better HCAHPS Patient Experience of Care results have fewer patients Left Without Being Seen. The data shows the relationship between OP-22 ED Patient Left Before Being Seen (percent) and HCAHPS Rate Hospital a 9 or 10.

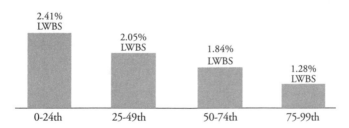

Hospital Score in "Rate Hospital a 9 or 10"
(Percentile)

Figure 1.11

Figure 1.12 shows that hospitals with higher quality Patience Experience of Care also have better efficiency ratios. The data shows hospital efficiency ratio by the "Percent of patients who rate the hospital a 9 or 10." In this case, the lower the percent, the better the results.

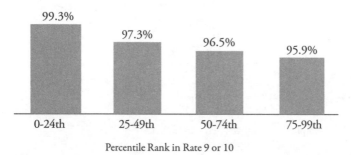

Percentile Rank in Rate 9 or 10

Figure 1.12

The data in figures 1.5 through 1.12 shows the improvement in specific quality of care performance measures when correlated to HCAHPS performance. These graphs represent just a few indicators of the connection between quality and perception of care. No matter how we cut the data, those organizations that perform better on their patient experience also have better outcomes, are more efficient, and have lower costs.

Here's the point: HCAHPS results go hand-in-hand with clinical quality metrics. So when we improve those results, we also improve our clinical care. And because the metrics that determine both are the metrics by which we'll be judged and compensated in the future, we also improve our likelihood of maximizing our reimbursement. In fact, your organization's HCAHPS data may well be a proxy for predicting your future reimbursement based on all value-based performance metrics. And it extends further to third party payers and community and national reputation.

We can create cultures of consistent excellence. We can become more efficient, more effective, and more transparent in order to not only deliver on our mission but also to meet the standards the government is going to hold us to in the future. We *can* get it right—not sometimes, but all the time—every day in every department with every patient. Every patient who comes to us for their healthcare needs deserves no less.

Why HCAHPS Is a Catalyst for Quality

HCAHPS results are a natural metric for determining what kind of job we're doing in caring for our patients—and pinpointing where we need improvement.

"Patient perception of care" is a whole lot more than making sure nurses and doctors are friendly and smiling. It's about saving lives and delivering safe healthcare. It's about quality in a very real, concrete way. It's about using HCAHPS results as a metric, a barometer for measuring clinical performance and improvement.

HCAHPS gives us a way to drill down into the details and discover what processes will positively and consistently impact the patient perception of quality but also better patient clinical outcomes: fewer falls, lower infection rates, fewer bedsores, fewer readmissions, and so forth.

It gives us a national benchmark by which to measure the quality we're seeking to achieve.

Yes, We *Can* Improve Quality

The best news is we know exactly how to achieve better outcomes. We know, right now, which tools and techniques make them happen. Why? Because we have research, conducted via our Learning Lab of hundreds of top hospitals, that clearly demonstrates what works.

When we talk to hospitals that consistently score high in the Responsiveness and Pain Management composites, we hear about hardwired Hourly Rounding® and Nurse Leader Rounding on patients. By checking on the patient every hour and communicating regarding pain and personal needs—and by having the nurse leader round to validate execution of the tools and tactics that work—you raise patients' perception of care. This translates to improved HCAHPS results and corresponding improvements in clinical outcomes.

The *American Journal of Nursing* reported on the effectiveness of Studer Group tactics, showing that Hourly Rounding leads to decreased falls by 50 percent and skin breakdown by 14 percent.[2] As organizations we coach implement Studer Group's evidence-based tools and techniques, they see a correlating improvement in hospital-acquired conditions as well. These improvements, as well as their improvement in HCAHPS results, position hospitals to be better prepared for health reform changes coming in the future.

Consistency Is Everything

Here's the reality: Many hospitals that focus a great deal of attention on something will see moderate improvements—unfortunately, they then shift their focus, and the results drop. We see this with key initiatives like Hourly Rounding. An organization will "roll out" Hourly Rounding, everyone will get trained, and leaders will focus heavily on the initiative. They will see jumps in their scores or sudden surges of improvement (which regress the next year). Some units may start to get great HCAHPS results while others lag behind.

These bursts of sporadic, partial, or temporary improvement aren't that difficult to achieve. But they also aren't good enough. To fulfill the mission and maximize pay-for-performance-related reimbursement, you need to deliver high-quality, efficient, and responsive care *consistently.*

Long-term, sustainable gains are much more difficult to achieve. It also could be said that if you are not getting better, you are getting worse—because every hospital in the country is focusing on this subject.

Organizations must put an infrastructure in place that allows them to quickly improve their HCAHPS results and consistently meet the high standards by which we will be judged and compensated in the future. They must create a high-performance culture.

The infrastructure proven to generate this level of efficiency and effectiveness is Evidence-Based Leadership.

EBL: A System for Creating a Culture of High Performance

Evidence-Based Leadership is an operational framework that establishes an infrastructure to improve execution and achieve outcomes. The framework provides the mechanism for leaders to ensure alignment of goals, behaviors, and processes; to get people engaged; and to hold them accountable for doing what they need to do. (Accountability is the foundation of EBL.)

Evidence-Based Leadership℠ Framework

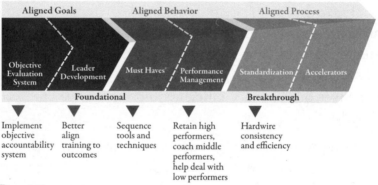

Figure 1.13

When this framework is implemented, organizations find a dynamic way to respond to the unique challenges of the industry today. It doesn't apply just to HCAHPS. If you have challenges with revenue cycle, quality outcomes, or employee turnover, the framework can guide you through problem solving your way to a better outcome.

Quint Studer's excellent book *A Culture of High Performance: Achieving Higher Quality at a Lower Cost* explains the pivotal role this framework plays in creating an organization that can stand up to the avalanche of challenges that might otherwise engulf you.

You might think of EBL as the strand that holds together the DNA of the high-performance culture. The DNA, of course, is a metaphor for the values that shape and define the organization.

To better understand this concept, take a look at the following graphic:

Aligned & Accountable Culture with Evidence-Based Leadership^SM Framework

Figure 1.14

Let's begin with the Engagement circle. Organizations that embrace EBL use proven tactics—rounding for outcomes, reward and recognition, focus/fix/follow-up, to name just a few—to get employees and physicians fully engaged. In turn, employees and physicians use other proven tactics—Bedside Shift Report, Hourly Rounding, Nurse Leader Rounding—to also get patients engaged in their own care.

Next, consider how this fits with the Safety circle. A study from the University of Alabama showed that employees with low engagement are more likely to work around safety protocols, while highly engaged ones are less likely to do so.[3] Obviously, we know that workarounds insert risk into a system. So when you improve engagement, you also improve safety.

This brings us to the Quality circle. It stands to reason that when you improve safety you also improve the quality of your clinical outcomes.

So what we see is that engagement improves safety, and safety improves quality. And when employees and physicians see that safety and quality outcomes are improving (and HCAHPS results along with them, of course), they become even more engaged. Engagement drives results, which drives more engagement, which drives more results. And so on.

Where the three circles intersect—well, that's the culture of high performance that Evidence-Based Leadership creates. That's the culture that organizations are going to have to develop in order to survive in our high-pressure external environment.

As healthcare delivery is increasingly impacted by reform, organizations that have embraced the EBL framework are able to incorporate or emphasize tactics proven to get results.

As different sections of the Patient Protection and Affordable Care Act are implemented, EBL becomes increasingly critical. It provides the foundation that allows our partners to respond faster and more effectively to industry changes.

Don't Forget the ED: Why a Patient's "First Impression" Sets the Stage for HCAHPS Success

You might find it odd that we would zero in on the Emergency Department in a book about an inpatient survey. But when you think about how your patients get to your hospital in the first place, it makes perfect sense.

For many organizations, the Emergency Department is the point of entry for the largest number of patients arriving at your hospital. Nationally, the ED accounts for 50 percent of inpatient admissions, 75 percent of plain radiographs, and 50 percent of CT scans and ultrasounds in the entire hospital.

First the bad news: Research performed during the HCAHPS testing period found that patients admitted through the Emergency Department rated care across all composites more negatively than those patients admitted through other avenues.

In our section on the new Care Transition Measures, you can read about two new "about you" questions, one of which is the addition of whether the patient was admitted via the Emergency Department. The inclusion of this question is most certainly to add to the pool of research that will help provide more accountability for the relationship that needs to exist between our EDs and our care of patients after admission.

The implication is clear. When a patient has a poor perception of the care he received in your Emergency Department, it's much harder to recover from it. That's why it's so critical to make a good first impression—to set the stage for a successful stay and, by extension, a favorable experience throughout the stay.

The good news is that Studer Group's own research shows that as ED perception of care results improve, so do inpatient results. Our partner data also indicates that by improving ED patient perception of care results, hospitals can also expect to see higher HCAHPS results in all ten composites. This chart shows the relationship between ED percentile rank and HCAHPS "overall" percentile rank.

Relationship between ED Percentile Rank and HCAHPS "Overall" Percentile Rank

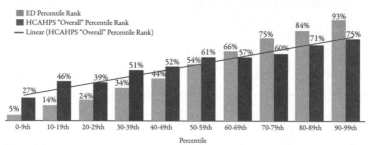

Figure 1.15

We reviewed the 180 hospitals for which Studer Group has both ED perception of care results and HCAHPS results. Our research found a statistically significant correlation between ED percentile ranking and HCAHPS percentile ranking for the "Patients who rated the hospital a 9 or 10" question (r= .486), meaning that as one goes up so does the other. (The likelihood that this occurs just by chance is less than 1 percent.)

We categorized each of the hospitals by their year-average ED percentile rank and then looked within each category at the hospital's HCAHPS "percent 9s and 10s" average percentile rank. Figure 1.13 shows that as a hospital's ED percentile ranking increases, so does the HCAHPS "percent 9s and 10s" percentile ranking. Therefore, organizations focused on improving their HCAHPS results would do well to focus on ensuring that ED patients have the best possible experience.

EBL tactics designed for the inpatient environment are easily modified for the ED setting to drive consistency of the patient experience. Studer Group has various resources devoted solely to this subject—among them the Fire Starter Publishing books *Advance Your Emergency Department: Leading in a New Era* by Stephanie J. Baker, RN, CEN, MBA, Regina Shupe, RN, MSN, CEN, and Dan Smith, MD, FACEP; *Excellence in the Emergency Department: How to Get Results* by Stephanie J. Baker, RN, CEN, MBA; and *Hardwiring Flow: Systems and Processes for Seamless Patient Care* by Thom Mayer, MD, FACEP, FAAP, and Kirk Jensen, MD, MBA, FACEP.

When you improve your Emergency Department, you improve your entire hospital—and your HCAHPS results, as well as your financial state, can only benefit.

A Desk Reference for Busy Professionals

You may not choose to read this book in one sitting. That's fine. We designed it to be a user-friendly "desk reference" of sorts—a trusted resource you reference to focus on specific opportunities for improvement with targeted strategies.

Of course, you may very well wish to read it cover to cover. And if you do, we hope you won't just put it on a shelf afterward and forget about it. We hope you'll return to it again and again, anytime you need to refresh your memory on a particular tactic.

You just read a section that briefly explains HCAHPS and puts it in context with health reform changes. And you're about to learn about a few foundational tactics you need to know in order to improve your HCAHPS results.

Nine tactical sections, each centered on a different HCAHPS composite or question, make up the heart of this book. (Most notable is a whole new section on the new Care Transition composite, as well as expanded information and how-to tactics we've refined since the first printing.) Within each section, a separate chapter is devoted to the survey questions that fall under that particular composite. Chapters feature detailed descriptions of a few tactics proven to increase the likelihood of an "always" (or comparable) response to the questions they spotlight.

This layout allows readers to quickly find the HCAHPS question they want to target for improvement. Once they've brought up that particular result, they can move on to the next problem area.

Finally, there's a chapter that helps you validate whether people are executing the tactics effectively and consistently.

Remember, the tactics and tools in this book have been field-tested by organizations that, coached by Studer Group, consistently enjoy HCAHPS results that are higher than those of peer organizations. Consistency is the key in creating a culture of every patient, every time, every interaction. That is hardwired excellence—or a culture of always.

CHAPTER TWO:

THE SURVEY: BASICS EVERYONE NEEDS TO KNOW

C hapter 1 was our "brief introduction" to HCAHPS. Now, we will dive a little deeper and provide more detail on how the survey is administered and scored. If you read the previous chapter thoroughly, some of this information may seem familiar to you. That's okay. Read what you need to know and skip the rest for now (you can always come back to it). Actually, that's the goal of this book—to be a quick and easy reference for busy health-care professionals.

How the Survey Is Administered

The HCAHPS survey, which takes about seven min-utes to complete, can be administered to patients in one of four ways:

- A mailed survey that is completed by the patient and sent back

- A phone call using a detailed script
- A combination of a mailed survey with a follow-up phone call
- An interactive voice response (IVR) survey, which is a system that allows people to communicate with a computerized voice either by answering verbally or by pressing touchtone numbers on the phone

Regardless of the survey's form, it must be administered via a CMS-certified vendor or by an organization that has been certified through CMS to administer it according to their guidelines. Most patient satisfaction survey vendors currently administer the HCAHPS survey.

The mailed version is available in English, Spanish, Chinese, Russian, and Vietnamese; the phone and IVR formats are available in English and Spanish.

Survey Sampling

Patients to be surveyed are selected randomly from all eligible discharges from the hospital each month. Hospitals must obtain at least 300 completed HCAHPS surveys for each 12-month reporting period. Small hospitals that do not have 300 eligible discharges in 12 months must survey all eligible discharged patients in order to get as many completed surveys as possible.

Discharged patients of all payer types are eligible to be surveyed, as long they meet the following criteria:

- 18 years or older at the time of admission
- At least one overnight stay in the hospital as an inpatient
- Non-psychiatric MS-DRG/principal diagnosis at discharge
- Alive at the time of discharge

Pediatric patients (under 18 years old at admission) and psychiatric patients are ineligible because the current HCAHPS survey is not designed to address the unique issues related to these populations. Patients whose MS-DRG/principal diagnosis is Medical, Surgical, or Maternity Care but who also have psychiatric comorbidities *are* eligible for the survey. Patients who did not stay overnight in the hospital are ineligible because they have fewer interactions with the staff. For more details on eligibility and exclusions, visit http://www.hcahpsonline.org.

Patients are surveyed between 48 hours and six weeks after discharge, regardless of which survey method is used. Interviewing or distributing surveys to patients while they are still in the hospital is not permitted.

Survey Questions and Scoring

One of the biggest differentiators between the CAHPS surveys and historic patient satisfaction surveys is the methodology for formatting the questions. Historically,

The Phone Survey Advantage?

Patients' responses to the survey can be affected by the method by which they were surveyed. For example, people speaking to another person on the phone tend to give somewhat more positive responses than those who complete a paper survey. Therefore, the results of these surveys can affect comparisons between hospitals.

CMS conducted a large-scale experiment to test for these effects. Based on the findings of that research, an adjustment has been built into the calculation of survey results to remove those effects from the scores.

More information about this experiment can be found under "Mode Adjustment" at http://www.hcahpsonline.org/home.aspx.

patient satisfaction questions queried patients regarding their feelings about the care they received and were more subjective in nature. The HCAHPS questions are now designed to measure the frequency of certain behaviors and processes that patients have determined are most important to them and their families, and that are known to drive high-quality healthcare.

As we discussed earlier, the questions are divided into ten categories, known as "composites." (This includes a composite made up of Overall Rating of This Hospital and Willingness to Recommend questions.) The composites, their scales, and how the results are reported are listed on the following page.

HCAHPS Composites and Scale for Reporting

Composite	Scale	Results Reported
Nurse Communication	Always, Usually, Sometimes, Never	Top Box % Always
Doctor Communication	Always, Usually, Sometimes, Never	Top Box % Always
Responsiveness of Staff	Always, Usually, Sometimes, Never	Top Box % Always
Pain Management	Always, Usually, Sometimes, Never	Top Box % Always
Communication about Medications	Always, Usually, Sometimes, Never	Top Box % Always
Discharge Information	Always, Usually, Sometimes, Never	% Yes
Quietness at Night of Hospital	Always, Usually, Sometimes, Never	Top Box % Always
Cleanliness of Hospital	Always, Usually, Sometimes, Never	Top Box % Always
Care Transition Measures	Strongly Agree, Agree, Disagree, Strongly Disagree or Don't Know/Don't Remember/Not Applicable	Likert Scale Score of 0-100
Overall Rating of Hospital	0-10	Top Box % 9s and 10s
Willingness to Recommend	Definitely no - Definitely yes	Definitely Yes

Figure 2.1

Patients are asked to provide some demographic information—such as education level, race, language spoken, and so forth—and to assess their overall health.

Also, there are several questions that are "screening" items meant to save patients from having to answer questions unrelated to their care. For example, the Pain composite asks if you received medicine for pain during your stay; if the answer is no, then the patient is instructed to skip the pain questions. The results of the question on willingness to recommend is not included in the value-based purchasing calculations due to some inherent biases that appear in the research.

How Percentile Rankings Are Calculated

Accurate comparisons across hospitals require that adjustments be made to factor in the data that are not directly related to the hospital performance but can affect how patients answer some survey items. CMS applies adjustments intended to eliminate any advantage or disadvantage in results that might be influenced by the survey mode or the characteristics of patients that are beyond the hospital's control.

CMS also performs quality and statistical analysis of the data submitted to assure that the HCAHPS survey is administered in a way that protects the validity and reliability of the data and reports. The adjustments made to submitted survey data explain the reason for the lag in timing of the publicly reported data.

Once the data is publicly reported, comparisons are the most accurate, and it is then that percentile rankings can be calculated. Many survey vendors provide interim (estimated) percentile comparisons, but it should be noted that these are generally estimates of the adjustment formulas and/or are vendor database-specific percentiles and the comparisons can change when the final, publicly reported data is published.

Top Box Rating

The "top box"—or most frequently reported *best* result in each composite—is the publicly reported data for each hospital. In other words, if 75 percent of your surveyed patients reported that their nurses always communicated well, 20 percent said they "sometimes" communicated well, and 5 percent said they "never" communicated well, 75 percent is reported in response to that question. It's important to note that only *always* counts—there is no partial credit for "almost" (like patient satisfaction vendors provide). See page 10 for more information.

Likert Scale

The new Care Transition Measure composite and the three questions associated with that are explained in further detail in Section 8. We mention it here because the scoring methodology differs from the other composites, and it will be important to understand that scoring method to properly analyze the results. The Likert Scale allows patients to report the degree of their agreement with the statement, using *strongly agree, agree, disagree,* and *strongly disagree* or *don't know/don't remember/not applicable.* Results are then reported on a 0-100 basis using those responses.

Tips for Analyzing and Improving Results

1. Leaders must be keenly aware of what the various numbers mean when analyzing their results. You must know if a result of 78 refers to 78 percent top box, or 78 on the Likert scale, or 78 percent "yes" response, or 78th percentile comparison based on your top box score.

2. Ask your vendors to provide percentage breakdowns of patient responses by unit, sometimes referred to as a frequency distribution. This information allows you to see how many patients respond in each category of the scale.

3. Focus first on moving *usually* to *always* and don't focus as much on the *nevers*—yet. Just as it's easier to move a B to an A than a C to an A, it's easier to move a *usually* to an *always* than to move a *never* to an *always*.

4. Focus first on units that are performing at mid-level and the ones that have the highest percentage of responses. This will give you the highest likelihood of moving the organizational results the fastest.

You *can* improve your HCAHPS results. When you follow the previous tips and hardwire the tactics provided in this book, you'll see the metrics begin to move. Even more important, you'll see evidence that you're providing better clinical care and better patient experiences—and that's what really matters in healthcare.

The Survey Itself

The next several pages provide an example of the current copy of the HCAHPS survey for your reference. We have also included the CMS web address so you can download your own copy. Please make sure your entire care team is familiar with this survey. The answers to these questions will comprise your patients' official "voice"... so it's important to know them well.

HCAHPS Survey

SURVEY INSTRUCTIONS

● You should only fill out this survey if you were the patient during the hospital stay named in the cover letter. Do not fill out this survey if you were not the patient.

● Answer all the questions by checking the box to the left of your answer.

● You are sometimes told to skip over some questions in this survey. When this happens you will see an arrow with a note that tells you what question to answer next, like this:

☐ Yes

☑ No → *If No, Go to Question 1*

> *You may notice a number on the survey. This number is used to let us know if you returned your survey so we don't have to send you reminders.*
> *Please note: Questions 1-25 in this survey are part of a national initiative to measure the quality of care in hospitals. OMB #0938-0981*

Please answer the questions in this survey about your stay at the hospital named on the cover letter. Do not include any other hospital stays in your answers.

YOUR CARE FROM NURSES

1. During this hospital stay, how often did nurses treat you with courtesy and respect?
   1 ☐ Never
   2 ☐ Sometimes
   3 ☐ Usually
   4 ☐ Always

2. During this hospital stay, how often did nurses listen carefully to you?
   1 ☐ Never
   2 ☐ Sometimes
   3 ☐ Usually
   4 ☐ Always

3. During this hospital stay, how often did nurses explain things in a way you could understand?
   1 ☐ Never
   2 ☐ Sometimes
   3 ☐ Usually
   4 ☐ Always

4. During this hospital stay, after you pressed the call button, how often did you get help as soon as you wanted it?
   1 ☐ Never
   2 ☐ Sometimes
   3 ☐ Usually
   4 ☐ Always
   9 ☐ I never pressed the call button

YOUR CARE FROM DOCTORS

5. During this hospital stay, how often did doctors treat you with <u>courtesy and respect</u>?

   ¹☐ Never
   ²☐ Sometimes
   ³☐ Usually
   ⁴☐ Always

6. During this hospital stay, how often did doctors <u>listen carefully to you</u>?

   ¹☐ Never
   ²☐ Sometimes
   ³☐ Usually
   ⁴☐ Always

7. During this hospital stay, how often did doctors <u>explain things</u> in a way you could understand?

   ¹☐ Never
   ²☐ Sometimes
   ³☐ Usually
   ⁴☐ Always

THE HOSPITAL ENVIRONMENT

8. During this hospital stay, how often were your room and bathroom kept clean?

   ¹☐ Never
   ²☐ Sometimes
   ³☐ Usually
   ⁴☐ Always

9. During this hospital stay, how often was the area around your room quiet at night?

   ¹☐ Never
   ²☐ Sometimes
   ³☐ Usually
   ⁴☐ Always

YOUR EXPERIENCES IN THIS HOSPITAL

10. During this hospital stay, did you need help from nurses or other hospital staff in getting to the bathroom or in using a bedpan?

    ¹☐ Yes
    ²☐ No ➔ If No, Go to Question 12

11. How often did you get help in getting to the bathroom or in using a bedpan as soon as you wanted?

    ¹☐ Never
    ²☐ Sometimes
    ³☐ Usually
    ⁴☐ Always

12. During this hospital stay, did you need medicine for pain?

    ¹☐ Yes
    ²☐ No ➔ If No, Go to Question 15

13. During this hospital stay, how often was your pain well controlled?

    ¹☐ Never
    ²☐ Sometimes
    ³☐ Usually
    ⁴☐ Always

14. During this hospital stay, how often did the hospital staff do everything they could to help you with your pain?

    ¹☐ Never
    ²☐ Sometimes
    ³☐ Usually
    ⁴☐ Always

15. During this hospital stay, were you given any medicine that you had not taken before?

    ¹☐ Yes

    ²☐ No ➔ If No, Go to Question 18

16. Before giving you any new medicine, how often did hospital staff tell you what the medicine was for?

    ¹☐ Never

    ²☐ Sometimes

    ³☐ Usually

    ⁴☐ Always

17. Before giving you any new medicine, how often did hospital staff describe possible side effects in a way you could understand?

    ¹☐ Never

    ²☐ Sometimes

    ³☐ Usually

    ⁴☐ Always

WHEN YOU LEFT THE HOSPITAL

18. After you left the hospital, did you go directly to your own home, to someone else's home, or to another health facility?

    ¹☐ Own home

    ²☐ Someone else's home

    ³☐ Another health facility ➔ **If Another, Go to Question 21**

19. During this hospital stay, did doctors, nurses or other hospital staff talk with you about whether you would have the help you needed when you left the hospital?

    ¹☐ Yes

    ²☐ No

20. During this hospital stay, did you get information in writing about what symptoms or health problems to look out for after you left the hospital?

    ¹☐ Yes

    ²☐ No

OVERALL RATING OF HOSPITAL

Please answer the following questions about your stay at the hospital named on the cover letter. Do not include any other hospital stays in your answers.

21. Using any number from 0 to 10, where 0 is the worst hospital possible and 10 is the best hospital possible, what number would you use to rate this hospital during your stay?

    ⁰☐ 0   Worst hospital possible

    ¹☐ 1

    ²☐ 2

    ³☐ 3

    ⁴☐ 4

    ⁵☐ 5

    ⁶☐ 6

    ⁷☐ 7

    ⁸☐ 8

    ⁹☐ 9

    ¹⁰☐ 10   Best hospital possible

22. Would you recommend this hospital to your friends and family?

   ¹☐ Definitely no
   ²☐ Probably no
   ³☐ Probably yes
   ⁴☐ Definitely yes

UNDERSTANDING YOUR CARE WHEN YOU LEFT THE HOSPITAL

23. During this hospital stay, staff took my preferences and those of my family or caregiver into account in deciding what my health care needs would be when I left.

   ¹☐ Strongly disagree
   ²☐ Disagree
   ³☐ Agree
   ⁴☐ Strongly agree

24. When I left the hospital, I had a good understanding of the things I was responsible for in managing my health.

   ¹☐ Strongly disagree
   ²☐ Disagree
   ³☐ Agree
   ⁴☐ Strongly agree

25. When I left the hospital, I clearly understood the purpose for taking each of my medications.

   ¹☐ Strongly disagree
   ²☐ Disagree
   ³☐ Agree
   ⁴☐ Strongly agree
   ⁵☐ I was not given any medication when I left the hospital

ABOUT YOU

There are only a few remaining items left.

26. During this hospital stay, were you admitted to this hospital through the Emergency Room?

   ¹☐ Yes
   ²☐ No

27. In general, how would you rate your overall health?

   ¹☐ Excellent
   ²☐ Very good
   ³☐ Good
   ⁴☐ Fair
   ⁵☐ Poor

28. In general, how would you rate your overall **mental or emotional health**?

   ¹☐ Excellent
   ²☐ Very good
   ³☐ Good
   ⁴☐ Fair
   ⁵☐ Poor

29. What is the highest grade or level of school that you have **completed**?

   ¹☐ 8th grade or less
   ²☐ Some high school, but did not graduate
   ³☐ High school graduate or GED
   ⁴☐ Some college or 2-year degree
   ⁵☐ 4-year college graduate
   ⁶☐ More than 4-year college degree

30. **Are you of Spanish, Hispanic or Latino origin or descent?**

    ¹☐ No, not Spanish/Hispanic/Latino

    ²☐ Yes, Puerto Rican

    ³☐ Yes, Mexican, Mexican American, Chicano

    ⁴☐ Yes, Cuban

    ⁵☐ Yes, other Spanish/Hispanic/Latino

31. **What is your race? Please choose one or more.**

    ¹☐ White

    ²☐ Black or African American

    ³☐ Asian

    ⁴☐ Native Hawaiian or other Pacific Islander

    ⁵☐ American Indian or Alaska Native

32. **What language do you <u>mainly</u> speak at home?**

    ¹☐ English

    ²☐ Spanish

    ³☐ Chinese

    ⁴☐ Russian

    ⁵☐ Vietnamese

    ⁶☐ Portuguese

    ⁹☐ Some other language (please print): _____

THANK YOU

Please return the completed survey in the postage-paid envelope.

[NAME OF SURVEY VENDOR OR SELF-ADMINISTERING HOSPITAL]

[RETURN ADDRESS OF SURVEY VENDOR OR SELF-ADMINISTERING HOSPITAL]

Questions 1-22 and 26-32 are part of the HCAHPS Survey and are works of the U.S. Government. These HCAHPS questions are in the public domain and therefore are NOT subject to U.S. copyright laws. The three Care Transitions Measure® questions (Questions 23-25) are copyright of The Care Transitions Program® (www.caretransitions.org).

To download your own copy of the survey, please visit the following website: http://www.hcahpsonline. org/files/HCAHPS%20V9.0%20Appendix%20A%20 -%20Mail%20Survey%20Materials%20(English)%20 March%202014.pdf

As CMS and AHRQ provide new information, Studer Group releases new insights, webinars, articles, and other timely tools aimed at helping organizations navigate our industry's changes. Please check our "Eye on the Industry" page at www.studergroup.com/HCAHPS periodically to see what's new and what you can do to maximize your performance.

CHAPTER THREE:

THE FUNDAMENTALS: WHAT YOU MUST KNOW AND DO TO IMPROVE YOUR HCAHPS RESULTS

A s you read *The HCAHPS Handbook*, you'll see that certain key behaviors show up over and over again. These are the "fundamentals"—evidence-based tactics that have significant impact on multiple patient experience metrics. Master them and you'll be able to tweak them to impact any HCAHPS composite you're trying to improve. Even more important, when practiced consistently across the organization, they will increase your likelihood of creating a culture of high performance.

Your entire staff will need to hardwire these tactics in order to deliver the quality of care that drives sustained results. Remember that to create a culture of *always* we must ensure that this proficiency is visible in every employee, every time, and with every interaction.

Before we start exploring the fundamentals, let's take a quick look at some of the forces that work against us. There are certain inherent barriers and challenges to hard-wiring these tactics that many organizations experience.

By becoming aware of them, we can plan and proceed in such a way that we can minimize or eliminate them.

Barriers and Challenges

1. **Not enough time in the day.** This is typically the most frequently cited barrier. Of course, there is no way to create more time. We must simply learn to make better use of the time we have. Leadership teams across the country continue to offer courses and education on time management and organizational skills. While they can be very helpful, we must also acknowledge that good general or leadership development and training create the foundation for effective time management. The more skilled you are at anything, the more efficient you become. A more skilled leader is a more efficient leader. Good leaders tend to lead more efficient teams. This is why we can't shortcut skill development—it ultimately lets us get more done in less time.

2. **Resistance to change.** People are naturally averse to change. Yet change we must. This is not a bad thing. Changes in governments, industries, and organizations challenge the status quo and force us to improve and innovate. As Ralph Waldo Emerson said, "People wish to be settled but only as far as they are unsettled is there any hope for them." Managing change is inherently part of the leader's role. They need the skills to help people

get comfortable with new ways of doing things—
or if not comfortable, inspired enough to face the
fear and make the leap anyway.

3. **Lack of performance management skills.**
A fundamental competency of leaders is managing performance—this includes both the reward
and recognition that needs to occur for those
who exceed expectations as well as accountability
in coaching and counseling for those who don't
meet them at all. If leaders are not highly skilled
in this competency, they will not be successful in
driving the change necessary to develop greater
skill sets in their team and, ultimately, to improve
HCAHPS results.

4. **Shortage of staffing resources.** Often, we
are asked how many staff it will take to get our
recommended strategies in place. We often hear,
"But we're reducing our staff!" or, "We're already
short-staffed!" Our response is, "Remember, each
of these evidence-based best practices is designed
to create efficiency." While it seems counterintui-
tive at first, many of our long-term partners will
attest to the fact that when leader and staff skills
are built, the tactics are hardwired, and the results
are achieved, they're able to accomplish more
with the same staffing levels.

5. **Lack of urgency or not understanding the**
why. If individuals or organizations don't have
a sense of urgency to change, they won't change.
The leader's ability to connect the dots on why the

change is important, not only to the organization or department but to the individual, corresponds to the staff's engagement level. In the reverse, staff members who understand and engage in the process become champions and make the leader's work much easier.

Actually, this last barrier contains the seeds of the solution to overcome all of them. Before your organization can master the critical skills covered in this book (and being proficient isn't enough—they must be hardwired), they must know *why* they need to master them. In turn, they must be able to convey the *why* to their team when introducing new tools and tactics to their team—to say to them, "This is needed for the well-being of the patient. If we implement this behavior 100 percent of the time, here is what it means to our patients, their family members, and the efficiency of our entire team."

What's more, leaders must be able to bring the right amount of urgency to the change they're asking people to make—enough to light a fire under them, but not so much that they are overwhelmed and paralyzed. Then, once people try out the tactic, they often see how impactful it can be. Often, understanding follows action.

Fundamental Tactic: Goal Setting

We cannot begin this chapter without underscoring the importance of leaders' goals as a method for ensuring accountability for the goals associated with driving HCAHPS results. This tactic and strategy will not be addressed specifically in each and every chapter, but it underscores all of them.

In Chapter 1 we introduced Evidence-Based Leadership[SM] as the framework for improving execution and creating a culture of high performance. You may recall that an objective, measurable, and weighted leader evaluation system is an important part of it—and it's fundamental to accountability and results.

In fact, the degree to which leaders are held accountable for achieving results corresponds to the likelihood that those results will be met. Whether leaders are held accountable for driving results on a specific question, for a composite, or for all composite results in aggregate, setting those goals ensures focus and urgency for achieving outcomes of any kind—for HCAHPS or any other important change.

HCAHPS goals can be set in a variety of ways. For example:

They can focus on accomplishing a specific percentile ranking.

HCAHPS Goal Sample – Department Specific

Goal Created from Template: HCAHPS - Doctor Communication - Dept Specific

Goal: Increase the HCAHPS Doctor Communication Composite from 54th %ile to the 75th %ile as measured by HCAHPS reporting.

Action ∨

Result: 65 for Jan - Mar
Calculation Method: Last
Units: Percentile

Higher is better
5 is 85 and above
4 is 80 to 84
3 is 75 to 79
2 is 54 to 74
1 is 53 and below

Scoring

		5
Weighted Value	15% ∨	4
Score	2	3
		2
Item Score	0.30	1

Notes ∨

Jan	Feb	Mar	Apr	May	Jun	Jul	Aug	Sep	Oct	Nov	Dec
54	60	65									

Figure 3.1

They can be written by way of improvement in a specific number of composites, such as 6 of 8 composites at the 75th percentile.

HCAHPS Goal Sample – Number of Composites at 75th Percentile

Goal Created from Template: HCAHPS Composite Bundle - Dept Specific

Goal: Increase the number of HCAHPS composites at or above the 75th %ile to 6 of 8 or more as measured by HCAHPS reporting.

Action ∨

Result: 5 for Jan - Mar
Calculation Method: Last
Units: # of composites

Higher is better
5 is 8 and above
4 is 7 to 7
3 is 6 to 6
2 is 4 to 5
1 is 3 and below

Scoring

		5
Weighted Value	15% ∨	4
Score	2	3
		2
Item Score	0.30	1

Notes ∨

Jan	Feb	Mar	Apr	May	Jun	Jul	Aug	Sep	Oct	Nov	Dec
3	3	5									

Figure 3.2

They can be written as a specific composite or question at a certain top box result or percentile level.

HCAHPS Goal Sample – Specific Question by Top Box Result

Goal Created from Template: HCAHPS - Discharge Communication - Dept Specific

Goal: Increase the HCAHPS composite Discharge Communication from 64% Top Box to 66% Top Box as measured by HCAHPS reporting.	**Result:** 66 for Jan - Mar **Calculation Method:** Last **Units:** % Top Box	**Scoring**
	Higher is better 5 is 68 and above 4 is 67 to 67.9 3 is 66 to 66.9 2 is 64 to 65.9 1 is 63.9 and below	Weighted Value 15% ∨ 5 / 4 Score 3 3 Item Score 0.45 2 / 1
Action ∨		Notes ∨

Jan	Feb	Mar	Apr	May	Jun	Jul	Aug	Sep	Oct	Nov	Dec
64.2	64.8	66									

Figure 3.3

The philosophy applied to goal setting is best determined by how your facility results are reported. Alignment with the reporting mechanism tends to make it easier to monitor and report progress toward the goals. This will create a culture that ensures appropriate priority is placed on accomplishing your objectives to create high-quality care and excellent patient experiences.

We strongly recommend weighting leader goals to prevent the "too many priorities" syndrome. Typically, a 10 percent weight means "Awareness," 20 percent means "Focus," and 30 percent means "Urgency."

10%	20%	30%
Awareness	Focus	Urgency

Let's say that a leader has five goals. If you want her to focus more heavily on one of them, you'll give it a weight of 30 percent. Another one might have a weight of 20 percent, and the other three might be divided up to equal the 100 percent total weight. This way, the leader will know which metrics will most powerfully drive their overall evaluation score (and most likely their compensation).

Not only should these weights reflect leader priority, they should also take into account the individual leader's performance and skill set development. When the right leader has the right goal at the right weight, amazing things can happen.

Fundamental Tactic: Nurse Leader Rounding

Nurse Leader Rounding is a *proactive* plan to engage, listen to, communicate with, build relationships with, and support patients and their families. While these actions are an inherent part of nursing, Nurse Leader Rounding provides a *structured* mechanism to ensure that quality, safe, and compassionate care is delivered to every patient, every time.

Essentially, leaders ask targeted questions to obtain *actionable* information. They can use this information to coach or reward and recognize staff in real time. When hardwired into your organization's processes, this tactic will drive better patient outcomes and results, as well as differentiate your organization from your competitors.

Ideally, nurse leaders—or their properly trained delegates—will round on every patient every day. At this level of rounding, you will see the biggest and most sustained impact. It allows nurse leaders to connect with patients to reinforce care, verify nursing behaviors, and recognize staff members who go above and beyond the call of duty. You may launch this strategy by rounding at least once during every patient's stay, but you should gain efficiency as competency builds and quickly be able to meet the best practice of rounding on every patient every day.

Nurse leaders can use questions strategically. In other words, they can design the questions they ask patients around the initiatives they're focusing on to improve care—managing pain, for instance.

Nurse Leader: *"Hello, Mr. Porter. My name is Jenny and I would like to ask you a couple quick questions to ensure you are receiving the best care. Is now a good time?"*

Patient: *"Sure."*

Nurse Leader: *"Good. Your pain is important to us, and I want to ensure we are managing it effectively. Can you tell me if the plan for your pain has been working well or if it isn't working and we need to try something different? Are the staff helpful in regards to managing your pain?"*

After the patient responds, the nurse leader would thank the patient for his time and let him know the follow-up he can expect.

You will find that Nurse Leader Rounding on patients is suggested as a key strategy to drive results in many of the composites that are nursing-sensitive. Figure 3.4 shows why. That said, the questions asked need to be aligned with the area of focus the unit or department is currently working on. Studer Group® has a library of questions that can be used as a guide to help ensure that effective rounding occurs.

Nurse Manager Patient Rounding Impact

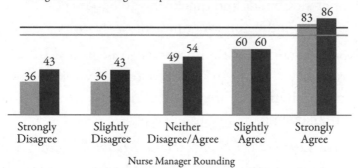

Patients who "strongly agree" that a nurse manager visited them daily have higher Overall Rating of Hospital and Nurse Communication results.

Survey Question: "A nurse manager or leader visited me about my care daily."
Data Source: Kaiser Permanente Program-wide ALL IP combined average results (Jan 2010 - Aug 2011)
National 75th percentile for Rate Hospital is 73% and for Nurse Communication is 80% (CMS 2010 Q1-Q4)

Figure 3.4

Now, take a look at Figure 3.5. It illustrates clearly that when patients answer yes to the question "Did a nurse manager visit you during your stay?" an organization's results in four HCAHPS composites—Overall Rating of Hospital, Nurse Communication, Responsiveness of Staff, and Willingness to Recommend—are likely to all be in the top quartile. It should also be obvious that when a nurse leader does not round on patients, the patients' perception of care is substantially lower.

Nurse Manager Rounding on Patients

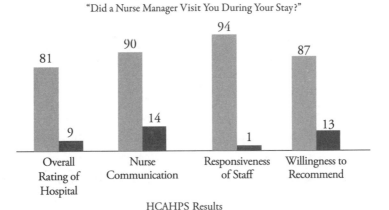

"Did a Nurse Manager Visit You During Your Stay?"

Source: Arizona Hospital, Total beds = 335, Employees = 4,000, Admissions = 10,188

Figure 3.5

In both of these figures, you can see that just the simple act of having the nurse leader visit the patient daily is in and of itself an important driver of perception of care results. The data demonstrates that when Nurse Leader Rounding is hardwired, organizations readily score in the top HCAHPS quartile—and when we don't, we are often in the bottom quartile.

After rounding has been completed, nurse leaders must use the information they obtained to ask themselves:

1. What have I learned about the care of my patients?

2. What must I do with this information?

The answers to these questions should be used to improve both individual caregiver opportunities and the collective performance of the unit as themes arise from the feedback obtained. If the leader learns that care is being delivered at the highest level, she can immediately reward the behaviors she was verifying. Alternately, she can take the opportunity to coach the staff on how to improve the care provided. Think of leader rounding as a catalyst for making lasting changes that will improve the care of all patients.

Please be aware: This tactic is not easy to implement. At first, it will unearth process improvement opportunities and require nurse leaders to spend additional time rewarding and recognizing staff as well as deal with subpar performers. In other words, it creates more work up front.

It will also take some time, especially on lower-performing units where there are multiple complaints. Again, this is exactly *why* nurse leaders should be rounding on every patient. If patients are complaining in the hospital, they certainly are not going to stop when they go home, and they are going to tell all their friends. Rounding provides an excellent opportunity for service recovery!

Once your nurse leaders have been diligent about getting it done for some time—after processes have been improved, systems are working well, and staff performance issues have been addressed—they'll find it to be one of the most enjoyable parts of their jobs. Why? Because it allows them to reconnect with patients, which is probably why they went into nursing in the first place. And they will hear about the excellent care the nurses are providing… and sharing these compliments from the patients is one of the best parts of this challenging job.

Fundamental Tactic: Key Words at Key Times

Key Words at Key Times (KWKT) is a strategy that triggers us to consider how we communicate with patients and whether we can do it better. Here are a couple examples of why, when left to our own devices, the words we choose may not be ideal:

Example 1:

OR nurse: "Operating Room, how can I help you?"

Elderly mother of a patient: "I would like an update on how my daughter is doing. She said someone would call me after her surgery, and I haven't heard anything yet."

OR nurse: "She's no longer with us."

The elderly woman gasps and hangs up the phone. Ten minutes later, the PACU calls with the previously arranged report and finds herself on the phone with the patient's distraught mother—who had interpreted the Operating Room nurse's words to mean that her daughter had died during surgery.

Example 2:

A patient receives a call from the physician's office with lab results. The nurse tells her that her biopsy results are negative and then goes on to describe the options for next steps to treat the patient's chief complaint, since the lab results didn't confirm any issue.

However, all the patient hears is the word "negative." She thinks it means the results are bad. Due to her high state of anxiety, she doesn't process anything else the nurse says. She spends the next week waiting for the physician to call with how they are going to treat her, and of course the call never comes. By the time the patient finally calls the office, she is quite upset.

In both of these examples, just a single word or phrase was instrumental in creating a poor outcome.

Words matter! Being conscious and strategic about what and how we communicate improves care, decreases anxiety, and creates better outcomes. It also saves time, since it often means caregivers don't have to go back and correct misunderstandings.

For these reasons, we at Studer Group have long recommended the use of Key Words at Key Times—carefully chosen words healthcare professionals use to "connect the dots" and help patients, families, and visitors better understand what we are doing—and most importantly, *why*.

Every day we deal with patients who are distracted, frightened, and often in pain. We may think we have communicated something, but in reality, what we thought we were communicating may not have been heard.

Key words are a simple way to solve that problem. They help patients understand their care better, they reduce anxiety and build trust, and they align the behavior of the staff to the needs of the patient. When we talk about key words, we are really talking about building relationships with our patients during their most vulnerable time of need. For example:

- When caregivers ask, "Do you have any questions?" the patient often says "no" as an automatic response. When caregivers ask, "What questions do you have for me?" the patient tends to give it more thought, and has the opportunity to bring up his or her concerns.

- Many organizations have found that the use of key words helps with co-pay collections. When reception staff ask, "Are you able to take care of your co-pay today?" the answer is often "no." However, when they say, "Your co-pay today is $40. We accept cash or credit—how would you like to pay?" the rate of collections is much higher.

- Using words that target areas for improvement can bring about the needed changes. If your pharmacy is getting low scores for accuracy on the Support Service Survey, pharmacy staff can include the word "accuracy" more often in conversations with clinicians. Saying, "Let me read this back to you to make sure it's accurate" puts both individuals' attention on the issue of accuracy, ensuring that the rate of accuracy is higher.

AIDET® (also called the Five Fundamentals of Communication) is a good platform for applying key words. More specifically, it's a communication framework that identifies five objectives to include in every interaction in order to improve patients' and customers' perception of their care or service, help reduce their anxiety (thus improving outcomes), build patient loyalty, and ensure that your staff is delivering the same consistent messages of concern and appreciation.

AIDET is an acronym that stands for **A**cknowledge, **I**ntroduce, **D**uration, **E**xplanation, and **T**hank You. When organizations incorporate AIDET into daily practices, the results are amazing.

Remember, in a culture of *always*, a patient is judging every employee and every interaction. The Radiology Department that standardizes and holds people accountable for using AIDET (along with the Nine Factors of Engagement, discussed later in this chapter) will impact the overall perception of the patient experience in a very positive way. Courtesy and respect applies to everyone, and AIDET can help promote these values.

Organizations that have leveraged the power of key words are exceptional at answering the following questions: What do our patients want to know? What do we need for our patients to know? How can we help patients/ visitors feel comfortable with our care and procedures? Are we communicating clear messages to everyone, every time?

Sample AIDET® Conversation

A Good morning, Mrs. Smith.

I I am Megan and I'm the radiology technician who will do your CT scan today. I've been at this hospital for 10 years, and I have done over 2,000 of these tests. You are in very good hands with our team.

D I am going to take about five minutes to explain this to you and then we will do the procedure. You should be ready to go back to your room in about 30 minutes. Shall we get started?

E First, we are going to start an IV. Are you right- or left-handed? Next we will…(explain the steps of the procedure). What questions do you have before I proceed?

T We are all finished. Thank you so much for holding so still; we got some very good information for the doctor to review. Are there any questions you have that I need to explain further? Is there anything I can do for you before I leave?

Fundamental Tactic: Managing Up

We can't move from these communication techniques without reinforcing the importance of managing up.

Simply put, managing up is a positioning statement. It helps us place ourselves and the next caregiver, department, or service provider in a positive light in order to reduce patients' anxiety.

In many cases, people are averse to managing up themselves because they feel like they are bragging. But at the end of the day, communicating confidence that you are the right person for the job has great benefit and meets a fundamental question that every patient or customer has: Do you know what you are doing and will you do it correctly?

Finding a way to manage up is essential. This is not a script to be robotically followed, but rather an opportunity to connect to the patient or customer in a way that makes him or her feel more at ease. This is not an optional part of the introduction part of AIDET but rather a required element that ensures that safety and competence are perceived by all.

Here are some examples of managing up statements:

"I know you got some difficult news yesterday. My whole purpose today will be to help you adjust to that news as I have helped many others in similar circumstances."

"I have been a NICU nurse for 20 years and I sing to all my babies."

"I am your transporter. If you feel up to it, I always have a 'joke of the day.' Let me know if you want me to make your ride more comfortable with my joke."

"Dr. Smith is so worth the wait. Patients wait weeks to see him. He's the best. He is absolutely who I would see if it were me or my family."

"Our Radiology Department is state of the art. You can trust they will be very accurate and work to get you your results as quickly as possible."

Each of these examples is designed to make the patient feel respected, comforted, and listened to. We must, of course, reinforce the need to be genuine. Find a way to word these reassurances that feels authentic to you, always keeping in mind that you're contributing to better patient care. There is almost always something that can be said to make patients feel better. Your challenge is to find that one thing.

Fundamental Tactic: Bedside Shift Report

This initiative refers to the process of transferring care delivery from one nurse to another at change of shift, at the patient bedside when appropriate. It incorporates other concepts such as AIDET, communication, teamwork, creating a safe patient environment, and managing up.

All necessary patient information is exchanged in the patient room: patient identifiers, safety checks, medications, tests, and so forth. This keeps patients informed and involved in their care, which is a basic patient right. It is also a nurse satisfier as it promotes teamwork, mentoring, and professional practice.

Bedside Shift Report will help hospitals demonstrate compliance with National Patient Safety Goals (NPSGs) regarding handoffs and transitions of care by allowing patients to hear their care plan and ask questions of their caregivers. This can be done in the IP, OP, and ED settings and can be adapted to *any* handoff or transition of care—meaning that every time a patient moves from one place to another or from one caregiver to another, the patient is included in his care.

Here is an example:

"Good morning, Mr. Jones. I am going home now to my family, and Karen is going to be your nurse today. Karen has been with us for three years and is one of our experts in caring for patients with pain after hip surgery. I'm leaving you in very good hands.

"You and I are going to share with her what we have been working on so she knows what's important to you, and so that she has all the information she needs to take very good care of you today. Can you tell Karen what we did last night that you feel helped with your pain?"

Here, the patient talks about his care. The offgoing nurse then fills in any pertinent clinical details, such as medication doses or frequency, that the patient might have left out. A similar conversation should occur for any part of the report for which the patient can offer input. Instead of the patient being the passive listener in the report, the report occurs between the oncoming caregiver and the patient, with the offgoing caregiver listening and offering additional details.

"Okay, Mr. Jones, can you tell Karen about the new medication you started today? Tell her why you are taking it and what common side effect we talked about.

"Do you have questions for me or Karen before we leave? Is there anything more that Karen needs to know in order to provide you with excellent care today?

"I'm heading home now. Thank you for allowing me to be part of your care team last night."

Handoff and Bedside Shift Report: Benefits

- Decrease potential for misses and mistakes

- Increase patient involvement and keep patients informed

- Increase patient trust through "managing up"

- Decrease patient wait times at change of shift and keep them from feeling forgotten or abandoned

- Decrease patient and family anxiety about oncoming caregivers' competency

- Transfer the "emotional bank account" from offgoing to oncoming caregiver

- Increase accountability for nurses as they report off visually in front of the patient and each other

- Increase new RN skill level—RNs can see and hear what the experienced RN is doing and why

- Increase teamwork between shifts

The Bedside Shift Report saves lives by ensuring safe handoffs. It also keeps patients informed about their care and reduces their anxiety by "managing up" the caregiver and decreasing the perception that "nobody is around at shift change." It is a real-time exchange of information that increases patient safety (sentinel events occur more often during change of shift), improves quality of care, increases accountability, and strengthens teamwork.

Fundamental Tactic: Post-Visit Patient Phone Calls

This tactic refers to a process in which the staff connects with patients following discharge to confirm compliance and understanding of discharge instructions, demonstrate empathy, and afford an opportunity for service recovery (if appropriate). Studer Group recommends that all organizations get a system in place for making post-visit calls—they should become a part of your culture and an extension of your care.

Outcomes of hardwiring post-visit calls into your everyday processes include:

- Reduced patient anxiety

- Increased compliance with discharge instructions

- Improved clinical outcomes

- Reduced readmissions

- Decreased complaints and claims

- Increased employee satisfaction

- Increased patient perception of care

There is much data that supports the need for aggressive use of post-visit patient calls. For instance:

- According to the Agency for Healthcare Research and Quality (AHRQ), heart failure represents $25 billion to $35 billion of healthcare expenditures each year; readmissions have tripled in the past 25 years and are expected to triple again over the next 30 years.

- According to AHRQ, the high rate of re-hospitalization for heart failure patients results from patients' inability to adequately self-manage the condition:

  - National average readmission rate 30 days post-discharge ranges from 18 to 20 percent depending on the region of the country.

  - Thirteen percent of these readmissions were "potentially avoidable," based on the IPPS rule, with major areas of concern including poor communication with patients at discharge, especially around medications, and inadequate post-discharge monitoring.

  - Prevention of these avoidable readmissions could save Medicare $12 billion per year.[1]

- Using interactive care, such as post-visit calls, organizations have been able to achieve a 74 percent reduction in heart failure readmission rate 30 days post-discharge, resulting in an overall readmission rate of 5 percent.

- At the same time, the organizations saw a 43 percent improvement in patient satisfaction.

Since we know that most adverse events will occur within 72 hours of discharge, Studer Group recommends that these calls be made prior to that timeframe. Ideally, calls take place within a 24- to 72-hour timeframe (or until the nurse has made three attempts).

While it is best for a clinical staff member to call the patient, any call is better than no call. It is valuable for staff to hear how the patients perceive their care.

Besides the fact that post-visit calls reduce readmissions, improve clinical outcomes, and save lives, they also reinforce a patient's perception of having received the very best care. And last but not least, they also offer staff members the chance to hear firsthand what a difference they make in the lives of their patients.

Post-Visit Phone Call Sample

Empathy and Concern	"Mrs. Smith? Hello, this is <name>. You were discharged from my unit yesterday. I just wanted to call and see how you are doing today."
Clinical Outcomes	"Do you have any questions about your medications?" "Do you understand what side effects you should watch for?" "How is your pain level today—is it better or worse than yesterday?" "Do you know what symptoms or other health problems to look out for?" "Have you scheduled your follow-up appointment?"
Reward and Recognition	"We like to recognize any employees who give our patients excellent care. Is there anyone who did an excellent job for you during your stay with us?" "Can you tell me what <name> did for you that was excellent?"
Service	"We want to make sure you were satisfied with your care. How were we, Mrs. Smith?"
Process Improvement	"Do you have any suggestions for what we could do to be even better?"
Appreciation	"Thank you so much for taking the time to tell me about your care. Do you have any questions for me?" "Is there anything else I can do for you?"

Figure 3.6

While we felt it was important to devote this section of the Fundamentals chapter to post-visit phone calls, we'd also like to briefly mention their counterpart: pre-visit phone calls. Both tactics—which Studer Group classifies as "care transition" calls—are immensely valuable in helping us coordinate care. They drive a focus on improving the continuum of care by extending it outside the four walls of the organization. Effective care transition calls (both pre- and post-visit) provide an opportunity to check clinical quality, harvest reward and recognition, and identify trends or areas of improvement through firsthand feedback from patients. We hope you will want to learn more about the impact of pre-visit phone calls. To do so, please visit www.studergroup.com/pcm.

Fundamental Tactic: Hourly Rounding®

Studer Group's Hourly Rounding® tactic has a tremendous impact on patient perception and quality of care. The September 2006 *American Journal of Nursing* published a study showing evidence that when implemented and hardwired, Hourly Rounding effectively decreases call lights by 37.8 percent, decreases falls by 50 percent, decreases hospital-acquired decubiti by 14 percent, and improves patient perception by 12 mean points.

Hourly Rounding also helps create work flow efficiency by keeping clinical staff from getting caught in the trap of reacting to so many call button requests, interruptions, and questions that could have been addressed had we been more proactive. Hourly Rounding reduces interruptions from patients to the nurses for non-urgent needs and requests, freeing them up to be more focused on urgent ones.

What *is* Hourly Rounding? Simply put, it's making a commitment to have a staff member visit every patient every hour during the day and every two hours during the night. This doesn't just mean "checking in," however—it means practicing a series of eight very specific behaviors.

Here are the eight behaviors and the composites they address:

Hourly Rounding Behavior	Expected Results	HCAHPS Composite
Use opening key words	Contributes to efficiency, decreases patient anxiety	Nurse Communication, Responsiveness, Pain Management, Cleanliness
Accomplish scheduled tasks	Contributes to efficiency	Responsiveness, Pain Management, Explanation, Communication About Medications
Address Three Ps (pain, potty, position)	Quality indicators: falls, decubitus, pain management	Nurse Communication, Responsiveness, Pain Management
Address additional comfort needs	Improved patient experience on pain, contributes to efficiency	Nurse Communication, Responsiveness, Pain Management
Conduct environmental assessment	Contributes to efficiency, teamwork, patient safety	Cleanliness, Responsiveness
Ask, "Is there anything else I can do for you before I go? I have time."	Contributes to efficiency, teamwork, patient experience	Nurse Communication, Responsiveness
Tell each patient when you will be back	Contributes to efficiency	Responsiveness, Pain Management
Document the round	Improves quality and accountability	Responsiveness

Figure 3.7

Following is an explanation of each behavior and what each one is designed to accomplish:

1. **Use opening key words to reduce anxiety (AIDET®).** For patients, the key words establish the expectation of what is going to happen next. This reduces anxiety since most people fear the unknown. These opening words are fully customizable to allow the staff to ensure they have focus in the right area. They should include AIDET and the key words "hourly round." They might sound like this on a unit that is focusing on improving pain: "Mr. Jones? [knocks on the door] This is Lynn, your nurse. I am back to do my hourly round and make sure your pain is under control."

2. **Perform scheduled tasks.** This behavior is included to recognize that Hourly Rounding is not something we do on top of everything else but rather integrated into everything we have to do. When staff understand how to organize all their tasks into the framework of Hourly Rounding, they really begin to feel the benefit of the structure this provides and the efficiency it creates.

3. **Address the "Three Ps"—pain, potty, position.** The Ps were identified by assessing the most frequent reasons for call lights, questions, or interruptions and then building them into the framework so we deal with them on a proactive basis. These will look different in various units or service lines.

4. **Assess any additional comfort needs.** We must proactively address the "little things" patients require, such as fluffing pillows, straightening sheets, filling water pitchers, answering questions—the back-to-basics, Nursing 101 techniques.

5. **Conduct an environmental assessment.** Ensure that the patient's area is clean, safe, and free of clutter. This is also designed to make sure the patient has everything within his reach and that all safety measures are in place, such as bed alarms, side rails, and Core Measure bundles. All staff who go in and out of a patient room, regardless of their department or position, can be trained to conduct this assessment before leaving the room.

6. **Ask, "Is there anything else I can do for you? I have time."** A genuine request to ensure that the patient does not have an unmet need will reduce further call lights. It also reminds staff to take one more look around to be sure they don't see anything left undone.

7. **Tell each patient when you will be back.** This behavior builds trust and reliability and will assist the patient in feeling confident that he can cluster his non-urgent requests until the next promised hourly round.

8. **Document the process in a rounding log posted in the patient's room.** The purpose of the logs, in addition to accountability, is to create a promise to the patient and family and to demonstrate that the promise has been fulfilled.

Also, what nurses are required to document establishes their priorities. Without the requirement to document the important process of Hourly Rounding, we inadvertently send the message that it is optional.

Each of these behaviors creates a specific desired outcome. Many times, staff and leaders are tempted to "modify" rounds by eliminating certain steps. But in doing so, you're reducing the impact and losing some of the successful outcomes you can achieve.

When presenting Hourly Rounding to nurses, focus on quality and safe patient care and the efficiency they will achieve. Refer them to the call-light statistic mentioned earlier and connect the dots on what is in it for them, in terms of helping them improve their efficiency and provide care more effectively. (That call-light study remains the largest study to date on the topic.)

Hourly Rounding® Results

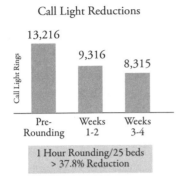

Call Light Reductions

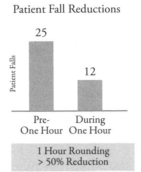

Patient Fall Reductions

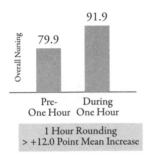

Patient Satisfaction Increase

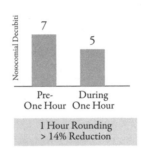

Pressure Ulcer Reductions

Figure 3.8

Quite simply, Hourly Rounding gets results. When staff members start seeing these results in their daily work lives, they'll naturally want to become more efficient and effective. While this tactic creates efficiency and focus for staff, it also provides a proactive framework in which patient needs are met before they have to call for them—and that is a "WOW" from a quality and experience standpoint.

Fundamental Tactic: Individualized Patient Care (IPC)

The term "patient-centered care" is pervasive in healthcare today. It is used to describe everything from nursing care models to broad philosophies. No one would argue that healthcare in general needs to be more patient-centered in its approach to care delivery—research suggests that when we accomplish this, not only does quality improve but so does the patients' and families' perception of their care.

Because of this focus on the patient as an individual, we have operationalized a process that has been successful in ensuring that the patient's preferences and priorities are known and acted upon: Individualized Patient Care (IPC).

The only one who can tell us what is truly important to the patient *is* the patient (and his or her family). IPC helps us ask them and then act on the answers. We take the technical/clinical aspects of care and link them to the individual patient via standardized communication with him or her. As a result, clinical outcomes and patient perception of care improve. More importantly, this provides a mechanism for our staff to get to know the patient as a person.

IPC allows us to gather a patient's thoughts on what excellent care means to him or her and to incorporate them into our interactions with that person. It also allows us to use this information to better connect with the patient and to "humanize" our care.

It's easy to come across as simply going through the motions when we assess patients—IPC helps alleviate that "robotic" effect. We recommend standardization and consistency in asking relevant questions, but those have to be balanced with what should be an honest desire to know what is really important to that individual patient, to make a positive difference in her view of the care she receives.

IPC means frequently reviewing your organization's performance on what's most important to a patient throughout her stay. Not only does this boost patient perception of care, it improves communication between the patient and hospital employees and encourages teamwork and efficiency. The only way we can truly deliver care that is important to the patient is to first understand what is important and then ask frequently how well we are doing.

Implement Individualized Patient Care at the time of admission assessment by discussing the following types of things with the patient:

- *"Our goal is to consistently provide excellent care to you. To do this we need to know what excellent care means to you."*

- *"Can you tell me two or three things that are most important to you that would make you feel we have provided exceptional care?"*

Write the patient's responses on her communication board or an Individualized Patient Care card. This is especially useful with Pain Management and Communication about Medications composites, as many patients answer those questions with statements such as "I am really worried about being in pain" or "I got very confused with all the medications I had to take last time. Could they be sure to write it all down for me?"

If these are the most important things to that patient, then it would be incumbent on the staff to ensure that the whole care team is aware of those priorities. As nurses and other staff enter the room, they can view the communication board to see what is important to her and customize their interactions based on this information. What's important to the patient should be considered during every interaction.

Implementing Individualized Patient Care

Action	How it works
1. Use key words.	Upon admission, the nurse says to the patient: "Our goal is to provide you with excellent care. (Use appropriate language from your patient satisfaction survey.) What three things can we do to make sure your care is excellent?" If the patient doesn't know, dig deeper using items from the survey. For instance, say: "How important is your pain management? How important is it that we keep you informed?"
2. Note items on the whiteboard.	There should be a whiteboard in every patient's room. Also, write the patient's pain goal and the next time medication is due.
3. Ask during daily rounds.	The nurse leader should ask, "How well are we doing with (each of the identified needs)?" and connect those to the survey questions.
4. Ask at shift change.	Nursing staff should repeat as above.
5. Ask at discharge.	Both nursing staff and case managers should ask, "How well have we done at (each of the identified needs)?"

Figure 3.9

IPC can be utilized in all care areas of the hospital, including Inpatient, Outpatient, Ambulatory Surgery, and Emergency Departments. By asking patients to tell you what excellent care means to them, you can avoid or immediately address situations that may create unnecessary anxiety and detract from the healing process.

Fundamental Tactic: M in the Box[SM]

This simple strategy was designed primarily to give staff a visual reminder, in each patient's room, to focus on new medications and their side effects. When we say simple, we mean *simple*. Here's how it works:

1. When the patient has a new medication ordered, the nurse draws a box on the communication board and writes an "M" inside it. This signals to other caregivers that a new medication was ordered and is being taught to the patient.

2. Each nurse or caregiver who enters the room and sees the M in the Box on the board asks the patient to articulate the purpose and potential side effects of the new medication.

3. Once the patient can easily teach back the information about the new medication, the M is erased.

Sometimes getting people to do simple things is hard. Nevertheless, in this case, just drawing a box and a letter and talking about it can be extremely effective. In fact, it can be lifesaving.

Fundamental Tactic: Engaging the Patient

Engagement may not be typically thought of as a tactic. Yet, in this case, we'd like to categorize it this way. In each of the aforementioned outlined processes, our attitude and demeanor have an influence on the overall outcome. If we follow all the steps of the processes but we do not make an effort to be kind, compassionate, or respectful in those interactions, we can still have a negative outcome.

When we make an effort to engage the patient—by communicating clearly and frequently, by actively listening, and by demonstrating other behaviors that show we care about patients and their concerns—we get the patient more involved in his or her care. And when patients understand their care and discharge plans, they are more likely to comply with those plans and therefore have better outcomes. Engagement isn't just important for your HCAHPS results—it's important to the health of your patients.

To ensure that positive attitude *and* behaviors are executed, we have established nine factors of engagement. This list identifies those elements that should also be assessed and considered important to successful implementation of any of the best practices identified previously.

Nine Factors of Engagement

Active listening	Pay close attention to the patient, avoiding distractions. Repeat their statements back to them to ensure that you understand what they are saying.
Non-multi-tasking	Focus only on the interaction at hand. More on how to do this can be found in the following chapter.
Eye contact	Look at the speaker.
Tone of voice	Use a kind and calming tone, not stern or commanding.
Appropriate speed of speech	Be careful not to talk too fast, so that patients have time to process the information you're giving them.
Appropriate use of touch	A gentle touch on the arm or shoulder can help demonstrate your interest in what a patient is saying and be comforting as well.
Appropriate use of humor/emotion	If the mood is right, gentle humor can build rapport with a patient. However, if the patient is feeling sad or distressed, a humorous comment can seem uncaring.
Physical positioning – sitting, kneeling, etc.	If possible, sit or kneel near the bedside so that the patient can better see you while you converse. Positioning yourself at the patient's torso is ideal.
Energy mirrors the needs of the patient	If the patient seems to need upbeat energy, try to provide that by being positive and cheerful. However, if the patient seems to need quiet and calm energy, try to speak more gently.

Figure 3.10

We know you and your team are busy. You don't need to add any more tasks to your already-full plates. The following chapters don't offer additional to-dos—they will show you new ways of doing the things you already do that will improve staff efficiency, communication with patients, and quality of care. When those improve, so do your HCAHPS results.

Tools & Resources

Studer Group offers a variety of tools and resources that support the tactics discussed in this chapter. To access the most up-to-date offerings, as well as to see what's new in healthcare, please visit www.studergroup.com/HCAHPS.

NURSE COMMUNICATION

I t's interesting to consider how the words we use evolve over time. Once, our industry talked about "patient satisfaction." Now, we talk more about "patient perception of care" and, increasingly, "patient experience." The evolution of these terms reflects the changes in the dynamic of how the care we provide is evaluated and how the transparent reporting of data has impacted how we view patient feedback and information.

Prior to HCAHPS and the public reporting of data by CMS, this measurement was confined to how a patient felt about his or her experience and was quantified by words such as "very good" or "excellent." As the industry began moving to a more patient-centered agenda, we were encouraged to talk less about "satisfaction scores" and frame the information as the patient's perception of his or her care. Today, we have ample evidence of the interconnected relationship between quality metrics and HCAHPS results—it has become evident that the patient experience needs to be our primary focus.

This is more than just semantics. "Perception" implies that the patient is observing her care while "experience" implies that she is fully immersed in it—not just receiving care but actively participating in it. When you consider where we are in this evolution (not just of wording but of the interactive nature of care itself), it's easy to see why the patients' view of the men and women who care for them is so critical—and why this composite matters so much.

HCAHPS correlation data indicates that Nurse Communication is the composite most highly correlated with overall hospital rating. As you learned in our introductory chapter, the genesis of HCAHPS and the questions being asked were developed by consumers. With this in mind, the following chapter outlines the strategies to help ensure that patients are able to give positive responses to those questions and have an overall positive experience in your hospital.

While this composite suggests that it is specific to nurses (later we will discuss this same topic for physicians), in reality it doesn't impact *only* them. Patients and their families often interact with dozens of healthcare professionals all dressed in scrubs. This can create an enormous amount of role confusion. (Many times, the only differentiation occurs due to our communication.) The result is that staff who "look" like nurses may end up being evaluated as such.

This chapter suggests strategies that all nurses should be required to implement, but you can see why it's wise to have *all* staff who interact with patients and families implement them too.

When we execute the best practices in this chapter, good things happen to both quality and patient experience, as you can see from these results. Our partners outperform the rest of the industry in this composite by nearly 20 percentile points.

Before we delve into the HCAHPS questions that encompass Nurse Communication, we'd like to share a story that shows how these tactics affect patients on a personal level—including impacting their clinical outcome:

Mrs. Jones was a 50-year-old patient on the Medical/Surgical Unit. The hospitalist in charge of her inpatient care had prescribed a blood-thinning medication for us to begin during her hospital stay. During handover at change of shift, Sandi, an RN, was reviewing Mrs. Jones's new medications, and asked her to tell Bill, the oncoming nurse, about the new meds the doctor had prescribed. During Mrs. Jones's explanation, she informed Bill that she had been on a daily regimen of low-dose aspirin, which she started after reading an article in a monthly periodical she receives.

Bill thanked Mrs. Jones for taking her health seriously and being well informed about current medications and best practices. He then explained about the effect of her blood-thinning medications and the effects that other aspirin products would have on her health if she were to continue taking them. Also, Bill reconnected Mrs. Jones to the pharmacist on call for a detailed explanation of the effects over-the-counter medications can have on prescriptions.

In this example, a number of strategies were used successfully. Bill and Sandi demonstrated very good *listening* skills, picking up on the fact that the patient was on an over-the-counter medication that could impact the newly prescribed blood thinner. They took the opportunity to bring in a pharmacist expert who could provide not just an explanation, but the "best" *explanation*. Bill's response (and the pharmacist's conversation) demonstrated *courtesy and respect* by not making the patient feel uninformed or guilty about having taken the additional aspirin.

This story also demonstrates that being a great nurse requires more than just technical/clinical abilities. Had the oncoming nurse (Bill) just read the medications on the chart or discussed them only with the departing nurse (Sandi), he would not have known about Mrs. Jones's daily intake of aspirin. Both Bill and Sandi truly engaged with the patient—and with each other—and thus were able to impact her health on a deeper level.

The more we interact with patients, the more we learn about them and the stronger the relationships are that we build with them—and the more likely we are to make the discoveries that lead to better clinical outcomes. The more we can understand the patient perception of the quality of care delivered, the better we can drive outcomes that impact results.

The Survey Questions

This aspect of the HCAHPS survey asks patients about their perception of nursing care during their hospital stay. Answers are given in frequency scale: *never, sometimes, usually,* or *always*. The percent of patients who respond *always* is publicly reported on www.hospitalcompare.hhs.gov.

1. **During this hospital stay, how often did nurses treat you with courtesy and respect?**

2. **During this hospital stay, how often did nurses listen carefully to you?**

3. **During this hospital stay, how often did nurses explain things in a way you could understand?**

In the following chapters, we will share several tactics for each question that positively impact the likelihood that patients will answer *always* to all three questions in the Nurse Communication composite.

CHAPTER FOUR:

COURTESY AND RESPECT (A GOAL FOR NURSES AND *ALL* STAFF MEMBERS)

The HCAHPS Question: During this hospital stay, how often did nurses treat you with courtesy and respect?

This question really addresses how successful we are at treating patients and their family members as individuals. It requires us to move from providing "task-oriented" care to holding memorable conversations and creating meaningful personal connections. In other words, we must take the time to find out what is important to a particular patient and fully partner with her and her family in the care we provide.

As a nurse, you can make or break a patient's experience with one encounter. Nurses help control pain, manage medications, ensure that patients receive help as soon as they request it, and help build relationships with physicians—all of which have a direct effect on the overall satisfaction and care of the patient. That is why when we look at HCAHPS, the Nurse Communication domain is the greatest influencer of the patient's overall experience and whether or not she feels respected.

While this question specifically singles out nurses, everyone in the organization owns the results. Remember, patients and families often mistake people functioning in other roles for a nurse.

...And the Tactics That Make "Always" Responses More Likely

Studer Group® draws from its work with a network of exceptional organizations to create videos, training tools, articles, and knowledge resources that will help you achieve results. This extensive online resource is called the Learning Lab.

Based on research from our Learning Lab, Studer Group has identified tactics that, when applied and customized appropriately, will have the most impact on improving staff members' ability to show courtesy and respect to patients. They're described here:

Tactic 1: Standardize Behaviors to Respect and Engage

If we are to be evaluated on treating patients with courtesy and respect, the reality is that behaviors matter. This means not just telling people to be courteous and respectful (this leaves behaviors up to interpretation) but to spell out exactly what it means. In most organizations, there is generally a set of defined behavior standards that outline how we are to act, and these generally tie to the mission and values of the organization.

For example, an organization's Standards of Behavior might include items such as:

- I will maintain eye contact with the client.

- I will ask an open-ended question, such as, "How may I be of help to you?"

- I will make every effort to answer calls within three rings.

- I will avoid phrases like "Okay," "Yeah," "Hold on," "Honey," and "See ya."

These are just a few examples used by organizations coached by Studer Group. To download a sample Standards of Behavior list, visit www.firestarterpublishing. com/HCAHPSHandbook.

It is incumbent on leaders to hold staff accountable for demonstrating these behaviors at all times in all interactions. By accountability, we mean rewarding and recognizing staff who demonstrate these behaviors routinely and coaching staff who do not.

It becomes abundantly clear that even one staff member who does not perform the best behaviors with a patient or family member will undo the great work that all the others have accomplished. It takes only one person not doing something well to keep you from getting an HCAHPS response of "always"—and, of course, to create the best possible experience for your patients.

In the Fundamentals chapter, we discussed the nine factors of engagement, and they have great application here. When those factors are consistently executed well and staff are used to being coached and evaluated on them, they become cultural norms of performance that ensure (along with the other tactics we will describe) that your patients feel they have been treated with courtesy and respect.

Nine Factors of Engagement

- Active listening
- Non-multi-tasking
- Eye contact
- Tone of voice
- Appropriate speed of speech
- Appropriate use of touch
- Appropriate use of humor/emotion
- Physical positioning—sitting, kneeling, etc.
- Energy mirrors the needs of the patient

Lastly, we need to be mindful of the cultural sensitivities of those we serve. Each culture has its own set of expectations regarding communication. When interacting with people from cultures different from your own, be aware and accommodating of these differences. It is important to remember we are here to meet the needs of our patients and their families, not our own.

Tactic 2: Key Words at Key Times (KWKT) and AIDET®

When patients enter the hospital, they are generally anxious and scared. Sometimes they're in pain. About half of them came from the ED and didn't even expect to be in the hospital. They have no control over where they stay, what they wear, and who is caring for them. What's more, hospitalists and other specialty physicians who will care for those patients may not have any prior relationship with them.

As a care provider, you can take specific steps to build positive relationships with patients and reduce their anxiety, as well as help them become more engaged in their own care. You make an impression on the patient starting the minute you walk into the room. AIDET® and use of Key Words at Key Times (KWKT) can help you alleviate this anxiety and in the process demonstrate courtesy and respect.

Everyone who interacts with patients and their families should be educated to acknowledge the patient in each and every patient encounter. They should address the patient by name, and if family or visitors are in the room, greet them as well.

AIDET was discussed in the Fundamentals chapter. However, it may be helpful to offer another example of how this framework can assist in communication, demonstrate courtesy and respect, and be seen by caregivers as an efficient strategy to improve relationships with patients and their families.

Jenni was a 28-year-old patient who was admitted following an elective surgery for a cyst removal near her kidney. During surgery, the cyst was found to be embedded in her diaphragm, and during the removal, air leaked into the chest cavity, which collapsed her lung. It was necessary to insert a chest tube.

After Jenni was admitted on the floor, and while they were still doing vital signs every 15 minutes, her nurse aide, Sara, went on break. The new nurse aide covering for Sara came into the room, stood at the end of the bed, looked at the patient, and promptly left the room without saying a word.

The patient then turned to her mother, who was at the bedside, and asked why that "nurse" just came in and stared at her.

The reality was that the aide did not "stare" at the patient, but rather looked at the blood pressure monitor to document the last recorded vitals. In other words, she did her task and left. However, the patient didn't know that and it made her feel uncomfortable. Think how much better this encounter would have gone if the care provider had used AIDET:

*Good morning, Jenni (**A**), my name is Bridget. I am a nurse aide covering for Sara while she is on break (**I**). I'm just here for a second (**D**) to get the reading of your vitals from the blood pressure machine (**E**). I don't need anything else from you at this time. Do you need anything from me? Okay. Thank you (**T**) and Sara will check on you next time.*

Certainly, this example of integrating AIDET would have made an important difference in how the patient and family felt about that interaction. Now you may be thinking, *That wouldn't happen in my unit*, but it happens more often than you think. If your courtesy and respect results aren't a perfect 100 percent always, this might be an area of opportunity.

A few additional tips:

- Be respectful of the patient's space and privacy. Knock—and wait for permission—before entering the patient's room.

- Be courteous and acknowledge everyone in the room.

- Respect the patient and assure the privacy of his body, his belongings, and his information.

- Demonstrate respect by making the patient a priority.

- Be respectful and ask, "What name would you like us to call you?"—and ensure this gets communicated to others.

Tactic 3: Manage Up

The term "managing up," discussed in the Fundamentals chapter, refers to statements made that position yourself, the next caregiver, another department, or anyone else in a positive light. This technique helps patients and their family members feel safe and confident that they are being cared for by competent and caring individuals who trust each other.

Managing up gets incorporated into the Introduction part of AIDET if you are introducing yourself, or into the handover component if you are in the process of handing over care to another caregiver or department. It is also very helpful to manage up physicians to patients.

In fact, this often can make or break the reputation of a physician with patients and their families.

Please realize: Managing up is not a "script" to follow. It can come in as many different forms as there are people. It is simply making a statement that the patient needs to hear that will make her feel positive about who and what she is about to experience.

Tactic 4: Individualized Patient Care (IPC)

After reading about IPC in the Fundamentals chapter, you have a sense of how this process can make our approach with patients more specific to their priorities and needs. Implementing this tactic along with caring behaviors and an attitude of kindness is the ultimate demonstration of courtesy and respect.

In one of our partner organizations, the nurse leader was rounding on patients. When reviewing the whiteboard, she noticed the IPC items written on it.

The first one was not unusual: *Pain.* The second one she had seen fairly often as well: *Warm blanket at night.* It was the third one that made her wonder: *Fishing.*

She laughed and asked the patient, "Will you please tell me about the fishing?" The patient explained that when they had asked for two to three things they could do to make his stay better, he couldn't think of a third thing. "So I just told them I really like fishing and that's where I wish I was," he said. "They wrote it on the board and now everybody comes in and asks me about fishing and we share fishing stories. It has been a lot of fun."

Clearly, this patient felt respected by the level of engagement the staff demonstrated, not just in his clinical outcomes, but in his life and interests overall.

Tactic 5: Nurse Leader Rounding

Nurse Leader Rounding is an important strategy for two reasons. First, it allows the nurse leader to validate that the staff have interacted with the patient and their family with courtesy and respect. The leader can do this by asking this simple question: "Have any of my staff done a very good job so that I can reward and recognize them?"

It would be highly unlikely that a patient would mention someone for recognition who had not treated them with the utmost courtesy and respect.

Additionally, the act of rounding itself creates positive perceptions for the patient and their family. Simply coming to the patient and showing her that you are invested in getting her feedback and input demonstrates your respect for her concerns and feelings. As long as this is done well by a trained and skilled nurse leader, Nurse Leader Rounding is a driver of improved results.

During the course of rounding as described in our Fundamentals chapter, the nurse leader can infuse key words into the interaction that will help support and underscore the topic. She can also manage up the staff, which will increase the impact. Here is an example:

*"Mrs. Jones, I see your nurse is Sharon. I have no doubt that you feel well cared for today. Sharon is one of my most experienced nurses and she takes excellent care of her patients (****Managing Up****). Are there any staff you have interacted with that I could recognize for doing a good job?"*

The patient responds by saying that the nurse aide Sheila was helpful by getting her back to bed when she wasn't feeling well. Mrs. Jones says she really appreciated Sheila's prompt response.

"Thank you for sharing that. I am not surprised to hear that Sheila was respectful of how you were feeling. I would be happy to acknowledge her for that.

"Mrs. Jones, I also want to be respectful of your time to rest. Is there anything else I can do for you before I go?"

Utilizing nurse leader rounds as an opportunity to reinforce key words and key messages will in and of itself be a driver of improved communication.

To be cared for with courtesy and respect is a basic patient right. And the vast majority of healthcare providers want to treat them this way. Not only does it help us engage with them in a way that yields better clinical outcomes, it simply feels good to treat patients the way we'd want *our* loved ones treated. These tactics help us make sure patients perceive the courtesy and respect we naturally want to provide.

A Few Additional Tips

Here are a few more tips to consider as you are hard-wiring the previous tactics.

Tip: Make Sacred Time

In these busy, challenging days in healthcare, it is easy for caregivers to get lost in what seems like a never-ending list of to-dos and interruptions. This busy pace requires caregivers to learn to multi-task in order to handle multiple priorities all at the same time. That said, multi-tasking in and of itself can interfere with effective communication—and especially courtesy and respect.

We do not want to tie the hands of our caregivers by saying it is not appropriate to multi-task, but we can offer some suggestions on how to keep it from being a barrier to our patient relationships. Specifically, we can offer guidelines on when it is and is not appropriate to multi-task. These guidelines focus on what we call "Sacred Time."

Sacred Time is the time spent focused solely on the patient. The staff person is ideally seated, making eye contact, demonstrating active listening, and not multi-tasking.

There are two occasions when it may be useful to have your staff eliminate multi-tasking and implement Sacred Time.

1. The first opportunity for Sacred Time is the first two minutes in which you are alone with the patient. In that time, you are beginning the relationship and establishing an emotional bank account. For many nurses, this might be when you return to a patient's room after report to do their assessment. For clinic nurses, it might be when you get the patient back to the exam room. In other words, take a moment to pause your activities and establish that rapport. The benefits are worth the investment.

2. The second occasion for Sacred Time is when the patient has asked a question. Because of our fast pace, we are often in the middle of another task when this occurs. Prior to responding, we must focus on the patient and ensure that our response is being internalized. We may need to say to the patient, *"Mr. Jones, that is a good question and I want to give you my full attention. Hold on for just one moment while I finish documenting your medication and I will be right with you to answer that."*

The implementation and suggestion of these guidelines to staff can be very helpful in mitigating the impact of appearing rushed or uncaring and will enhance the feeling of value and presence, translating to courtesy and respect.

Tip: Narrate Care

When Studer Group coaches are in the field, in hundreds of organizations day in and day out, we are often in units, departments, and clinics observing staff and leaders. It is not unusual to see staff members approach patients and families with no communication. But when care providers complete tasks in silence, it can be confusing and even upsetting to patients. This is why we must narrate care.

Narrating care simply means verbalizing the what, why, and how of our care processes so that the patient is more informed and feels well communicated with. The AIDET section earlier in this chapter highlights one such example, in which the nurse aide could have simply narrated what she was doing and why she was doing it—which would have gone a long way to improve the interaction.

Many times nurses are so focused on the task that they miss the opportunity to explain what they are doing, when that important and relevant information would probably make patients feel better and more secure.

As you read some examples of simple tasks that we might sometimes miss the opportunity to narrate, try to picture the physical act that the nurse might be performing. Challenge yourself to remember whether you have ever seen these done without any explanation or narration:

IV status checks: *"Your IV site looks good. The tubing was changed yesterday so we don't have to do that today. Your pump is programmed just right and it shouldn't alarm until 2 p.m. this afternoon, so it is all set."*

Medical assistant in clinic taking a patient back to the exam room: *"Mr. Jones, welcome to Dr. Smith's practice. As I walk you back to the exam room, we have a few things to do, such as get your weight and blood pressure, and then we will review your medications and health history. All of this will help Dr. Smith be well prepared for your time with him."*

Lab tech preparing to draw blood: *"Mr. Jones, I'm getting my supplies all set so once I draw your blood I can be as efficient as possible. I need to draw two different tubes of blood to get the specific tests your physician ordered, and of course, I will use each of these supplies only once for your safety. I also want to check and for you to double-check the labels so we are both confident they are correct."*

In each of the previous examples, the staff are merely talking out loud as they perform the specific task and as they remind themselves of what they are checking or doing—but saying it in a way that the patient gets the information as well. It is a win-win.

Tools & Resources

Studer Group offers a variety of tools and resources that support the tactics discussed in this chapter. To access the most up-to-date offerings, as well as to see what's new in healthcare, please visit www.studergroup.com/ HCAHPS.

CHAPTER FIVE:

CAREFUL LISTENING

The HCAHPS Question: During this hospital stay, how often did nurses listen carefully to you?

When we enter a patient's room, we almost always bring with us physical and mental checklists detailing what we need to accomplish. As we go through the lists of everything we need to accomplish for the patient in front of us, we are often mentally reviewing our to-do lists for all of the patients in our care.

It's not surprising that patients and their families can get the impression that we are not listening. Sometimes, despite our best intentions, they are right. And that's a problem—when our minds are focused on our tasks, we may miss cues that could allow us to provide better care.

It is only through *actively listening* to the patient that we can build relationships, which allows us to individualize his or her care to achieve the best outcomes. In the nurse-patient relationship, communication involves more than the transmission of information; it also involves transmitting feelings, recognizing these feelings, and letting the patient know that his or her feelings have been recognized.[1]

This HCAHPS question addresses just how closely we are listening to our patients. Getting an *always* response requires that we not just listen, but also demonstrate that we have truly heard what they said and acknowledged how they feel. Of course, this is easier said than done. As caregivers we must balance many patients' needs, so taking the time to consistently listen and seek patient input—to hardwire this behavior—can be a challenge.

In other words, being a good listener doesn't happen automatically. It requires intentional effort and constant diligence. Yet it is an essential skill worth mastering.

...And the Tactics That Make "Always" Responses More Likely

Following are some new approaches to key Studer Group® tactics that you may already be using. It's impossible to focus on too many tactics at once. That's why we suggest you start with the first three key tactics, then add the others (which are also impactful) after the first three are hardwired. The idea is to perform the "fundamentals" of these tactics while you also demonstrate to patients that you are actively listening to them.

Tactic 1: Individualize Care for Each Patient

As care providers, we recognize that patient anxiety can adversely impact the healing process. Therefore, we are constantly looking for ways to alleviate it—as well as to improve our patients' ability to engage in their own care, understand their care plan, and understand what to do once they return home. This leads to improved quality of care *and* perception of care.

Of course, "care" is a subjective term. That's why Individualized Patient Care, or IPC, is so valuable: It helps us understand exactly what excellent care means to each patient. As we discussed in Chapter 3, it requires care providers to frequently check back in with patients to ensure that we truly are meeting their needs. That's the very heart and soul of careful listening!

Here are helpful hints:

Prepare for your visit before entering the room. Organize what you want to communicate and what you need to accomplish with the patient.

Use the name the patient prefers to be called. Demonstrate that we have listened to his or her preferences or ask if you are unsure.

Remove any distractions. Ask to turn off the television and pull the privacy curtain.

Start the conversation on a personal note. Connect with the person, not just the patient. Assuming that the patient approves, put individualized information on the communication board, such as

"I love the Cowboys." This allows staff members to notice the patient's interests and interact accordingly with him or her.

Recap patient responses and concerns. One of the most effective ways of demonstrating that you are listening to the patient is to recap important aspects of the conversation.

Sit at the bedside whenever possible. Research indicates that sitting down increases the patient's perception that you're listening, as well as her perception of the time you spent with her. Make every effort to be at eye level. Look patients in the eye and smile. Patients are seeking physical cues, so make sure yours are reassuring and positive.

Stay on topic. When the patient provides input, you can be a good listener by making comments about the same subject. If you change the topic suddenly, she may think you were not listening. If the patient asks a question, your answer can demonstrate you were paying attention.

Consider cultural sensitivities. Each culture has its own set of expectations regarding communication. When you are interacting with patients from cultures different from your own, try to be aware and accommodating of these variations. It may be helpful to know the demographics of your community and review the cultural needs of the different groups. Also, be aware of your own biases. The key is to not let them get in the way of what others have to say. Try to fully understand the person and her context versus relying on just your personal experience to guide her.

Recognize the impact of family. Remember to listen to these individuals and include them in the patient's care. This is also an opportunity to thank the family members for their support.

Avoid finishing the patients' thoughts or sentences. It diminishes what they're trying to say and tells them that you are waiting to talk more than you are listening.

Tactic 2: Use Key Words to Demonstrate That You Are Listening Carefully

Key Words at Key Times (KWKT) are generally used to explain the care we are providing. They are most commonly used to explain why we are doing something in a way that the patient will understand. They can also demonstrate to patients that we are carefully listening to them. Here are some examples.

To show a patient or family member that you are considering what they say as you plan their care:

"Mrs. Jones, as I was listening *to you talk about your husband's pain, it occurred to me that we might try repositioning him more frequently. How do you feel that would work for him?"*

To show a patient that your note-taking does not mean you are not listening, but rather ensuring that his information is well documented:

"Mr. Jones, it's very important that you have a say in your care. As we talk, I will be listening and taking notes, so I can enter them into your record and share them with everyone else who is caring for you. Putting this information into the computer will make certain the care team knows what is important to you and how you are progressing."

To clarify a patient's statements and gain more information by asking probing, open-ended questions:

"I've heard you say several times how nervous you are about going home. Can you tell me more to help me understand what is causing you to worry?"

Tactic 3: Patient Communication Boards (Whiteboards)

This is an effective tool to show evidence of listening—but only if we update the information and use it as a reference to ensure that the patient-specific information has been heard and the patient's needs addressed.

Make sure every shift reviews with the patient the list of individualized needs written on the communication board and updates it as needed. For example, we may know a patient is extremely hard of hearing and we need to always be on the patient's right side where she hears well. Putting this information on the communication board and using it accordingly demonstrates that we have listened and are ensuring the entire care team will also be aware of the patient's specific concerns or needs.

Additional Tips and Tactics

Once you've hardwired the previous tactics, you can start implementing others that will improve your results even more. The following tips and tactics will help improve your listening skills and your patient's perception of feeling listened to.

Tactic 4: Hourly Rounding®

This tactic is very versatile, so you will find it mentioned consistently throughout the book. In the case of using Hourly Rounding® as a tool for listening, we must remember that every time we interact with a patient, we have the opportunity to assess their needs.

We listen to what the patient says. We listen to what their body is telling us. We listen to what their lab work says. So it stands to reason that Hourly Rounding is a great opportunity to show patients that we are listening to them. Staff should be prepared to listen to the patient with each interaction, assess, and respond.

More overtly, the specific Hourly Rounding behaviors that have a direct influence on listening are performance of the Ps, additional comfort measures, and closing key words such as "Is there anything else I can do for you before I go?" Each of these behaviors provides the opportunity for messages to be sent and received and needs to be accompanied by careful listening.

Tactic 5: Bedside Shift Report

The Bedside Shift Report (BSR) is a powerful opportunity for careful listening. Two to three times a day, two nurses provide undivided attention to a single patient and his or her family. The sole purpose of this exchange is to ensure that we have met the patient's clinical quality and safety needs.

When properly executed, this best practice is more of a conversation between the offgoing nurse and the patient, with the oncoming nurse listening in. Yet the offgoing nurse needs to listen carefully as well. If both nurses have listened effectively, both will come away from this exchange well prepared to continue to meet and exceed the patient's needs.

The conversation could sound something like this:

Offgoing nurse: *"Mr. Jones, can you tell Sharon [the oncoming nurse] what we have been working on today to progress your diet?"*

Mr. Jones: *"We started out with just ice chips but I was starving, so I tried some clear liquids. The apple juice tasted best. I got a little nauseated because I think I drank too much too fast so then I tried sipping a little every five minutes. That really worked well. This afternoon, I had some popsicles and 7-Up and those were just fine, so I had some crackers about an hour ago and those were good too. I think I am ready for some food."*

Offgoing nurse: *"That's exactly right, Sharon. His orders are to progress to normal diet as tolerated, so I would advance him to a soft diet for dinner, and if he does okay, he can have a general diet tomorrow."*

Oncoming nurse: *"So, Mr. Jones, if I heard you correctly, after your crackers you have not had any nausea?"*

Mr. Jones: *"Right."*

Oncoming nurse: *"Fantastic. I'm glad to hear things are going so well. Solid food, here we come!"*

As this exchange demonstrates, Bedside Shift Report is an effective "listening post." It's a great opportunity to not just make sure we've listened carefully to patients, but to make sure they realize we've done so. BSR can be a powerful relationship-builder between caregivers and patients.

Tactic 6: Nurse Leader Rounding

Dynamic by design, Nurse Leader Rounding (NLR) allows you to shift focus as necessary when addressing various aspects of quality and care initiatives. In this case, we want to use it as a listening post in and of itself. Therefore, regardless of the questions we choose to ask patients and families, we need to be sure nurse leaders are demonstrating all the active listening skills described earlier.

In addition, we can also use NLR to see if patients and their families have felt listened to and if we have been successful in our approach with other strategies. Some insightful questions that might be included are:

Nurse leader: *"Mrs. Jones, yesterday you described to me in my rounds that you were concerned about the lack of responsiveness to the call button. I heard you loud and clear and I would like to know if things have improved since we talked."*

Patient: *"Oh yes! They have been right here. I hate to complain but they have done really well since we talked."*

Nurse leader: *"Wonderful. I appreciate your bringing it to my attention. We want to exceed your expectations. I just want to be sure you feel listened to."*

Using nurse leader rounds to validate the key behaviors the team is focused on as they care for the patient demonstrates active listening and ensures good follow-through. This powerful tactic addresses a variety of needs. Listening more carefully to our patients and families is, of course, a deeply important one.

Tip: Manage Pain

This book includes an entire chapter dedicated to strategies to improve pain. Still, it's important to mention here the relationship between pain and how a patient feels about whether we are listening to their needs. Certainly, if we have not done everything we can to address the patient's pain from his perspective, or at least offered some improvement in his pain control, he will not feel listened to.

Through active listening, we can indicate to patients that we understand their pain issues and they will understand what we're doing to help.

All of the tactics identified in this chapter will provide a solid platform of communication with an emphasis on careful listening. When they are executed well, your patients will feel well cared for because they know that they are being heard and that their concerns are being addressed. By using careful, intentional, and active listening with our patients, we are able to build trust and strengthen our relationships with them.

We should also acknowledge that clinicians listen just as much with our eyes as we do our ears. We must not only hear the spoken messages but be tuned into those subtle but important non-verbal cues patients and their family members send. Many times, these messages communicate with more honesty than the verbal ones. A patient may say she is not in pain but the grimaced facial expression and clenched fist may tell a different story. We must be prepared to "listen" to all the messages our patients communicate.

Listening carefully is a cornerstone of our responsibility to our patients. It is our way of saying, "Your perceptions, opinions, and well-being matter to us. We want to hear how you feel, what you need, and what we can do to better serve you." The ability to send this message, and mean it, is a big part of what it means to be a healthcare professional.

Tools & Resources

Studer Group offers a variety of tools and resources that support the tactics discussed in this chapter. To access the most up-to-date offerings, as well as to see what's new in healthcare, please visit www.studergroup.com/HCAHPS.

CHAPTER SIX:

UNDERSTANDABLE EXPLANATIONS

The HCAHPS Question: During this hospital stay, how often did nurses explain things in a way you could understand?

Healthcare terminology can be as confusing to patients as texting lingo is to the typical grandparent. We use a lot of large words, clinical phrases, and acronyms that make perfect sense to us, but to patients, family members, and other industry outsiders, they come across as an inexplicable flavor of "alphabet soup."

This is true of most industries, of course. In ours, however, the customer is often sick, distressed, and frightened, so we have more reason than most to try to avoid exclusionary language. Not understanding what the caregiver is talking about can leave an already-anxious patient feeling very alienated. Taking the time to explain our actions to patients and their family members in a way they understand helps alleviate stress and makes it more likely that they will partner in their own care.

When patients understand the *what* and *why* behind the care they are receiving, they feel better about the process. And obviously, when they have a thorough understanding, they are more likely to comply with our directives.

Of course, the patient is the only one who can determine whether an explanation is understandable. Too often it just isn't. We've all heard, "Well, I told her three times about that already!" from a frustrated staff member. Clearly, we need to do a better job of not just "telling" the patient, but making sure she truly gets the message.

As you will see, a big part of helping patients understand comes down to patience and compassion on the part of the caregiver. By helping staff members empathize with the patient and her stress level, we will improve the patient's perception of what we're striving to communicate.

...And the Tactics That Make "Always" Responses More Likely

Before we get into the specific tactics, we'd like to discuss a technique that applies to all of them. We call it DNS (Describe, Narrate, Summarize), and it's an extra measure that helps ensure patients get what you're trying to tell them.

No doubt about it: The explanations caregivers provide patients can often be pretty complex. Layer on top of that complexity a good dose of anxiety, not to mention the effects of medication, and you can see why fully grasping the message might be difficult. The following three steps can ensure that you are giving good explanations:

1. Describe what you are going to do before you do it.

2. Narrate the care again while you are doing it.

3. Summarize what you have just done.

While this may sound repetitious and cumbersome, it is actually just what the doctor ordered. It greatly increases the likelihood that our explanations will penetrate the anxiety and medication effects that keep patients from comprehending our information. (The "tell 'em three times" strategy has been used with great success by teachers, journalists, and others who have to convey important details in an easy-to-understand manner.)

Here is a simple example of this based on a medical assistant's walking a patient from the reception area to the exam room:

"Mr. Jones, it's good to see you again. Thanks for being so prompt with your appointment time. My name is Sharon and I'll take you back and get you ready for Dr. Smith's exam. On our way back, let me explain what you can expect. We will get your weight and blood pressure and I will check the accuracy of your medications. We'll also discuss what brought you in today so I can make some notes to prepare Dr. Smith.

"Please have a seat on the exam table and we will get started. (The medical assistant will now repeat each of these as she

completes each task.) Mr. Jones, let me get your blood pressure. Okay, now let's review your medications....

"Well, Mr. Jones, I have completed everything we talked about. I have your weight, blood pressure, medications, and the notes for Dr. Smith. He will have these when he comes in, which should be in about 15 minutes, but if it is longer I will keep you updated. Do you have any further questions or need anything before I go?"

Following these tips on a regular basis as you use each of the strategies identified in this chapter will help you be more effective in transferring important information to patients.

Organizations coached by Studer Group® find that the following tactics have the most impact on helping providers explain care to patients in a way they understand.

Tactic 1: Implement Hourly Rounding®

The first and most obvious way to increase patient understanding is to make sure we have Hourly Rounding® framework in place. This is actually one of the most often missed opportunities to have patients understand the promise we are making—*to provide safe, effective care that proactively seeks to address their needs.*

We need to explain up front to patients what Hourly Rounding is and what they can expect from it. This is essential to creating a reliable system that patients and families can trust.

The Hourly Rounding framework places us at the patient bedside every hour. When we perform the behaviors appropriately, we help ensure that patients are getting their needs met and their questions answered. The behaviors that influence explanations most are:

- Behavior 1: Opening key words—we can target key words in AIDET® and highlight explanation.

- Behavior 2: Perform scheduled tasks and ensure that we narrate those so the patient knows what we are doing and why.

- Behavior 3: Environmental assessment of the room—be sure to narrate this so the patient knows that you are assessing whether the call light is in reach and the safety of their environment.

- Behavior 4: Closing key words—these can include asking if there are questions, concerns, or anything they didn't understand.

Tactic 2: Focus on the "E" in AIDET®

When used properly, AIDET® is a valuable tool for helping nurses meet the criteria required for positive responses to all three HCAHPS questions in this composite. A focus on the "E" will yield significant impact on the "understandable explanations" question.

Here are some tips as you focus on the "E":

Be aware that AIDET is scalable. AIDET doesn't need to be implemented all at once. You have the option of focusing on one letter at a time. To improve patient response to this particular HCAHPS question, focus just on the "E." If you are already using AIDET, you may want to pay particularly close attention to how you are explaining the care.

"Good morning, Mr. Johnson. I wanted to share with you what to expect when you go to radiology later this morning. The transporter is going to take you down on a gurney. Your physician ordered a test called a CAT scan. This test requires no needles. You will simply lie still in a large tube-like machine. The test will last only about 15 minutes if you lie still really well. You'll probably be gone from your room for about 45 minutes by the time we count the transport time back and forth and getting you checked in and ready in their department. Now, when you come back to the room, you'll be able to have lunch. We'll get that ordered. What questions do you have for me regarding this test?"

You'll note that this example not only explains what is going to happen, but also seeks to alleviate worries that we know patients typically have—for instance, the fear that needles may be involved and the concern that lunch may be missed. Not only are we showing compassion, we're reducing the patient's anxiety so that he will be more able to process what we're telling him and comply with what we need him to do.

Narrate the care you are providing. As you are caring for the patient, explain what you are doing and why. You are already mentally noting these items. Simply saying them out loud will greatly ease your patient's worry and increase his understanding of the care you provide.

- Wrong: *As you walk into the patient room, the IV alarm is going off. You walk over to check the monitor. Shut it off. You check the bag and see it is full. Then you say, "All right, I'll check back in a little bit."*

- Right: *"Hi, Mr. Rodriguez. I know this alarm can create concern but it is doing its job. Let me check a couple of things quickly for you. The bag looks full and your IV site looks good. Sometimes when you bend your arm like that, the flow gets disrupted and that causes the alarm to go off. Everything looks okay, so let's just reset this alarm. What questions do you have for me before I leave? Great. I'll check back in an hour to see how you are doing. Is there anything I can do for you now? Thank you."*

Again, we're anticipating patient concerns and relieving them.

Tactic 3: Use Bedside Shift Report

Although details vary from facility to facility, successful implementation of this tactic provides a real-time exchange of information that increases patient safety (including fewer medication errors), improves quality of care, increases accountability, and strengthens teamwork. It also reaffirms what is important to the patient at every shift change and reduces end-of-shift overtime for your nurses.

The Bedside Shift Report not only makes the patient feel more informed, she hears that she is being listened to and feels that she is a part of her care. She also gains confidence in her care providers by hearing them discuss her care.

One note of caution: If bedside report merely involves two nurses standing at the bedside sharing the usual array of clinical jargon at one another, while the patient lies silently by, you may actually be increasing her confusion and anxiety rather than alleviating it. Staff must involve the patient in this conversation. They ensure that they are speaking in terms the patient understands, that they urge the patient to describe the care herself as often as possible, that they use Teach Back methods to validate understanding, and that they ask clarifying questions of the patient and family members.

Tactic 4: Nurse Leader Rounding

In Nurse Leader Rounding, there are several opportunities to validate that the patient and family have received explanations in a way they can understand.

The first can simply be to focus on information that is presented on the patient communication board (whiteboard) and ask some key questions to ensure the patient has fully understood it. We can also ask if they have been told about various aspects of the care process such as use of the board or the benefits of Hourly Rounding.

Some examples of questions that could be asked:

"Have you received any information from the staff that you have not fully understood or that needs clarifying?"

"Hourly Rounding is an important quality framework for the care we provide. Did anyone share with you what Hourly Rounding is and why it is so important?"

"I see the information on your communication board about your pain. Has this information and how we use it been explained to you? Has that been helpful to you?"

Once again, Nurse Leader Rounding is a valuable tool for ensuring that the strategies we put in place are effective and having the expected impact on patients and their families.

Tactic 5: M in the Box[SM]

Many of the organizations we coach use and recommend this communication strategy, which increases compliance with explanations of medication and conversations about side effects. This best practice is described in detail in the Fundamentals chapter. It's a great example of how simple it can be to provide excellent explanations—even on subjects that can have serious health implications.

Being able to provide understandable explanations is a skill that's non-negotiable for nurses. Please make sure your staff masters it and works to become better and better.

Indeed, it is our hope that the tactics throughout this Nurse Communication section will help your staff make deeper, more meaningful connections with patients. It is impossible to overemphasize the clarity and thoroughness with which nurses and, indeed, all staff members must communicate. These are the interactions by which many patients will judge their entire hospital stay. And, of course, how well these critical staff members communicate directly connects to the quality of care patients receive.

Tools & Resources

Studer Group offers a variety of tools and resources that support the tactics discussed in this chapter. To access the most up-to-date offerings, to see what's new in healthcare, and to download a worksheet that will help you create a plan to improve patient perception of care in the "Nurse Communication" arena, please visit www.studergroup.com/HCAHPS.

SECTION TWO:

DOCTOR COMMUNICATION

The name of this section, which is also the name of the HCAHPS composite it explores, contains the word "Doctor." However, we'd like to say up front that the suggestions in this chapter also apply to physician extenders such as physician assistants and nurse practitioners (even if we don't mention them by profession every time). These men and women diagnose and treat patients in much the same way as doctors, and thus they have the same opportunities to impact quality and perception of care.

First things first: When we as an industry seek to help physicians become better communicators, we need to let them know why. And we need to not only be clear on why this issue matters *to them*—obviously, providing excellent care is at the top of the list—but also make them understand that there is room for improvement.

If asked, many physicians say they are communicating well with their patients. In reality, though, fewer than

20 percent of them have been trained on how to communicate with patients.[1]

The Accreditation Council for Graduate Medical Education recommends that physicians become competent in five key communication skills: (1) listening effectively; (2) eliciting information using effective questioning skills; (3) providing information using effective explanatory skills; (4) counseling and educating patients; and (5) making informed decisions based on patient information and preference.[2]

The HCAHPS survey provides them with a valuable opportunity to get feedback from patients about their perception of the care they receive. It can also provide a great incentive to move the results upward. Data shows that when HCAHPS performance improves, so do clinical outcomes and patients' relationships with providers.

Healthcare leadership can partner with physicians to support their efforts by providing education and tools to help them be successful. In fact, improving the HCAHPS Doctor Communication composite requires positive collaborative relationships between operational leadership, physicians, and the clinical care team. These respectful, trusting relationships will lay the foundation for a physician's willingness to partner in the tactics covered in this section of *The HCAHPS Handbook*.

The good news is that these tactics don't add more work to physicians' already-jam-packed schedules. Instead, they help physicians improve their efficiency and effectiveness and maximize the impact of work they are already doing. In addition to saving valuable time, better physician-patient communication skills also improve:

- Patient and physician satisfaction
- Clinical outcomes
- Treatment adherence/patient compliance
- Patient self-management
- Diagnostic accuracy

Physicians care about all of these benefits. That's why it's a good idea to help them connect back to the *why* as you help them master these tactics.

Following is a story that demonstrates the importance of patient/physician communication. It shows how getting to really know a patient can greatly impact clinical outcomes.

Roger had been a patient of mine for 10 years and was in regularly for blood pressure checks. He was a very quiet man. In order to draw him out and ensure I was getting the complete picture, I would always ask if there was anything else I should know to help care for him. By asking probing questions, I was making a conscious effort to get to know him better, and I'm glad I did.

During one visit as we sat and talked, I noticed he was a bit more hesitant than usual. As it turned out, his hesitation was masking a troubling symptom. After some time, Roger felt comfortable enough to share that he was having rectal bleeding. (My gut reaction was to think: I've been his physician for 10 years. Shouldn't I be the first person he called when these symptoms started? *Of course, I immediately reminded myself that when scary symptoms appear, it's natural for people to go into avoidance mode.)*

It turned out Roger's father had experienced the same symptoms when he was about Roger's age—and his diagnosis had been terminal. Roger was certain his prognosis was the same.

Building from our earlier relationship, I was able to talk to Roger a bit more. I wanted him to know I felt empathy for the loss of his father, understood his worry, and wanted him to be completely tested as soon as possible to figure out exactly what was causing this symptom. I listened carefully. I assured him that I had time to hear and discuss all his concerns and questions.

I am happy to report that Roger is here and fine today. The bleeding was caused by polyps that were able to be surgically removed.

I am thankful I spent a bit of extra time with Roger and engaged myself completely in the conversation. It could have been different, and Roger could have walked out anxious and thinking there was no hope. Had I not been able to convince him to act quickly, the next time I saw him those polyps could have turned into the cancer Roger was so worried about.

Knowing Roger as a person made all the difference.

- Barbara Loeb, MD

Stories like these happen every day—and not just with patients who have known their doctor for years. It's very important for doctors to fully engage with their patients.

The manner in which a physician communicates information to a patient is as important as the information being communicated. It influences all sorts of outcomes including emotional health; symptom resolution; function; pain control; and physiologic measures, such as blood pressure level or blood sugar level.

When doctors communicate well, patients are more likely to acknowledge health problems, understand their treatment options, modify their behavior accordingly, and follow their medication schedules.

Research has shown that effective patient-physician communication can improve a patient's health as quantifiably as many drugs—perhaps providing a partial explanation for the powerful placebo effect seen in clinical trials. [3, 4, 5, 6]

It stands to reason that the vast majority of physicians *intend* to be effective communicators. But for all their good intentions, many of them are not. Consider Figure ii.1, which compares physicians' perspectives of their own communications with patients' perspectives of those same communications.

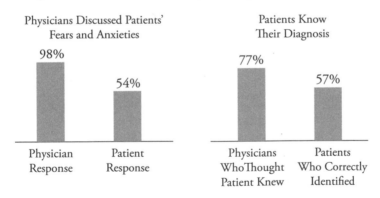

Recognize Differences in Patient and Physician Perspectives

Physicians Discussed Patients' Fears and Anxieties
98%
54%
Physician Response
Patient Response

Patients Know Their Diagnosis
77%
57%
Physicians Who Thought Patient Knew
Patients Who Correctly Identified

Percentage of Respondents Who Answered Yes

Figure ii.1

In the study depicted in Figure ii.1, 98 percent of physicians thought they had discussed patients' fears and anxieties, while only 54 percent of those same patients agreed. Likewise, 77 percent of physicians thought their patients knew their diagnosis, but only 57 percent of the same patients could correctly identify it. Clearly, physician perception is *not* always reality.

When we contemplate this data, it becomes clear why we need to focus on the quality of physician communication—and perhaps why our clinical outcomes are not where we want them to be. Our HCAHPS results can serve as the eye-opener we need to motivate us to improve our processes and skills.

A physician needs good communication skills at every phase of the patient encounter. This chart summarizes what they look like in action.

Communication and Phases of the Encounter

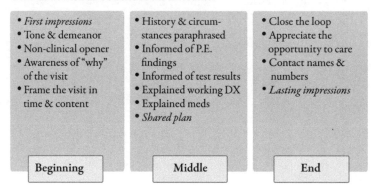

Figure ii.2

When we understand how best to leverage particular skills at each phase of our encounter with patients, we can see the path to better results.

Of course, all physician/patient communication must be paired with a healthy dose of empathy, which is an important subject we'll discuss later in this section. Physicians and others need to constantly seek to convey that powerful unspoken message that says: "I understand what you are going through, I care about your well-being, and I want to make your stay as comfortable as I possibly can."

In the following pages, you'll learn more about how to build the kind of engaged physician/patient relationships that lead to outcomes like the one in the story at the beginning of this section.

The Survey Questions

This aspect of the HCAHPS survey asks patients about care received from doctors at the hospital. Answers are given in frequency scale: *never, sometimes, usually,* or *always.* The percent of patients who responded *always* is publicly reported on this composite at www.hospitalcompare.hhs.gov.

1. **During this hospital stay, how often did doctors treat you with courtesy and respect?**

2. **During this hospital stay, how often did doctors listen carefully to you?**

3. During this hospital stay, how often did doctors explain things in a way you could understand?

This section is divided into three chapters, each based on one of the questions in the HCAHPS Doctor Communication composite. Each chapter shares two to three specific tactics that positively impact the likelihood that patients will answer *always* to the respective question.

As with other chapters in this book, these do not contain a "laundry list" of all possible tactics. Rather, they convey a few carefully targeted specific actions you can take to immediately impact patient perception of how well your doctors communicate. We've also included some tips you can use to further improve once the main tactics are hardwired.

CHAPTER SEVEN:

DOCTOR COURTESY
AND RESPECT

The HCAHPS Question: During this hospital stay, how often did doctors treat you with courtesy and respect?

Patients have come to assume quality care. In fact, it has been demonstrated that the principal predictor of patients' perception of quality has little correlation to objective clinical quality markers. Patients' rating of quality is more predicted by their rating of the quality of communication between the healthcare team and the patient.[1]

In other words, Core Measures probably don't differentiate one hospital from another in the eyes of most patients. Rather, effective communication is what separates the good from the great in today's consumer healthcare marketplace. Certainly, communication with doctors—courteous, respectful communication that conveys empathy—is a key piece of this picture.

Yet hospitals often fail at high-quality communication even when providing high-quality care. Consider the following statistics:

- Seventy-five percent of patients admitted to the hospital were unable to name a single doctor assigned to their care.[2]

- A study found that 91 percent of patients want to be addressed by name and 78 percent of patients wanted their physician to shake hands. While physicians seem to be doing a good job with the handshaking (the study found they did so in 82.9 percent of visits), they use the patients' name less than 50 percent of the time during initial encounters.[3]

- Communication is one of the root causes in *more than 63 percent of The Joint Commission sentinel event occurrences.*[4]

Take a closer look at the second statistic in this list. Addressing a patient by name shows that you respect him. Shaking his hand is an act of courtesy. Clearly, patients crave and deserve courtesy and respect—and they notice whether physicians provide it or not.

The rising premium on delivering effective communication with patients can be demanding and at times frustrating for physicians. Much of that frustration comes down to the reality of compressed time and patients' expectations. This is understandable. Yet what physicians need to realize is that improved communication doesn't have to add a lot of time to patient visits. Best of all, it can make them more impactful and yield better clinical outcomes.

The patient-centered model—characterized by patient involvement and inclusion in clinical decisions—is how care will be delivered going forward. Patient-centered communication skills, including those that specifically convey courtesy and respect, can optimize the physician-patient relationship. When doctors master these skills, patients feel more at ease and are more engaged; therefore they listen more closely, therefore they are more likely to comply, therefore they enjoy better outcomes.

As the volume of patients physicians must see continues to increase—due to our nation's aging population, marketplace changes related to the ACA, hospital mergers, and other factors—great communication skills are more vital than they've ever been. Indeed, HCAHPS "doctor" questions are becoming a transparent verification tool for critically important physician behaviors.

Finally, while this HCAHPS question focuses on doctor courtesy and respect, we need to remind ourselves that communication is not just a doctor issue. Nurses and other care providers also impact responses to this question (much in the same way that ancillary employees impact the Nurse Communication results). There is plenty that nurses and other care providers can do to boost the patient's perception of the physician, and we'll discuss some of these issues in the next several pages.

...And the Tactics That Make "Always" Responses More Likely

As always, there are a few actions to consider even before we address the tactics that are foundational for courtesy and respect. Behaviors matter, and just as we outlined in the Nurse Communication chapters, it is vital for physicians to follow your organization's standards of behavior and use the nine factors of engagement.

Members of the medical staff also generally have a written credo or code of conduct that establishes expectations for behaviors during their interactions with patients and team members. (This is in addition to the hospital's standards of behavior.) These must be respected and coached, and providers must be held accountable for adhering to them.

Tactic 1: Strengthen Nurse/Physician Relationships

The way nurses and providers interact says a lot to a patient. If a patient detects a disjointed connection between members of her care team—for instance, if a nurse says something like, "The consulting doctor didn't know you were going home today," or, "Your doctor didn't tell me that"—the patient feels anxious and stressed. On the other hand, when the chain of communication is unbroken, she feels soothed and confident. She feels that she is being well cared for by a strong team.

A collaborative relationship will put patients at ease. When such a relationship is in place, patients feel the atmosphere of teamwork and respect that results. Nurses are able to better keep patients informed because the doctors have kept *them* informed. This creates a safer environment for patients as well.

Here are a few proven tips on fostering good nurse/physician relationships to communicate respect:

- **Foster two-way communication.** Effective communication between caregivers can strengthen a collaborative approach to care and prevent negative patient outcomes. Two-way communication demonstrates teamwork and respect for the nursing assessment and critical thinking skills.

- **Have nurses round with physicians.** Nurses can truly impact the perception of teamwork between themselves and physicians by rounding *with* physicians on their patients. The team then participates in the collaboration with the physician and can reinforce the communication in later patient teaching opportunities.

  At a minimum, it is helpful for the nurse to share his observations and assessments in a quick huddle with the doctor prior to rounds. This ensures the physician has the latest information and demonstrates teamwork to the patient.

- **Use a consistent framework for communication.** When the conversations do not convey critical components or provide information needed to make decisions, the implementation and the results may fall short.

Many hospitals have adopted the evidence-based SBAR model to communicate important messages. It is highly adaptable for all-important conversations that require a decision to be made and an action to be taken. SBAR is an acronym in which S = Situation, B = Background, A = Assessment, and R = Recommendation. While it is only a framework, it does help communicate messages in a consistent and reliable way. Physicians will appreciate this, and patients will feel like a collaborative team cares for them.

Tactic 2: Encourage Members of the Care Team to "Manage Up" Each Other

We can show courtesy and respect to our patients by sharing positive information about their other care providers. The subtle message to patients is "You are worthy of the best care and the best care team." Managing up takes very little time and is proven to reduce patient anxiety and improve perception of care.

An added benefit is that patients will often share these positive comments with other staff members. For instance, a patient will say to a nurse, "Dr. Jones mentioned that he is always confident and comfortable with you as his patients' nurse." Managing up can change the environment and help create a collaborative and cooperative team that works together to take great care of patients.

Here are examples to show how each care provider can manage up the other:

Nurse manages up physician: "Ms. Kind, I see Dr. Jones will be visiting you today. He is one of the best physicians at this hospital. He has been practicing for more than 20 years and has an excellent reputation."

Physician manages up nurse: "Ms. Kind, you are fortunate to have Florence as your nurse. Her clinical judgment and assessments are a real asset to our team. I feel comfortable knowing she is caring for you."

Here are some additional examples on how to manage up in circumstances when it can be challenging:

"Mr. Woods, Dr. Jones will be making rounds tomorrow at 6 a.m. I know this is early, but he is going into surgery and wants to make sure there is no delay in your care. He is one of our finest surgeons, as you know from your own surgery."

"Dr. Jones has a wonderful physician assistant who rounds early in the morning. She will usually review all the tests and have them ready for Dr. Jones to review with you when he comes to see you around noon. They make a great team and together provide excellent care."

"Mrs. James, I know you wanted to take a shower, but I just saw Dr. Jones, and he will be making his rounds soon. I know you will want to talk with him about the questions you wrote down, so perhaps you can wait to take your shower until after he rounds so you don't miss the opportunity to speak with him personally."

"Mrs. Jones, I apologize but Dr. Smith was just called to do an emergency C-section at the hospital. We will have to reschedule your appointment. While I know this is inconvenient, I also know you

would want him to be available for you if the need arose. Thank you for understanding."

Tactic 3: Focus on Acknowledging the Patient and Introducing Care Providers (the "A" & "I" of AIDET®)

AIDET® was introduced in our Fundamentals chapter and has the same application and relevance for use by providers. Here are a few tips that help underscore the relevance and dynamic ways providers can use this with their patients.

A—Acknowledge: Greet patients and establish a positive first impression.

I—Introduce: Introduce yourself to patients while describing your role in the patients' care and the experience you bring.

D—Duration: Keep the patient informed on wait times, admission length, test turnaround times, therapeutic effect, or symptom resolution.

E—Explanation: Provide patients with information on treatment, medications, diagnosis, and therapy options.

T—Thank You: Thank patients for trusting you with their care and closing the clinical encounter.

As we discussed at the start of this section, more than three-quarters of patients admitted to the hospital are unable to name a single doctor assigned to their care.

Of the remaining quarter who were able to give a name, only 40 percent of those patients were correct. This is a real shame.

What's more, with the increased use of hospitalists, there's good probability that the physician caring for the patient in the hospital will not be the physician who's treated him or her for years. Focusing on the "A" and "I" of AIDET will not only help make a stronger personal connection, but it will give the patient confidence in his or her new care provider.

The way a physician greets the patient and introduces himself (and his specialty or role in the care) will set the stage for every encounter. Done properly, it will demonstrate courtesy and respect as well as expressing empathy for the patient. This, in turn, will put the patient at ease and make him comfortable enough to partner in his care.

This is especially important in the inpatient setting where a patient may meet several doctors, including hospitalists, consultants, residents, and even student doctors.

Some examples:

- Physician: *"Mr. Werner, my name is Dr. Cooper. Your primary care physician, Dr. Roberts, and I work together often. He asked me to do an assessment of your breathing today. My specialty is Pulmonology and that means I deal mostly with patients who have trouble breathing or issues with their lungs. I have been doing this for 10 years. My experience with this is why Dr. Roberts asked me to see you. Let me tell you a little about the assessment, and I'll share the results with Dr. Roberts by the end of the day."*

- Nurse (visiting after Dr. Cooper's visit): *"Hello again, Mr. Werner. I'm Kate, and I'm stopping back to see how you are doing. I see Dr. Cooper has come in. He is one of our best specialists in dealing with your condition. Dr. Roberts refers to him frequently. What questions can I answer for you or what questions do you want to write down for when the doctors visit you tomorrow?"*

Following are additional strategies that will help physicians achieve optimal patient-physician communication. Some of these connect directly to AIDET. Others indirectly support the communication framework. All of them go a long way toward helping us meet our commitment to treat patients with empathy—saying, in effect, "I understand how you feel and I want to make this experience as easy for you as possible."

- **Describe your exact role in the care of the patient.** The average patient can encounter nearly 30 care providers following surgical admission and 20 providers in a medical case. The absence of clear introductions to patients and families can instill confusion and anxiety and can diminish trust.

- **Communicate experience and expertise.** Patients want to know that a physician has experience and that they are in competent, expert hands. If a physician explains that he has been caring for patients with similar conditions for 15 years and has treated thousands of them successfully, it reassures the patient. Not only is the patient's anxiety certainly reduced, but he also feels respected because the physician took the time to share this information with him.

- **Ask permission to begin an exam or assessment.** In any other setting, it would be considered rude to invade a person's space and especially to touch him. It is a clear sign of respect to ask the patient for permission to begin the exam. Then, to make the patient comfortable, narrate the exam. Let the patient know the *what* and *why* behind the exam. And, tell him the results of the physical exam when possible (i.e., "This looks normal.").

- **Sit whenever possible.** Sitting conveys to the patient that you have some time to spend. Patients perceive the amount of time a physician spends with them as an indicator of respect. Research has shown that patients involved in seated interactions overestimated the time providers spent performing exams by an average of 1.3 minutes.[5]

While the patient may perceive the time spent as longer, this alone will not compensate for other communication gaps, such as interrupting and closed body language. There is also evidence that shows that some patients assess physicians as being more compassionate when they sit at the bedside, especially when sharing bad news.[6]

Ultimately, when physicians and other care providers implement these strategies, quality and the patient experience improve together. Courtesy and respect, built on a foundation of empathy, can be extremely powerful forces. As individuals *we* want to be treated with courtesy and respect. Making sure our patients receive the same type of care from the men and women they've put their trust in is simply the right thing to do…and it must be a cornerstone of our mission.

Tools & Resources

Studer Group offers a variety of tools and resources that support the tactics discussed in this chapter. To access the most up-to-date offerings, as well as to see what's new in healthcare, please visit www.studergroup.com/HCAHPS.

CHAPTER EIGHT:

CAREFUL LISTENING BY DOCTORS

The HCAHPS Question: During this hospital stay, how often did doctors listen carefully to you?

Listening counts. It counts even more than having access to the latest technology and most sophisticated equipment. It is through carefully listening to what the patient is saying that we provide the best care and create meaningful patient/physician relationships. Plus, to connect back to the subject of the last chapter, it's a marker of courtesy and respect. In order to demonstrate those qualities, we must be willing to listen to what the patient has to say.

Yet it's clear that some physicians, like other health-care professionals, need to work on their listening skills. According to Dr. Jerome Groopman, author of *How Doctors Think*, physicians interrupt their patients within 18 seconds of the start of the conversation. Imagine how patients feel when this happens. They surely don't feel listened to, they don't feel respected, and they probably assume the physician isn't hearing the symptoms they're describing.

It just makes sense that careful listening leads to good diagnoses, good treatments, and good outcomes. And the converse is true as well: Doctors who don't listen carefully tend to have less than desirable outcomes (and less than satisfied patients).

Listening and empathy are intertwined. When we listen to our patients, we are more likely to understand how they feel. This creates a powerful connection that, in turn, builds trust. And when patients trust us, they are more likely to comply with their treatment plans, which means they are more likely to experience better clinical outcomes.

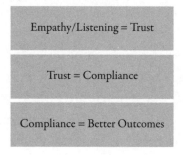

Consider the following evidence graphics. In Figure 8.1 we see that as HCAHPS results in the Doctor Communication composite decrease, the prevalence of poor adherence to medications increases.

We know that listening is a very strong influencer of results in the Overall Communication composites (both

Doctor and Nurse). It makes logical sense that when we improve our listening skills we are better able to identify concerns or barriers that keep patients from adhering to their medication regimens. Thus, we are able to help patients address these barriers and improve their overall outcomes.

Medication Adherence

For each 10-point decrease in HCAHPS Doctor Communication rating, the prevalence of poor adherence to medications increased.

Compared with patient offering higher ratings, patients had poorer adherence when they gave healthcare providers lower ratings:
- involving patients in decisions
- understanding patients' problems with treatment
- eliciting confidence and trust

Source: Communication and Medication Refill Adherence; The Diabetes Study of Northern California; Ratanawangsa, N. MD, et al

Figure 8.1

Obviously, when patients don't adhere to medication treatment, their clinical outcomes suffer. Figure 8.2, depicting the results of a Studer Group analysis of publicly reported data, shows that the likelihood of poor glycemic control increases as HCAHPS Doctor Communication results decrease.

Hospital Rating for Doctor Communication

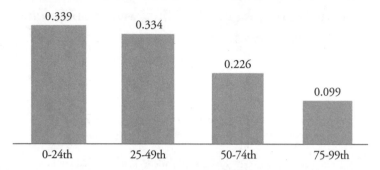

Manifestations of poor glycemic control (per 1,000 medical and surgical discharges) by Hospital Rating for Doctor Communication

0.339 0.334 0.226 0.099

0-24th   25-49th   50-74th   75-99th

Hospital Rating for Doctor Communication

Figure 8.2

The information here demonstrates that when doctors listen well they are likely to capture information from the patient, family, and other members of the care team that reduce the incidence of poor glycemic control. For example, let's say a patient's blood sugars have been high since hospitalization and the patient states, "At home I usually eat breakfast at 5 a.m., and since I have been here they make me wait until 8 a.m." What seems like a minor detail—the patient complaining about the timing of his meals—actually has implications for the care plan as well as for the patient's outcomes, since the meal time is also directly attached to the timing of his insulin dose.

Being able to listen for those kinds of details can enhance both the quality outcome and the patient experience. The converse, of course, is also true: Poor listening skills on the part of physicians can have very real negative consequences for patient health.

Beyond the clinical quality and patient experience impact of these strategies, poor execution can harm the reputation and financial well-being of healthcare providers and the organizations that partner with them.

One study found that some of the most common reasons cited for malpractice claims are that providers[1]:

- Didn't listen

- Didn't return phone calls

- Showed little concern or respect for the patient's condition

- Were rude

- Didn't spend enough time

- Didn't answer questions adequately

It's no coincidence that "didn't listen" appears at the top of the list. You'll notice, also, that all of the other complaints are related to poor listening as well. Physicians have the same obligation as nurses to use both eyes and ears to take in all the messages our patients and their families send to us if they are to perceive caregivers as good listeners.

...And the Tactics That Make "Always" Responses More Likely

Studer Group® examined the evidence we have gathered via research in our Learning Lab and identified some tactics that have the most impact on improving patients' responses to the "doctors listen carefully" HCAHPS question.

Tactic 1: Practice Reflective Listening (Paraphrasing)

Reflective listening, also known as parallel talk and paraphrasing, is a critical physician skill. It involves paying close attention to what you are hearing so you can repeat it back to the speaker. When you practice this skill, you convey to the patient that you are listening and that you care about getting the story right.

Reflective listening can accomplish all of the top six attributes patients want in physicians[2]. These attributes are listed in order here. Essentially, patients are saying *I want my physician to:*

1. Treat me with dignity and respect

2. Listen carefully to my health concerns

3. Be easy to talk to

4. Take my concerns seriously

5. Be willing to spend enough time with me

6. Truly care about me and my health

Here are a few tips for using reflective listening:

- **Pay attention to your tone of voice.** Take a few deep breaths to calm your pace prior to talking with patients. Slow down and use a calm, even tone. You'll come across as unrushed and interested. One study found voice tone alone could differentiate no-malpractice claim surgeons from high-claim ones. High-claim surgeons were judged to be dominant, fast-paced, and less concerned for patients compared to no-claim surgeons[3].

- **Use open-ended questions.** Open-ended questions are designed to encourage full, meaningful answers using the patient's own knowledge and/or feelings. These inquiries allow physicians to gather as much information as possible. For example, if a patient comes in with chest pains, the physician would say, "Tell me about your chest pain." A closed question would be, "Where exactly is your chest pain?" which pulls only limited information from the patient.

- **Follow the two-minute rule and establish Sacred Time (described in Chapter 4).** Allow the patient to talk for at least two minutes uninterrupted. Maintain eye contact for 80 percent of the encounter. This takes practice—it is very difficult to allow someone to talk for two minutes uninterrupted. But it is an important habit to master when you're striving to listen carefully. When providers allow this time, the information gleaned is usually very insightful, and in many cases, will further the accuracy and the efficiency of the overall exam.

- **Paraphrase with key words.** Key words are phrased to evoke a predictable positive impression. Here are some examples of key words to demonstrate listening:

  ○ *"I want to make sure I heard you correctly..."*

  ○ *"As I was listening to you, it occurred to me that we might need to..."*

  ○ *"Let me see if I understand..."*

Tactic 2: Demonstrate Empathy

Physicians certainly feel empathy for their patients, but in a hurried environment they may not always come across that way. In fact, one study found that, without training, doctors took advantage of less than 10 percent of the opportunities to convey empathy[4].

When a patient believes you feel her pain, so to speak, she also believes you are hearing her. The two go hand-in-hand.

As Figure 8.3 demonstrates, one study found that providers with high empathy scores have better clinical outcomes than other providers with low results.

Physician Empathy

"Our results show that physicians with high empathy scores had better clinical outcomes than other physicians with lower empathy scores."

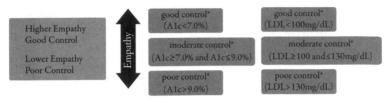

Source: *Thomas Jefferson University, Physician Empathy Directly Associated With Positive Clinical Outcomes in Diabetic Patients*

Figure 8.3

The expression of empathy is a conscious behavior. The physician who chooses to seize an empathic opportunity can make a critical difference in a patient's perception of him. It can lead a patient to think, *Wow, this physician cared about me, listened to me, and treated me with respect!*

Let's say, for example, that a patient who had a big summer trip planned comes in with chest pain and finds herself in the ICU with an acute MI. After gathering the patient's history, the physician might just acknowledge the patient's personal situation: *"I'm so sorry you are here and not enjoying that fun vacation you planned. I'm sure this must be really, really tough. We're going to do everything we can to take care of you."*

Demonstrating empathy takes virtually no time, and it can make a big difference in the patient's perception of whether the physician is listening. When opportunities aren't seized, the patient thinks, *That doctor didn't care about me as a person. He didn't listen to a thing I said.*

Empathy diffuses tension and fear. It says, *I understand. I care.* Empathy creates the space for the comfort in asking questions. Questions promote dialogue. And dialogue promotes a better understanding of the patient's real concerns and expectations and leads to increased compliance with physician orders.

A few tips for showing empathy:

- **Imagine yourself in the patient's shoes.** As you listen, place yourself in that person's situation. You'll naturally want to make her feel better. (Remember, empathy is all about understanding and sharing the feelings of others, so this strategy makes perfect sense.)

- **Say, "I'm sorry."** You can't always understand exactly what a patient is experiencing, but you can always tell her you are sorry she is in that situation, feeling this pain, or experiencing such loss.

- **Actively listen.** Completely engage yourself in listening. Practice the 60/40 rule: Listen 60 percent of the time and talk 40 percent. Hear the words but also try to feel the emotion the patient is showing. Be aware of the non-verbal signs she is showing.

- **Offer help or a suggestion.** Put the patient at ease with key words that offer a solution or at least move her toward a solution. *"I am so sorry you are spending your birthday in pain in the hospital. Let me start by helping to reduce the pain you are feeling."*

- **Recognize the impact of family.** Due to pain and medication effects, family members often act on a patient's behalf. Remember to listen to them and include them in the patient's care.

Sometimes it feels like listening—*really* listening—is a lost art. The same is true of showing empathy. The good news is that the two can go hand-in-hand—and doctors are in the perfect position to practice both. When we listen and show empathy, we not only build stronger relationships with our patients, we gain clues that help us provide proper diagnoses and better care.

Tactic 3: Collaborate with the Rest of the Care Team to Maximize Listening

The nurses on the care team will already be using a variety of strategies to enhance their ability to listen. As partners in this process, physicians can enhance their effectiveness by being aware of those tools and supporting their use with patients and families. For example, doctors making rounds on patients will notice whiteboards in the rooms bearing important patient information. Responding to and referencing this information says to the patient, "We are all listening and working together to meet your needs."

Physicians can also support the nursing staff's execution of Hourly Rounding® and Bedside Shift Report. Both are effective listening posts, and when a physician can manage up their importance, it helps ensure open participation by the patient. For example, a doctor might say to his patient: "*Sharon, I see you are doing better today. That must be because your nurse is Faye. I have worked with Faye for years. She is excellent at managing pain and I see by your communi-cation board you are reducing the frequency of your pain medication. Is that right? Well, I know the staff round on you hourly to check that your pain is managed so it must be working!"*

Tactic 4: Manage Pain

Just as we discussed in the nursing chapters, pain management is critical to a patient's perception of our listening. If the reason the patient came to us was illness that is causing pain and we have not fully or adequately addressed that pain, he will not perceive that we are listening to his concerns. We will discuss pain in great detail in a future chapter, but for now, consider the following tips:

- Remind patients and family members that you are listening to what they say and taking it into account as you plan care: *"Mrs. Jones, as I was listening to you talk about your husband's pain, it occurred to me that we might try repositioning him more frequently. How do you feel that would work for him?"*

- Explain why you are taking notes. When visiting a patient, it is highly likely you will need to document what he or she is saying. However, the patient may perceive your notetaking as a sign you are not lis-tening. Use key words to explain why:

"Mr. Simmons, as we talk I may look down and take notes to document the points you are making and what is important to you. It is very important to me that you have a say in your

care and that you stay as comfortable as possible. I am taking notes to be sure that I capture everything. I am listening to you."

- Recap patient responses and concerns. One of the most effective ways of demonstrating that you are listening to the patient is to recap important aspects of the conversation. For example:

"Let me recap our discussion about your pain and our plan. I heard you when you shared that your abdominal pain was rated at 5 to 7. Given it is two days after surgery and you have not yet had a bowel movement, your pain is likely gas pain. Our plan will be to add a laxative and stool softener as well as to increase your activity. I want you to walk at least three to four times a day around the unit for at least two or three laps. I am changing your pain medication to one that is less likely to cause constipation and I think that will also help you get more comfortable. Are you in agreement and comfortable with this plan? What questions do you have for me?"

The research is clear: Careful listening creates trust, and gaining trust with patients can make the difference in their health status. As physicians do better with communication, outcomes improve. That's really the only "call to action" we need to take steps to ensure that our patients are truly heard.

Tools & Resources

Studer Group offers a variety of tools and resources that support the tactics discussed in this chapter. To access the most up-to-date offerings, as well as to see what's new in healthcare, please visit www.studergroup.com/HCAHPS.

CHAPTER NINE:

DOCTOR EXPLANATION
OF CARE

THE HCAHPS QUESTION: During this hospital stay, how often did doctors explain things in a way you could understand?

Being in the hospital is often a deeply confusing experience. Patients are sick or injured, in pain, and anxious. They're out of their normal environment and routine, which in itself can be disorienting. Their mental state may be affected by medications. Add to this diminished capacity the fact that they're probably unfamiliar with medical terminology and processes and it's easy to see why patients have a hard time grasping what physicians are trying to tell them.

It's no surprise, then, that studies show too many patients are not processing the information they need to get well.

One Mayo Clinic study suggests that 58 percent of patients discharged from the hospital don't know their own diagnosis. Another study states that "a substantial number of hospitalized patients do not understand their care plan. Patients' limited understanding of their plan of care may adversely affect their ability to provide informed consent for hospital treatments and to assume their care after discharge."[1]

The quality of information patients receive and the level of understanding they have regarding their diagnosis and treatment plan can improve adherence to treatment regimens. And nonadherence is an area that desperately needs improving.

"The Challenge of Patient Adherence," a 2005 *Therapeutics and Clinical Risk Management* article, describes the problem this way:

"Patient nonadherence (sometimes called noncompliance) can take many forms; the advice given to patients by their healthcare professionals to cure or control disease is too often misunderstood, carried out incorrectly, forgotten, or even completely ignored."[2]

The article goes on to detail the costs of nonadherence:

- Yearly expenditures for the consequences of nonadherence have been estimated to be in the hundreds of billions of U.S. dollars.[3]

- Estimates of hospitalization costs due to medication nonadherence are as high as $13.35 billion annually in the U.S. alone.[4]

- In addition to the most obvious direct costs, nonadherence is also a risk factor for a variety of subsequent poor health outcomes, including as many as 125,000 deaths each year.[5]

- One large study of over 2,500 patients found that nearly one third had marginal or inadequate health literacy. Of these, 42 percent misunderstood directions for taking medications on an empty stomach, 25 percent misunderstood the scheduling of their next appointment, and nearly 60 percent were unable to read and understand a typical informed consent document.[6]

These findings certainly provide a strong call to action for all of us in healthcare to improve the way we educate patients about their conditions and treatment. Physicians, of course, have an especially vital role to play.

This HCAHPS question gives physicians an opportunity to see *how well* we are explaining our care to patients in a way they understand. It is a frequency question (possible responses are *never, sometimes, usually,* or *always*) that reflects *how often* doctors explained things in ways patients could understand.

Of course, the answer we want to achieve is *always*. When we *always* make sure patients understand their diagnosis and treatment, we *always* give them the best chance to recover once they leave the hospital.

...And the Tactics That Make "Always" Responses More Likely

Following are some tactics that will help improve outcomes in this area:

Tactic 1: Use Physician Notepads

These notepads are given to patients so they can write questions to the doctors or nurses. They're a great example of how the simplest of tools (paper and pen) can have a huge impact. Not only do they help patients feel informed and included in their plans of care, they serve as a visual representation to both patients and families that we invite their questions and involvement.

Here's how physician notepads work: As he is reviewing the care plan for the day, the nurse asks if the patient has any questions for the doctor. The nurse then writes the questions down on the notepad and asks the patient to add more questions as she thinks of them. (If the patient is incapacitated, a family member is encouraged to write the questions.)

When the doctor rounds on the patient, she can ask, "What questions do you have since I saw you yesterday?" Then they can review the questions together. If the nurse has already answered a question, it can be crossed off but left on the notepad, so the doctor can see what it was. As the nurse rounds on patients, he can use the notepads as a vehicle for managing up the physician. For example:

"Ms. Garrido, I see that Dr. Lee was here this morning. Was she able to answer all of your questions? That's good. She does such a nice job of using these notepads to ensure you feel comfortable asking questions."

Tactic 2: Focus on the "E" in AIDET®

As we've already discussed, AIDET® is an acronym that represents the framework for effective communication with patients. It has been proven to not only improve the patient experience but also to positively impact clinical outcomes. AIDET alleviates anxiety and makes patients more likely to comply with medications and treatment regimens and follow the recommendations of their care providers after they leave the hospital. What's more, this level of solid communication goes a long way toward creating patient loyalty.

Organizations get great results when they focus on key elements of AIDET in order to drive outcomes in specific areas. If data analysis indicates the question with the most opportunity for improvement is the explanation of care, the obvious choice would be to zero in on the "E."

Explanation involves providing patients with information on treatment, medications, diagnosis, and therapy options in ways they can understand. Explaining clinical information to patients is at the core of quality and safety. In the following pages, we will articulate tips specific to explanation regarding diagnosis and treatment. (In a later chapter we will go into more depth on the "E" as it relates to medications.)

Explaining the Diagnosis and Treatment

Conveying a clear *explanation* of the diagnosis and treatment will help patients partner in their care and improve their perception that their physicians have explained things in a way they understood. It will also help maximize patient compliance and create more positive outcomes.

Here are some tips physicians can use to better explain diagnoses and treatments and gain patient partnership in their care plans:

- **Provide the diagnosis and treatment information in a clear, logical order.** Provide the information in the following order with clear transitions:

    1. Share the diagnosis OR what you are attempting to clarify or rule out.

    2. Share the recommendations for treatment.

    3. Share the expected clinical course of the condition.

    4. Explain what the patient needs to do.

    5. Address symptom management.

- **Share the name of the diagnosis.** Patients want to know what they have. Let them know the name and write it out for them. If you are not certain, then provide a list of possibilities based on presenting symptoms and exam findings. By the way, it's equally important to mention serious diseases they *don't* have to relieve the "worst case scenario" many patients are already imagining.

- **Use language the patient understands.** Medical terminology is acceptable but must also be followed by a clear explanation of *what the terms mean.* Use appropriate terms; avoid jargon. If you are talking about side effects, say "side effects." (Too often, physicians just say, "Look for this," or, "Call me if this happens," rather than actually calling the symptoms side effects.)

- **Let him know about diagnostic testing.** If there is a list of diagnostic possibilities and further information is needed to clarify the diagnosis, physicians should explain this in detail. Explain the nature of the test, what will be done, what specifically is being looked for. Let the patient know how long the test will take, if it will be noisy, if there will be pain, or if it may be uncomfortable. Give him as much information as possible to prepare him. Don't forget to share how long it will take for the results to come back.

- **Share the recommendations for treatment.** Provide a clear summary of the treatment plan. Let the patient know what will happen next. What tests are needed? What are you looking for or ruling out? Are there any appointments or other physician consults? Be clear and thorough.

- **Share the clinical course of the diagnosis.**
  Patients want to know what they should expect.
  They will need to know the timing of a therapeutic
  improvement and if and when things will get better.
  Patients value this information, even if it isn't what
  they want to hear.

- **Share the information several times.** We often need to hear information several times to gain
  a complete understanding and retention. Share
  it *multiple times* and *in multiple ways*. Use the Teach
  Back method to check for understanding (see the
  next point), and if questions persist, approach the
  information in a different way. It may trigger a new
  question from the patient that will help gain his
  compliance in his care.

- **Check for understanding.** Of course, you'll
  want to explain in a way that aligns with a patient's
  education and intellect. Use Teach Back methodology, such as "I have given you a fair bit of information today. Would you mind telling me what
  you understand about this illness?" You'll be able
  to evaluate if the patient has effectively understood
  what has been shared; if not, explain again.

- **Get commitment to adhere to the treatment plan.** Patients need to be partners with their
  providers and that means making sure they agree to
  uphold their end of the deal. Before a patient leaves
  your office or you leave his hospital room, ask, "Are
  you comfortable with the plan of care I described?
  What questions do you have?" The way the last

question is worded is important because it will elicit a deeper thought process than some other similar versions of the questions such as "You don't have any questions, do you?" or "Do you have any questions?" Then say to the patient, "Will you please repeat back to me what you will do to care for yourself after you leave the hospital?" When human beings promise out loud to do something, we are more likely to actually follow through with it.

- **Give patients a central location for important information.** Some of Studer Group's highest achievers keep a folder at the patient bedside. This simple tool will go a long way toward helping patients keep track of their medications and all the information they have received. This folder can be an excellent reference tool for the patient when a nurse makes her post-visit calls to his home.

Tactic 3: Provide a "Patient Care Card"

This card should include a simple explanation of the condition, self-treatment responsibilities, and side effects or symptoms to look out for. The earlier in the hospital stay you can give this information to the patient, the better. Encourage her to read and highlight information she doesn't understand (or may need to reference later) so it can be discussed and clarified.

Divide the patient care card into four sections:

1. Diagnosis/Condition

2. Possible Side-Effects

3. Treatment Plan/Self-Treatment Responsibilities

4. Future Course of Action

Patient Care Card

Patient Care Card	
Diagnosis:	Treatment Plan/Self-Treatment Responsibilities: 1. 2. 3.
Symptoms/Side Effects of Associated Medicines:	Future Course of Action: Follow Up Appointment:

Figure 9.1

When a doctor focuses on providing a thorough explanation of diagnoses, the plan of care, and medications, his or her patients are more likely to understand their conditions and their own roles in treating them. This will lead to better compliance and better clinical outcomes. Plus, it will give patients a more favorable impression of the physician—and most likely, by extension, your hospital.

Once you put the tactics you've learned in this section into place, not only may your HCAHPS results improve right along with patient care, your entire staff is likely to enjoy stronger, more rewarding relationships with your physician partners. And that will benefit your organization in immeasurable ways.

Tools & Resources

Studer Group offers a variety of tools and resources that support the tactics discussed in this chapter. To access the most up-to-date offerings, to see what's new in healthcare, and to download a worksheet that will help you create a plan to improve patient perception of care in the "Doctor Communication" arena, please visit www. studergroup.com/HCAHPS.

SECTION THREE:

RESPONSIVENESS OF STAFF

W e are a time-oriented society. How long things take matters, and we have become accustomed to getting our needs met quickly. Drive-thru restaurants, Google searches for information, overnight Amazon deliveries. You name it, when we want or need something, we want it quickly. When we perceive an urgent or emergent need, our expectations rise even further.

It is that perspective that patients and families bring to their perception of whether we meet the intention of this composite. When we understand the relative importance of responsiveness and how patients will perceive it, we can better understand what gets in the way of doing it well.

A study by Deitrick and Associates examined problems related to answering patient call lights in acute inpatient care settings and found that the most frequent concerns of patients were:

- Delays in getting call lights answered

- Variation in the call light response time from a low of less than a minute to a high of 20 minutes

- The amount of time it took to handle the patient's request once the light was answered

- The patient's request not being fulfilled once the call light was answered

Frustration over delays in answering call lights is one of the most frequent comments that patients make.[1]

We suspect that none of that is a surprise. Those are the same general complaints anyone would have when needing any service. That said, at the end of every call light request is a potential risk or emergency. So the need to respond quickly could have life-or-death consequences in some cases.

According to another study, the primary reasons for patient-initiated calls are (1) pain medication and management (the most often identified reason), (2) bathroom assistance, (3) intravenous problems or pump alarm, (4) personal assistance, (5) accidental pressing of the call light, and (6) repositioning or transfer.[2]

Take a look at Figure iii.1. It shows conclusively that the better organizations perform on responsiveness, the better the clinical outcomes will be. While this data demonstrates this connection for falls, the same trend applies to all Core Measure data available, such as CLABSI rates, pressure ulcers, etc.

Falls and Trauma Decrease as Responsiveness of Staff HCAHPS Rating Increases

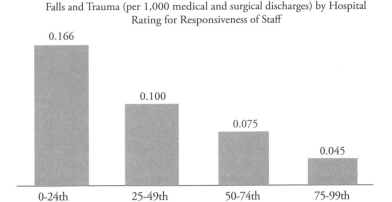

Falls and Trauma (per 1,000 medical and surgical discharges) by Hospital
Rating for Responsiveness of Staff

Hospital Rating for Responsiveness of Staff

Figure iii.1

Finally, a *Journal of Nursing Care Quality* article by HM Tzeng and CY Yin has shown that when the average response time to call lights are longer, the patient satisfaction scores are lower.[3,4,5] It's as simple as that.

Now, here is another interesting chart. The data in the following Figure iii.2 demonstrates that there are important correlations not only between HCAHPS results and quality metrics but also between results in various HCAHPS composites. In this case it is clear to see the relationship between the Responsiveness and Doctor and Nurse Communication composites. When Responsiveness results go up, so do Nurse and Doctor Communication results...and vice versa. (Much like the "chicken or the egg" debate, no one has definitively determined which comes first.)

Relationship between Communication and Responsiveness of Staff Ratings

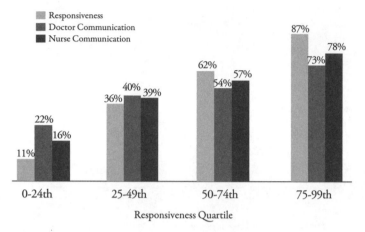

Figure iii.2

Remember that one of the questions relating to both Nurse and Doctor Communication centers on courtesy and respect. This makes perfect sense. Any patient who is not getting her needs met in a "responsive" fashion will very likely feel that we don't respect her nor will she likely feel listened to. When you respect someone, you listen and respond to her needs.

As leaders prioritize their action plans, it should be reassuring to know that if we perform well in one composite, it will likely have a positive impact on others.

Consider the following scenario that illustrates the influence Nurse Communication has on Responsiveness:

A patient (let's call him "Eric") has been experiencing intermittent alarms from his IV pump all day. Each time the alarm went off he would press the call light button and wait for a staff member

to arrive. Several minutes later a nurse would silence the annoying alarm without discussion and walk back out of the room. He assumed that if something were wrong the nurse would share it with him, so he did not ask any questions.

That evening Eric was introduced to a roommate (previously he had been in the room alone). What had started as mere annoyance now turned into anxiety. As nightfall set in, the IV alarm began to seem extraordinarily louder. His anxiety over the alarm was exacerbated because of the fact that it now impacted another patient as well.

Eric rang for the nurse again, feeling that the wait was forever and the jarring sound just kept getting louder. Why does this thing keep alarming? *he fretted.* Why does it take them so long to respond? Why don't they figure out how to keep it from happening again? Why, Why, Why? *In the midst of his turmoil, the staff finally came in and pushed the alarm to silence it—again without much investigation—and, not wanting to further interrupt his roommate, Eric chose not to address it.*

Later the next day, a nurse leader was rounding in her unit and asking patients how promptly staff members were answering their call lights. The patient responded that it took a while on the night shift when he rang his call light button because his IV alarm was beeping and he hated that it would wake up his roommate. When the nurse leader asked how long it took for the staff to respond, he answered, "I don't know, but it beeped 156 times."

The patient was actually counting the alarms. When the nurse leader timed it out, she found that the patient had actually waited about eight minutes—but you can imagine how slowly that eight minutes passed for a patient lying in the dark worrying about the impact the noise was having on someone else.

Why Don't We Respond to Call Lights?

Many nurse leaders work very hard to implement specific behavioral and process changes to improve results. They're puzzled when execution is less than desired. Often, this is because leaders have not addressed some underlying attitudes that staff may have. In the case of Responsiveness—specifically as it relates to call button response—it helps to look at some research.

A recent study by *Health Services Research* found that although the majority of the staff (79 percent) agreed that call lights were meaningful, only 49 percent of the staff members perceived that call lights mattered to patient safety and required nursing staff attention. What's more, 53 percent of nursing staff thought that answering call lights prevented them from doing critical aspects of their role.[6]

Nursing staff's perceptions about the nature of calls varied across hospitals. Junior staff tended to overlook the importance of answering calls. A nurse participant tended to perceive calls as more likely requiring nursing staff's attention than a nurse aide participant.[7]

Answering calls should not be perceived as preventing staff from performing the critical aspects of their role. Rather, it should be considered meaningful and a high priority. We need to share research with our staff that underscores this point.

Consider this study, for example: The University of Michigan School of Nursing found that patients were more satisfied with nurses' responsiveness when they perceived that nurses often answered call lights in person, that their problems were resolved after pushing the call light, and that their call lights less frequently involved safety issues.[8]

When we understand the attitudes and perceptions that keep staff from answering call lights, we can begin to change them. We can help people "connect the dots." And when they know the *why* behind what we're asking them to do, they're far more likely to do it.

In order to ensure timely response to call lights, it is helpful to have as many resources as possible participate in assisting the patient with these needs. It may not always fall solely to nurses and nursing assistants. In many cases ancillary departments can help. Later we will address some ideas on specifically how to manage this, such as a "No Pass Zone."

When the nursing staff and ancillary departments work together to respond quickly to patient needs, it's a combination that can't be beat. And the winner is the patient.

Before we get into specific tactics, consider the following story that was shared by a nursing director as she rounded with a nurse:

We went into this young man's room. His name was Akeem and he was about 26. His nurse Candace introduced me and explained that we were rounding together.

"Tell us a little about how your day is going," said Candace.

"Well, it's been pretty good," he responded.

"Just pretty good—it's not excellent?" Candace pressed.

"Oh no, no, it's been excellent."

"Why is that?"

"I gotta tell you, I don't know what's going on in this hospital, but this is my second time here," said Akeem. "Last time, I got taken care of, but it's so much different now. When I hit my call light, it's almost like they know I am going to hit it because they are in the room right away. It's like they have ESP."

(It should be noted that Studer Group had helped the hospital implement Hourly Rounding®—which we'll discuss further in Chapter 10—in the interim between Akeem's first and second stays.)

"That's good. Who's been so good to you?" asked Candace.

"Josh."

"Why is that?"

"Well, because he comes in and checks on me every hour like clockwork, and he tells me what is going on. It's almost like déjà vu. Like I said, before I even hit that light, in comes Josh to check on me."

"It sounds like we have been very responsive and keeping right on top of things," noted Candace.

"Absolutely!" the patient beamed.

It was clear Akeem felt cared for. The key? Responsiveness. We were able to immediately let Josh know the difference he was making.

—Shawnda, Nursing Director

The Survey Questions

This aspect of the HCAHPS survey asks patients about their perception of the responsiveness of staff during their hospital stay. Answers are given in the frequency scale: *never, sometimes, usually,* or *always.* The percent of patients who responded *always* is publicly reported on www. hospitalcompare.hhs.gov.

Screening Question: During this hospital stay, did you need help from nurses or other hospital staff in getting to the bathroom or in using the bedpan?

1. **How often did you get help in getting to the bathroom or in using a bedpan as soon as you wanted?**

2. **During this hospital stay, after you pressed the call button, how often did you get help as soon as you wanted it?**

This chapter does not cover all possible tactics. Rather, it conveys a few carefully targeted specific actions you can take to immediately impact patient perception of how well your hospital staff responds to their needs.

CHAPTER TEN:

BATHROOM ASSISTANCE

THE HCAHPS QUESTION: How often did you get help in getting to the bathroom or in using a bedpan as soon as you wanted?

Imagine that you are a patient lying in bed and you have to use the restroom. How long will you wait, wondering when someone is going to come in and help, before you take the risk and try it on your own? Patients will eventually take risks to get to the restroom when they need to go badly enough.

When they take these risks, serious injuries can occur—injuries that adversely impact clinical outcomes and, obviously, patient perception of care. What's more, such injuries are financially costly.

Between 700,000 and 1 million patients fall in hospitals each year, according to the Agency for Healthcare Research and Quality. While the majority of patients who fall are not seriously injured, the toll of fall-related injuries is hefty. The Joint Commission reports that the average increase in a hospital's operational costs for a serious fall-related injury is more than $13,000, and the patient's length of stay increases by an average of 6.27 days.[1]

It's true that Medicare has not reimbursed hospitals for these costs for some time. But now, as a result of the Patient Protection and Affordable Care Act, hospitals failing to meet certain hospital-acquired condition (HAC) performance criteria (including falls) will be subjected to a new reimbursement penalty. By statute, the HAC reduction program will impose a 1 percent reduction to total inpatient payments for hospitals that rank in the lowest-performing quartile of hospital-acquired conditions.

Of course, cost is not the primary concern. Most healthcare organizations have missions that center on providing the best possible care—and putting patients in a position where they feel they must take risks is antithetical to that mission.

...And the Tactics That Make "Always" Responses More Likely

Through partnering with organizations across the country, we at Studer Group® find that the tactics that follow have the greatest impact on patients' perception that they received help as soon as they wanted it.

Please note that while this question focuses specifically on bathroom assistance, these tactics will overlap with those of the call button assistance chapter. From the patient's perspective and hopefully yours as well, it's all about responsiveness.

Tactic 1: Ask Open-Ended Questions During the Bedside Shift Report

The Bedside Shift Report is a great opportunity to reassess and engage the patient in regard to how the staff is responding to her bathroom needs. The offgoing nurse asks the patient to report to the oncoming nurse what kind of assistance she has had over the last shift by asking engaging, open-ended questions:

"Tell Sheila, the oncoming nurse, how we are doing in helping you to the bathroom as you need it or if there is anything we need to do differently during her shift."

"Is there anything else you would like Ryan to know about how he can best help you with your bathroom needs?"

Also, be sure to schedule extra coverage around peak times, or at minimum raise awareness of the staff to stay vigilant about bathroom needs during peak times. Bedside Shift Report is designed to assist with this issue during shift change, but there are other times of the day that need this focused attention, such as mealtimes and bedtime. Identify staff to address bathroom needs, answer call lights, and respond to patients' needs during these times.

Tactic 2: Use Hourly Rounding® to Be Responsive to Bathroom Needs

We already know that Hourly Rounding® can have a powerful impact on many components of the patient's perception of quality care. As presented in the Fundamentals chapter, Studer Group's national call light study discovered that when participants implemented Hourly Rounding, they were able to reduce call lights by 38 percent. This rounding model places the emphasis on proactively meeting patient needs rather than providing care in a reactionary mode.

In other words, Hourly Rounding presents the perfect opportunity to proactively meet patients' needs for restroom assistance and therefore improve call light response. First, make sure staff understand the framework's eight behaviors (including, of course, the third one regarding the Three Ps—Pain, Potty, and Position). Then, follow these tips:

- **Explain to staff members that Hourly Rounding reduces bathroom calls.** At first, it can be hard to realize that this tactic really does save nurses time, so help them connect the dots. Explain that when they address "call of nature" needs proactively, they won't be called into patient rooms as often. Once Hourly Rounding is hardwired, they'll see the difference for themselves, but by emphasizing up front how efficient the tactic is, you can get enthusiastic buy-in.

- **Change your wording when you ask about the "Potty."** Don't ask if the patient needs to go to the bathroom. Instead, tell him you have time to take him to the restroom. This more assertive approach reduces the likelihood that a patient will say no to the question you ask and then 10 minutes later call for help to the bathroom.

- **Be timely in responding to patient needs around getting back from the restroom.** It's not just getting them to the restroom that counts. Getting stranded in the restroom has a negative impact on their perception as well.

- **Work as a team.** Quicker call light response takes teamwork, which negates the "not my patient" syndrome. If you are going to be unavailable for longer than 15 minutes, whether it is at shift change or a need to be in an isolation room, ask a staff member to watch your rooms for call lights. It is a good practice to identify people to cross-cover responsibility and monitor rooms during busy times and formalize a buddy system as part of shift assignments.[2]

- **Keep "bathroom" items within reach.** When performing Hourly Rounding Behavior #5—conduct an environmental assessment of the room—check to ensure that, if needed, urinals or bedpans are within reach of all patients. Many call lights go off because a patient cannot reach a needed item.

- **Implement a check-before-you-go policy.** Ask nurses and staff from other departments to do a bathroom check before they take patients to another location.

"I'm Mike from Radiology. I'm here to take you for an MRI. We are going to be gone for about two hours. Do you need to use the restroom before we go?"

"I know you have several tests scheduled today. If someone comes by to transfer you to these, please let them know you need to use the restroom before you go."

- **During leader rounds, make sure bathroom needs are being met.** Research has proven that leader rounds are key to verifying and validating that a behavior is being done. The leader should actively listen and ask probing questions.

  "It's important for me to know how we are doing at helping with your needs. How many times in the last eight hours or so have you had to use your call light to get help getting up to go to the bathroom?"

- **Set the expectation with the patient.** During the admission assessment, let the patient know that one of the staff members will be checking on him hourly during the day and every two hours through the night. Use key words such as:

  "For your safety, we do Hourly Rounds on this unit. There are several things we check on during these visits. We check your need to use the restroom and your comfort level as it relates to pain and position. We also check to make sure everything you need is within your reach. We check on you so frequently because we don't want you to have to use your call light. If you need something in between our regular Hourly

Rounds, of course we will respond to your call light in a timely manner."

- **Communicate the goals of Hourly Rounding to patients.** Explain to patients that the goal of Hourly Rounding is to be proactive in their care and to keep them safe. This will help the patient to view care as extremely responsive, perhaps even to state, "I never had to wait to go to the bathroom. I never even had to push the call light for help."

- **Use the key words "risky behavior" with both staff and patients.** We have found that this term engages both the hospital staff and the patients. When the purpose of Hourly Rounding is explained as the best way to help a patient avoid a dangerous situation like going to the restroom on his own, staff are more likely to get on board. Using the term "risky behavior" with patients reduces the chance that they will try to go to the restroom on their own and makes them a partner in their care. It also explains the *why*.

"One side effect of your medication is dizziness. Remember, I am going to come by every hour to check and see if you need to use the restroom. While you are on this medication, going to the bathroom on your own can be risky behavior. I want to help you when you need to go, so make sure not to try to go to the bathroom on your own."

- **Combine bathroom needs with medication administration. (This is part of Behavior #2 in Hourly Rounding: perform scheduled tasks.)** Some medications require large amounts of fluid or have a side effect that puts the patient in a less ambulatory state. Be aware of this and address it up front.

"Before I give you these meds, I'd like to help you up to see if you can use the restroom. Here's why..."

Also, remember how the medications work. If you give a diuretic to a patient at 9 a.m., there is a good chance he will need to use the restroom by 9:30 a.m. Make sure and communicate this to all caregivers, so they can proactively address medication effects.

- **Be consistent and build confidence.** If you have been practicing Hourly Rounding and haven't seen your call lights fall and patient perception of care rise, look at your consistency with executing all eight behaviors. If the tactic is not done consistently and fully as prescribed, the patient won't trust that you'll be back when you say you will or you will be leaving out key components that impact your results. In our Learning Lab of partner hospitals, we have found it takes 90 percent compliance or better to have patients consistently believe we are always responsive.

Using the bathroom is, of course, a basic human function, but it can be more complicated than one might expect. That's because it's associated with issues like privacy, sensitivity, cultural norms, age issues, gender issues, and health concerns. When we take away a patient's independence by telling her she must have help using the bathroom because of all the risk factors we have discussed, she may feel anxious, uncomfortable, and embarrassed.

With all this in mind, our obligation is to then be as responsive as possible to offset the impact of all those issues. It is what any of us would want and will most likely eventually need when it is our turn to fill a hospital bed.

Besides, being responsive to patient needs is the right thing to do. We are demonstrating that we understand what is important to them. We are demonstrating that we care. When we practice the tactics that show responsiveness, we can improve quality and ensure that patients, families, and physicians feel great about the care being provided.

Tools & Resources

Studer Group offers a variety of tools and resources that support the tactics discussed in this chapter. To access the most up-to-date offerings, as well as to see what's new in healthcare, please visit www.studergroup.com/HCAHPS.

CHAPTER ELEVEN

CALL BUTTON RESPONSE

THE HCAHPS QUESTION: During this hospital stay, after you pressed the call button, how often did you get help as soon as you wanted it?

Time seems to move much more slowly when you are waiting for something. Have you ever seen family members standing in the patient's doorway with worried looks on their faces? Often these families are acting as call lights. Their daughter or father or grandmother is in the room in pain or experiencing a specific need. The family is concerned and looking for a care provider to help.

Many times, the *actual* call light has been on, and nobody has physically come into the room. Someone might have asked, "May I help you?" from the desk, but nobody has actually addressed the need. Or they talked to their nurse but it has now been 15 minutes and she has not come back with the information they requested.

Meanwhile, the family member's and the patient's anxiety continue to rise.

The call light is a vital patient communication link during hospital stays. In fact, it is one of the few tools patients have access to that let them exercise meaningful control over their care. That's why it's so important to respond to it quickly and in the right spirit—it symbolizes your willingness to communicate and partner with the patient and her family in her care.

There will always be a need for call lights in healthcare. Still, we don't want patients overusing them. That's where tactics like Hourly Rounding® come in. We described this tactic in the Fundamentals chapter and further refined it in several others. In this chapter, where it most intuitively lies as a strategy of success, we will identify why Hourly Rounding becomes so essential to our responsiveness to call button strategy.

We are about to describe several tactics that allow caregivers to improve their response to call lights. However, before we review them, we'd like to share a few important tips to consider.

Create response time goals and hold staff accountable for them. One organization coached by Studer Group® has created the expectation that every call light be answered within two minutes. Every week, each nurse leader posts a list of nurses, along with the number of call lights they are responsible for that exceeded two minutes. The CNO also hosts a weekly meeting with all nurse leaders and reviews the list.

This organization's leaders realize there can be valid exceptions to the two-minute rule, but they are just that: exceptions. If a nurse is consistently taking longer to answer call lights, training is in order.

It's clear that this practice is working. For the last two quarters, the organization has been in the 99th percentile for response to call lights. And call lights are responded to not in two minutes, but in one minute.

How Data Can Help

It's important to know the capability of your current call light system to provide data and reports. Many nurse leaders do not. If you are one of them, it is worth asking your system administrator and product representatives if the system is capable of providing data on frequency of calls and time from call to cancel. Even these basic pieces of information can be helpful in monitoring performance on an overall basis.

In one organization in the southeast U.S., a nurse leader was able to review call light data by individual nurse. She reported each staff person's average number of call lights per shift per week. In the review, it became very clear that some of her staff regularly had very few call lights per shift while others consistently had many.

Therefore, the nurse leader established the Top 10 Club, made up of staff who averaged 10 or fewer call lights per shift per week. In their busy med-surg unit, they consistently had 7-8 nurses with 5-6 patients under their care who met the Top 10 Club requirement. It was also no surprise that those were the staff members who were most frequently recognized by patients and families in the leader's rounds.

In contrast, some staff members were averaging upwards of 40 call lights per shift. The data was a powerful tool for showing staff what can be done. It allowed the unit to begin breaking down how the efficient staff were working so that they could share their "best practices" with others—and so that ultimately, all staff could get the same results.

If you can obtain that kind of valuable data, you too can reevaluate your current processes for call light response, including who, how, when, where, and why. Also, be sure call light response time is incorporated into standards of behavior so the expectation is set for responsiveness.

Don't shortcut the training process. Clinicians don't automatically know how to prevent and respond to call lights. They must be trained in Hourly Rounding as well as in proper standards of behavior for call light response; organizations rarely devote enough time to ensuring that staff understand and can competently perform these tactics. Training should include why this is important, how to accomplish it, what the expectations of performance are, and how success will be measured and validated. It's crucial to provide demonstration of the skill in a skill lab or live demonstration format.

Train all staff to respond to call lights (not just nurses). All staff members—physical therapy employees, radiology employees, transporters, coordinators, housekeepers, and so forth—should be trained to respond to call lights. This means walking into the patient's room, acknowledging the patient, and either assisting (if possible) or letting the patient know the nurse is coming.

When patients press their call button and watch employees walk past their door, again and again, it sends a disheartening message: "Other patients and tasks are more important than you." Of course, this is not true! To achieve *always* on this HCAHPS question, we must take deliberate action to ensure that patients are not kept waiting. The tactics in this chapter will help.

...And the Tactics That Make "Always" Responses More Likely

Once your staff are aligned and thoroughly trained in how to respond to call lights, there are several tactics you can hardwire to help minimize them, and, when they do occur, to keep patients as safe as possible.

Tactic 1: Use Hourly Rounding to Minimize Call Button Use and Impact Responsiveness

Hourly Rounding involves staff (nurses, nurse assistants, and appropriate team members) rounding on patients every hour during the day and every two hours at night. As you've already read, this tactic is the product of a Studer Group study on call lights. It was determined that call lights occurred most often due to bathroom/bedpan assistance, IV/pump alarm, pain medication, monitoring/device alarm, needed a nurse, and position assistance. (Of course, they can also occur because a patient can't reach her phone, book, water, and so forth.)

In addition, call lights can happen just because we said they should. It is not unusual for staff to say to patients, "Call me if you need me." When we say that (with no qualifying key words to make it clear that calls are for urgent needs only), some patients will take us at our word. Imagine your community's 911 operators being inundated with all kinds of calls and questions—about restaurant suggestions or where to take a pet for a veterinarian visit, for instance. If, all of a sudden, the community used the 911 operators like a Google search function, what would happen to the response time of the emergency team? Of course it would decline rapidly.

That is just what occurs when we tell patients to use their call lights for all needs. Suddenly, what was designed to be the hospital's 911 system becomes clogged with non-urgent requests, impacting our overall ability to respond.

This reality certainly contributes to the staff attitude that call lights don't represent essential or critical tasks.

All that said, of course we want patients to feel free to call us if they *really* need us. We want to seem accessible and caring. We just don't want them to "need" us for unnecessary things. This is why it's so important that we meet all of their needs before they have to ask—and that we use key words to make sure we're sending the message that call lights are for urgent needs only.

Hourly Rounding helps provide consistent proactive care by bundling a patient's needs into one visit and setting expectations about frequency of visits. To maximize the impact of this tactic, there are specific behaviors that must occur during each round. These behaviors were developed as a result of the aforementioned Studer Group call light study. (Because this study helped us understand why call lights go off, we are able to recommend behaviors we know prevent them.)

Just checking in on patients every hour is helpful, but you will not see the maximum results until all eight behaviors are hardwired with all staff.

A few tips for implementing Hourly Rounding to minimize call button use and impact responsiveness:

Customize the Ps to reflect the needs or requests of your unit or service line. You read about the Ps in the Fundamentals chapter, but those were developed in our study for specific service lines such as med/surg, orthopedics, and telemetry units. In other service lines, patients' routine needs are different—therefore, in those areas, the Ps need to be customized to reflect the needs of those patients.

For example, in women's services or OB, it is not uncommon to add "supplies" to the list, since often mothers call for more formula, diapers, pads, etc. By customizing the Ps effectively, you reduce call lights, proactively ensure that needs are met, and continue to exceed expectations for responsiveness.

Explain the purpose of Hourly Rounding. Let the patient know that your goal is to be so responsive she doesn't even have to use the call light. For example:

"One of our staff members will round on you every hour during the day because we want to make sure we are meeting your needs before you have to use the call light. Of course we want you to feel free to use the call light if you have a truly urgent need, but you probably won't need to since you know we'll be back in an hour, at the latest."

Setting the expectation of when someone will be back in to check on her helps reduce anxiety. Patients also tend to store small requests they may have if they know someone will come soon.

Share rounding hours with the patient. Many organizations round every hour from 6 a.m. to 10 p.m., then every two hours through the night. Use key words to let the patient know why rounding occurs only every two hours at night. For example:

"I'll be back to check on you at midnight. Remember, at night I check on you every two hours so that I don't disturb you as often and you can get better rest."

Be consistent. If Hourly Rounding isn't practiced every hour, patients won't be confident that someone will round and they will use their call lights. If events prevent a caregiver from being able to round, implement a buddy system so that there is coverage to reassure patients that they are not being forgotten. The staff members who are covering may not be able to do the full scope of the round, but minimally they can inform the patient that their nurse or patient care team will be back on track after they get freed up.

Tactic 2: Create a "No-Pass Zone"

Before we discuss the No-Pass Zone, let's "connect the dots" to a part of Hourly Rounding that can be helpful in creating an environment or culture that makes accomplishing it easier. In our Fundamentals chapter on Hourly Rounding, we discuss Behavior #5—conducting an environmental assessment of the room. As previously discussed, we know that if we look around the patient's space, we can ensure that the items they need within reach are there. This is an important safety strategy.

Behavior #5 is also central to getting ancillary and support staff involved in assisting the clinical team with care. Any staff member who goes in and out of patient rooms for any reason can be trained to do the brief environmental assessment of the room as described in the Fundamentals chapter. (This policy greatly increases the hospital's resources for helping patients keep items close and safety in mind.) At this point, the staff member will (obviously) notice if a call light is going off.

Besides this visual scan, the staff should use the key words, *"Is there anything you need before I go? I have time."* If the patient asks for something beyond the scope of the person's skill set, the staff member should inform a caregiver.

This practice sets the stage for our No-Pass Zone strategy. From here, it's just a hop, skip, and jump to creating a standard that anyone (leader or staff member) who even walks by a patient's room and sees a call light must get involved. No one—and that means *no one*—walks past a patient's room where a call light is going off without going in and offering assistance to the patient or their family.

As you can imagine, when you apply the collective resources of every staff person walking the halls or nursing units during the day and night, you should have excellent response time.

Following are some tips for creating a No-Pass Zone to improve responsiveness to call lights:

- **Use the patient communication board to minimize call light use.** Train staff to update, review, and check the information on the communication whiteboard as they respond to the patient. It will hold clues as to what matters to that patient. Staff can then use that information to provide better care. For example:

"Mr. Smith, I see on your whiteboard that your pain medication is due in the next 30 minutes. I am here to do your physical therapy and it would probably be better if we do it after you have your next dose. How about if I come back in an hour? I will talk with your nurse to be sure she brings that in right on time so we can have a really good session. Now, before I leave, is there anything else I can do to make you more comfortable?"

- **Teach staff this: When a patient seems to be in need, act as if he had hit a call light.** A patient may not be able to hit a call light in physical therapy or in pre-op, but he may still have a need that requires assistance. Proactively offer assistance when a patient—any patient, anywhere—seems to need it. This is a sign of courtesy and respect. If a patient looks like he needs assistance, do not wait to be asked; offer help. If a patient is waiting in physical therapy and can't get help, it will impact his perception of responsiveness by staff overall.

- **Modify and verify behavior standards to account for the No-Pass Zone.** Behavior standards should include "Don't walk past a call light that is going off" and "Staff members are not to say, 'That is not my patient.'" If items like these are in behavior standards, verification needs to occur to ensure that staff members are complying with them.

  Staff should also be trained to politely confront their colleagues who walk past call lights. They will learn to hold each other accountable for this lapse.

To make this positive and non-punitive, come up with a fun way to say, "Remember our No-Pass Zone."

Many hospitals conduct actual audits on the No-Pass Zone. Directors or other staff are assigned to monitor hallways during random hours and note if any staff member passes a call light. Offenders can get a "passing in the No-Pass Zone" ticket for the first two offenses, but after that they get a verbal reprimand from their leaders. There has to be some accountability for this rule to be effective.

Tactic 3: Conduct Unit Clerk Introduction Rounds

This is a very simple strategy that pays big dividends in patient perception regarding both call light response and courtesy and respect. If your hospital has a centralized call system with unit clerks who answer the call lights from the nursing stations, have these individuals round at the beginning of the shift and introduce themselves to the patients by using AIDET®.

"Hi, Mr. Jones. My name is Sara and I am the unit clerk today. Mine will be the voice you hear when you push your call light. I have been on this unit five years and I am here to ensure your safety by getting your call button answered right away. I just wanted to take a moment to help you connect my voice with my face. Thank you and do you need anything from me before I go?"

Most patients don't hit the call light unless they really have to. When they do, it may mean they waited as long as they could or that they tried but just couldn't do or reach something by themselves. More importantly, it may mean a life-threatening emergency. The more effective the Hourly Rounding is, the more likely call lights will truly reflect urgent and emergent needs. You will know this has happened when you start seeing a "drop and run" response by staff to call lights.

Do not underestimate the power of responsiveness. You *can* get to the point where you are not only responding quickly and efficiently to patient needs, but actually anticipating most of them and "heading them off at the pass."

When that happens, you'll reap many more benefits than just improved HCAHPS results. You'll create an organization that's known for great clinical outcomes, engaged and fulfilled employees, and, best of all, satisfied, loyal patients who receive care in a safer environment.

Tools & Resources

Studer Group offers a variety of tools and resources that support the tactics discussed in this chapter. To access the most up-to-date offerings, to see what's new in healthcare, and to download a worksheet that will help you create a plan to improve patient perception of care in the "Responsiveness of Staff" arena, please visit www.studergroup.com/HCAHPS.

SECTION FOUR:

PAIN MANAGEMENT

Imagine living your life in pain. Unfortunately, millions of people don't have to imagine. They are all too familiar with the toll chronic pain takes on not just the body, but also on the mind and spirit. That, in turn, affects perception. No doubt about it: A person in pain is likely to view the same day that others perceive as gorgeous and sunny as grim and depressing. It's not hard to see how this translates to the way they view their care experience.

Pain is a big problem for our nation. More than 116 million Americans struggle with it—more than the total affected by heart disease, cancer, and diabetes combined—according to a 2011 report from the Institute of Medicine. Pain also costs the nation up to $635 billion each year in medical treatment and lost productivity.[1]

With that perspective as a backdrop, you can guess what happens when any of those millions of people in pain is suddenly hospitalized, whether for a condition related to their pain or not. Regardless of what put them in the hospital, their pain will likely be exacerbated by the illness, procedure, or just being out of their normal environments and routines. It will color the way they perceive their entire stay. Yes, for this reason as well as all of the "human" reasons, managing our patients' pain is critical.

The following data shows that hospitals that rank high in pain management also rank high in overall patient ratings:

Relationship Between Patients' Willingness to Recommend and Pain Management Results

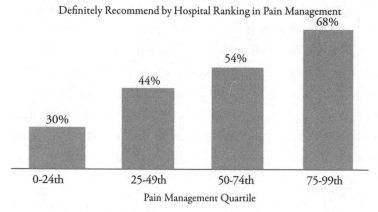

Definitely Recommend by Hospital Ranking in Pain Management

Figure iv.1

Relationship Between Percent of Patients Who Rate the Hospital a 9 or 10
and Pain Management Results

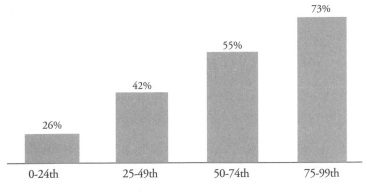

Patients Who Rate the Hospital a 9 or 10 and Pain Management Results

Pain Management Quartile

Figure iv.2

Patients' perception of the quality of pain management is *not* dependent only on the level of pain they are feeling. It can be affected by many factors, including:

- Effective communication with physicians and nurses, which means:

  ○ Being candid about what to expect and keeping patients informed

  ○ Building patient and family partnerships

  ○ Controlling patient anxiety

- Responsiveness, which means:

  ○ Discussing patient preferences

- Developing pain goals and a plan; using whiteboard to show next scheduled medication

• Empathy, which means:

- Patient must believe that staff is doing everything they can to help with pain

Let's take a look at a couple more graphics that provide evidence for the connection between pain management and communication:

Relationship Between Nurse Communication and Pain Management Results

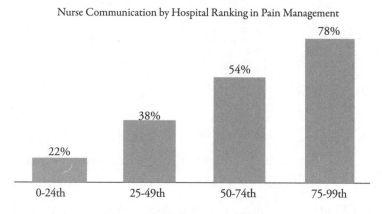

Nurse Communication by Hospital Ranking in Pain Management

Pain Management Quartile

Figure iv.3

Relationship Between Doctor Communication and Pain Management Results

Doctor Communication by Hospital Ranking in Pain Management

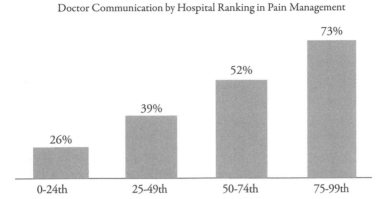

Figure iv.4

All of this means it's crucial to implement not only the tactics connected to pain management, but also those connected to the Communication composites. These factors all work together to help us control pain. It makes sense that when a patient's pain is under control she is comfortable, more compliant in her care, and likely to have better clinical outcomes.

With all that said, what does it mean to have pain under control? In general, it means that pain is prevented and reduced *to a degree that facilitates function and quality of life*—and the specifics depend on the individual patient.

Pain is primarily measured by a subjective self-evaluation by the patient. The standard of practice for this is the pain scale where patients rate their pain on a scale of

1-10. In other words, measuring pain is quite subjective. Many clinicians find it all too easy to challenge the integrity of this self-report, often second guessing the amount of pain the patient is truly experiencing. But in order to truly make progress in the results being measured by HCAHPS, organizations will find it necessary to challenge our attitudes regarding this and adjust to the reality that if the patient says it is pain, it is pain.

This section is not intended to discuss modalities of pain control. Rather, we will share how to build a relationship with each patient that improves her perception of how frequently we always did everything we could to help her control her pain.

We will also share tactics that keep communication about pain front and center with the patient. We know these tactics work because our partners outperform the nation by 21 percentile points in the "Pain Management" composite.

Interestingly, it's not necessary to completely eradicate pain in order to change patient perception. An article in the *Gallup Business Journal* indicates that there are times a certain level of pain is necessary to properly diagnose and treat a condition. However, staying in constant communication with the patient to explain properly and manage expectations, along with other actions such as anticipating the pain medication schedule, can have a positive impact on the patient's experience.[2]

In other words, patients are more satisfied if they feel the staff cared and did everything they could to help control their pain, even if it was not completely gone.

The following story, from a nurse at one of our partner organizations, demonstrates the impact we have on patients when we work with them to manage their pain (even when they aren't sure they want help). It also shows the impact our efforts have on patients' loved ones.

Chase was a 22-year-old male who had just been admitted following a motorcycle accident.

His doctor and I (his nurse) were in his room along with his mother. We were all concerned about his pain. However, when asked, Chase denied being in much pain. His tone said something different. He was speaking in a "macho/tough guy" fashion.

The doctor explained, "Chase, in order for us to keep your wound free of infection, your nurse and I need to 'debride and clean' it. This is basically scraping out any debris in the wound, and it's painful. I'd like to give you something for pain control prior to the procedure."

The patient rejected the medication saying, "I'm fine. I can handle it. I don't need the drugs." As he said this, the doctor noticed the patient's mom's face crinkle in worry.

The doctor decided to give it one more chance. He said, "Your mom knows you better than anyone, and the look on her face tells me you are in more pain than you are admitting. It is so hard for moms to see their sons in pain. Let's try this again, for your mom's sake. I think it's best for you to have some pain medication before we begin. Is it okay with you if we give you some?"

This resulted in a shoulder shrug and a nod of yes from the patient. It also resulted in a large smile from the mother. She was deeply relieved…and I suspect Chase was too, now that he had his mother's well-being as an "excuse" to accept the medication.

—Hannah, RN

It's true that uncontrolled pain impacts a patient's ability to heal. And as this story demonstrates, it also impacts the loved ones supporting him. When we do everything we can to control a patient's pain—and let him and his family know that we're doing it—we can make everyone feel better.

The Survey Questions

This aspect of the HCAHPS survey asks patients about their perception of the management of their pain during their hospital stay. Answers are given in the frequency scale: *never, sometimes, usually,* or *always.* The percent of patients who responded *always* is publicly reported on www.hospitalcompare.hhs.gov.

Screening Question: During this hospital stay, did you need medicine for pain? If patients select yes to this screening question, then they are asked to respond to the next two questions.

1. **During this hospital stay, how often was your pain well controlled?**

2. **During this hospital stay, how often did the hospital staff do everything they could to help you with your pain?**

In the chapter that follows, we will share specific tactics that positively impact the likelihood that patients will answer *always* to these two questions.

CHAPTER TWELVE:

CONTROL OF PAIN/HELPFULNESS OF STAFF

THE HCAHPS QUESTION: During this hospital stay, how often was your pain well controlled?

As care providers we have a tremendous opportunity to make a difference in people's lives. This is especially the case with pain relief. Pain management is more than giving a medication to a patient. High-performing organizations have learned that managing a patient's pain includes building a relationship with her and doing everything we can to address her specific pain needs.

In many cases, it is pain alone that drives patients to seek treatment in the first place. People are willing to be sick at home and try self-treatment until which time their pain becomes uncontrollable. If at the very moment they seek our help we are unresponsive to their needs, it will create the impression of poor quality and result in a lack of satisfaction with their experience.

Caring for the patient means caring about her pain and doing all we can to keep it under control. When we do this, it resonates with the patient and her family.

THE HCAHPS QUESTION: During this hospital stay, how often did the hospital staff do everything they could to help you with your pain?

If we are to do everything we can, then we must first explore clinician attitudes about pain. There is a great deal of subjectivity in how we collect pain information from patients, leading clinical scientists to challenge the lack of objective data related to pain. This phenomenon, over time, has led many to develop attitudes about pain and pain management ranging from skeptical to downright dismissive. At the same time, access to more addictive pain regimens has increased dramatically, along with health conditions that exacerbate pain—diabetes, obesity, orthopedic problems, and cancer, to name just a few.

Additionally, the incidence of opiate-tolerant and addicted patients is increasing. We must ensure that the care team is open to listening to the concerns of *all* patients in pain, even those with chronic pain conditions and those who might unkindly be called "drug seekers" so that we can continue to find ways to respectfully care for their needs. Anything less will automatically ensure that a patient does not feel we are doing everything we can to help with their pain or assist in getting it better under control.

We have to get inside the patient's mind and understand what "everything" means to her, specifically. We need to tailor our care to her particular definition of "everything."

How we communicate with our patients is a big part of the Pain Management composite. Studies show that frequent communication, shared goals, shared knowledge, and mutual respect among clinicians were associated with not just patient perception, but can actually decrease pain. Time spent with the patient communicates empathy and concern that may go a long way in providing patient comfort and reducing anxiety.

Also, while talking with the patient, the nurse may uncover factors contributing to discomfort, such as uncomfortable position, thirst, or the need to urinate, that influence patient perception of pain management. [1,2,3]

If we approach the patients' pain with an openness to doing everything we can to help, then the following best practices, consistently executed, will provide a framework to address their needs.

...And the Tactics That Make "Always" Responses More Likely for Both Questions

Tactic 1: Use Nurse Leader Rounding and Hourly Rounding® to Provide Focus and Discipline to Address Pain Management

Nurse Leader Rounding provides an excellent framework to evaluate how the patients individually and collectively are responding to our strategies and practices to help with and control their pain. If our focus is on improving our results in this composite, we may suggest that the nurse leader include some specific questions during their rounds to elicit feedback on pain management. Some suggested questions:

- *"In the last 24 hours have you needed to use your call light to request pain medications?"*

- *"Can you describe for me what actions the staff have taken that have helped control your pain—or if there have been any that haven't worked and we need to try to do something different?"*

- *"Has the information on your communication board regarding your pain been kept updated consistently, and is this information useful to you?"*

Each of these questions is designed to obtain actionable information validating whether staff members are executing specific best practices and whether they are having the desired impact on the patient.

While Nurse Leader Rounding allows us to assess how the staff is managing pain overall, Hourly Rounding® similarly allows us to frequently assess and reassess the patient's pain status and the effectiveness of any measures we have taken. The specific behaviors of the rounds that apply are:

- Opening key words such as *"Your pain is my priority. I am back to do my hourly round and be sure your pain is under control."*

- Performing scheduled tasks—repositioning, pain medication administration.

- The Three Ps—One of the Ps is always "Pain" and includes pain assessment and reassessment.

- Additional comfort measures—This can include fluffing pillows, alternative pain measures, etc.

- Closing key words such as *"I will be back to be sure our plan for your pain is working."*

Tactic 2: Focus on Pain Management during the Bedside Shift Report (BSR)

The handover process is an ideal time to summarize what has worked well with the pain plan, how well the patient understands it, and how effectively pain has been controlled. The patient is present and ideally takes a very active role in the transfer of information to the oncoming caregiver. This is a good opportunity to have the patient communicate in detail about how well his pain is being controlled so staff can respond appropriately. When possible, it's a good idea to include the patient's family as well.

Besides sharing clinical details such as the current pain level and stated pain goal, the Bedside Shift Report increases the patient's engagement in his care. The offgoing nurse might ask the patient to describe to the oncoming nurse what has happened over the last shift that has helped with his pain. For example:

"Mr. Smith, can you share with Kim what we have been work-ing on this shift that has helped with your pain so she knows what you think has been the most effective? Has that been effective enough in controlling your pain?

"Can you share with Kim your understanding of the medicines we have been using to help manage your pain? Are there any of those medications you feel work better than others? Can you share the side effects we have discussed with Kim so she knows you are aware of what we are watching for?

"Are there any concerns you have about your pain control at this point that Kim needs to be aware of?

"Is your pain being well controlled right now?"

These examples are not meant to be an exhaustive list, but they should trigger ideas on how to include pa-tients and families in the report discussion and provide a sense of how effective it can be when they are regularly engaged in the process. Their plan will be well under-stood, and caregivers will obtain the feedback they need to ensure that they are making patients as comfortable as possible. Meanwhile, they will be reassured continuously that we are working hard to help control their pain.

Tactic 3: Use Individualized Patient Care (IPC) to Communicate Personal Pain Levels and Con-trol

As described in our Fundamentals chapter, IPC is asking the patient what two or three things we can do to ensure that quality care is achieved *for them*. Many times, a patient who is experiencing pain will respond to this question by asking that her pain be well managed. If so, this will be reflected as one of her priorities and will be documented on her whiteboard for the entire care team to see. It is generally written in the patient's own words so it might read "manage my pain" or "be on time with pain medication." It is then incumbent on the team to ensure excellent execution of all the previously mentioned strategies.

The whiteboard will serve as a cue to all members of the care team, such as respiratory therapists, physical therapists, transporters, physicians, and others, to be tuned into this priority and to assess the patient's pain whenever they interact with her. This further reinforces our teamwork to the patient, as well as the level of interest the whole team has in addressing the things that are most important to her.

These priorities are also reinforced or reevaluated at each shift change during BSR.

Tactic 4: Make Use of Complex Pain Control Strategies

Many organizations may find they have variation in their results on the "pain well controlled" question versus the "they tried to help" question. Typically the pain control question is the more lagging result. In some cases, achieving good patient pain outcomes (and receiving favorable HCAHPS results on both the pain management questions) requires more complex, interdisciplinary strategies. Addressing pain control requires that the appropriate strategies are in place and fully executed. Here are just a few of them:

1. Bring in multi-disciplinary pain teams. The teams will help analyze information and develop a plan designed to address patients with complex conditions or patients with unresolved pain.

2. Create and standardize definitions and processes to respond to unresolved pain events and elevate these to the same level of priority and response as other sentinel events in the organization.

3. Educate staff and provide evidence to support handling of opiate-tolerant patients so that they will respond to patient needs in an appropriate and evidence-based way.

4. Remove any tolerance for use of the term "drug seeking" or the attitudes that allow that. "Drug seeking" is a judgment, not a diagnosis. There is no room for judgment—only respectful treatment.

5. Create plans with patients and families that acknowledge their specific challenges and include some of the following tactics:

   - Setting reasonable expectations
   - Being candid about the level of pain to be expected
   - Keeping the patient informed

- Respecting the patient's expertise and involving him in selection of pain scale

- Discussing options, tradeoffs, and preferences, including what has worked previously

- Developing pain goals and a plan

- Keeping the pain goal and plan visible, as well as the next scheduled medication

- Tracking progress[4]

Tactic 5: Include Pain Management Questions in Post-Visit Calls

If the calls effectively assess the patient's pain control progress, they can help drive quality and ensure that the care was (and is) working well. They can also alert us to any changes we need to make in the future.

Here are some potential questions to ask:

- *"Were you able to fill your prescriptions for your pain medication and have you been taking them as prescribed?"*

- *"Is your pain improving the way you would expect it to since you have returned home?"*

- *"Are you experiencing any of the side effects of the pain medication?"*

- *"Do you have any questions or concerns about your pain medications?"*

Often, pain is the primary symptom that makes patients come to us for care. We need to respect that reality and do all that we can to help. We cannot always resolve their pain completely, but we can make sure they know that we are doing everything possible to control it.

Using these tactics to not only control patients' pain but also communicate with them about what we are doing goes a long way toward building strong patient-caregiver relationships. That relationship is one of the most important drivers of positive HCAHPS results... and the backbone of a positive patient care experience.

A Few Additional Tips

Here are a few more tips to consider as you are hard-wiring the previous tactics.

Tip: "Alternative" (Non-Drug) Measures That Control Pain

While pharmacology and pain medication regimens are an integral part of good pain management, they do not make up the entire plan. In the complex world of pain management, alternative pain measures are important as well. These non-pharmacological interventions can be an important adjunct to potentiate the effects of the pain medication and they generally have no negative side effects!

Nurses in particular should be advocates for maximizing these opportunities as part of a well-rounded, individualized pain plan. Some of these include:

- Music therapy

- Repositioning

- Isolation/elevation

- Heat/ice

- Massage

- Aromatherapy

- Distraction techniques such as reading, television, games, visitors, exercise, etc.

Here is an example of how pain-related communication during Hourly Rounding might sound:

"Mrs. Jones, since your pain was already at a level 6 last hour when I rounded and you are currently due for another dose, I went ahead and brought your pain medication with me. (scheduled task, pain management)

"Can you rate your pain for me now? (Three Ps)

"Would you like to go back to bed now from being in the chair? This might help you relax and help this dose of medication work faster. (position)

"Let me fluff those pillows for you so you can get comfortable back in bed. I can also dim the lights so you can rest a bit before physical therapy comes next hour. This should help you do better during your therapy if you are more relaxed. (additional comfort measures)

"Managing your pain is a priority for me." (closing key words)

While this is not a full example of an hourly round, it does highlight how you can take specific behaviors and highlight them to focus on an area of opportunity.

Tip: Use Patient Communication Boards or Pain Posters, Including Pain Scale and Pain Goal

The patient communication board (sometimes also called a whiteboard) is a common tool used in many patient care settings to help convey important patient information. Pain is, of course, one of those important aspects of care commonly included on the board.

The pain poster is typically used when there's not enough space on the communication board to include the information.

Regardless of which you use, board or poster, it's highly suggested that you regularly include the following elements:

- Current pain level on 1-10 scale

- The patient's pain goal (tolerable pain level that indicates control has been achieved)

- The next dose of pain medication available

These essential elements ensure that patients know we're taking every possible action to help manage their pain.

Tools & Resources

Studer Group offers a variety of tools and resources that support the tactics discussed in this chapter. To access the most up-to-date offerings, as well as to see what's new in healthcare, please visit www.studergroup.com/HCAHPS.

Communication About Medications

M edication can be an amazing force for good. It can stop an infection in its path, help the body heal itself, relieve pain, calm anxiety, and lift the darkness of depression. Medication brings hope and saves lives. It is, perhaps, the most powerful weapon in a care provider's arsenal.

And yet, like any tool, medication has a potential dark side. When it's misused or misunderstood, it can cause great harm, even death. Sometimes, too, undesirable drug reactions are beyond anyone's control. Medication doesn't always work in the way we expected. What works very well for one patient may not work at all for another. As with life itself, there are no guarantees.

We all know these realities. Yet all of us can benefit from frequent reminders to always treat medications— all medications—with the respect and vigilance they deserve. We must always be clear and thorough when we talk to our patients about the medications we prescribe for them.

Nearly one in every five patients experiences an adverse event after being discharged from the hospital.[1] And according to the *Annals of Internal Medicine*, 66 percent of these events are medication related.[2] When we don't communicate and communicate often regarding all of the necessary details about a medication and its side effects, we are putting our patients in danger.

Here are some more disturbing statistics:

- An adverse drug event (ADE) is defined as harm experienced by a patient as a result of exposure to a medication, and ADEs account for nearly 700,000 Emergency Department visits and 100,000 hospitalizations each year. ADEs affect nearly 5 percent of hospitalized patients, making them one of the most common types of inpatient errors; ambulatory patients may experience ADEs at even higher rates.[3]

- ADEs occur frequently, are often preventable, and are usually caused by physicians.[4]

- ADEs are likely the most common source of preventable harm in both hospitalized and ambulatory patients, and preventing them is a major priority for accrediting bodies and regulatory agencies. ADEs are responsible for an estimated one-third of all hospital adverse events, affect approximately two million hospital stays annually, and prolong hospital length of stay by approximately 1.7 to 4.6 days.[5]

- Inpatient preventable medication errors cost approximately $16.4 billion annually. Outpatient preventable medication errors cost approximately $4.2 billion annually.[6]

- Nationally, serious preventable medication errors occur in 3.8 million inpatient admissions and 3.3 million outpatient visits each year.[7,8]

Medication errors can be made by healthcare professionals, home caregivers, or the patient him or herself. Better communication can help prevent all types of errors.

Understanding the causes of medication errors can provide insight into strategies to prevent them. Some of these causes include:

- **Prescription mistakes:** Studies have shown that unintended medication discrepancies occur in nearly one-third of patients at admission, a similar proportion at the time of transfer from one site of care within a hospital, and in 14 percent of patients at hospital discharge.[9]

- **Poor communication:** A *JAMA* study found that 77 percent of medical errors and adverse events were medication related, and that standardizing verbal and written communications between members of the care team reduced medical errors by more than 45 percent and adverse events by more than 54 percent.[10]

- **Lack of pharmacist follow-up:** Patients who received pharmacist follow-up calls were 88 percent less likely to have a preventable medication error resulting in an ED visit or hospitalization.[11]

- **Fragmentation of care:**
  - Direct communication between hospital physicians and primary care physicians occurs infrequently (in 3-20 percent of cases studied), and the availability of a discharge summary at the first post-discharge visit is low (12-34 percent).[12]
  - An oft-cited study found that including a pharmacist on routine medical rounds led to a 78 percent reduction in medication errors.[13]

- **Lack of information technology infrastructure:**
  - Twenty-seven percent of all prescribing errors that occur in the hospital result from incomplete medication histories at the time of admission.[14]
  - Only 4 percent of physicians reported having EMR systems that were described as fully functional and had a prescribing function.[15]
  - Numerous studies have shown that use of electronic prescribing, barcode electronic medication administration system (eMAR) technology, and computerized physician order entry systems can reduce medication errors by as much as 85 percent.[16,17,18,19]

In addition to the causes of medication errors listed previously, there are other risk factors that can lead to mistakes. For instance:

- **Polypharmacy (Patients taking more medications than are clinically indicated).** This affects:

  ○ Elderly patients, who take more medications and are more vulnerable to specific medication adverse effects

  ○ Pediatric patients, since many medications for children must be dosed according to their weight

  ○ Patients with limited health literacy and numeracy (the ability to use arithmetic operations for daily tasks)

- **High-alert medications.** For example:

  ○ Medications that have dangerous adverse effects

  ○ Look-alike, sound-alike medications, which have similar names and physical appearance but completely different pharmaceutical properties (Patients get confused and take the wrong one)

  ○ Antidiabetic agents (e.g., insulin), oral anticoagulants (e.g., warfarin), and antiplatelet agents (such as aspirin and clopidogrel): Together, these medications account for nearly 50 percent of

Emergency Department visits for ADEs in Medicare patients.[20]

Improving our communication in this critical area is about *always* letting patients and their families know what medications have been prescribed—and why. It's about discussing these medications in a communication style and at a level that the patient and her family understand. It's about *always* sharing with patients the side effects that may impact them. It's about *always* conveying the *why* to patients so they are more likely to comply with treatments and get better outcomes.

Making sure they understand their medication and hear the explanation more than once is essential to patient care—not just to raise HCAHPS scores, but also to do everything we possibly can to ensure their safety and well-being.

The following story, which relays the experience of a quality assurance nurse, demonstrates why communicating about medications is the absolute right thing to do for the patient.

During quality checks on a hospital unit, I asked if we could walk into a nearby patient's room in order to round. The nurses protested. They said, in essence, that we shouldn't go into that particular patient's room because "he's not very nice."

Of course, the minute I heard this, my mind was made up—I was absolutely going in that room. Again, the nurses expressed their hesitation. They said, "He's crabby, he's mean, and he doesn't like us." Naturally, this only strengthened my resolve.

I went into the patient's room, introduced myself, and asked, "How has your stay been?"

"It's been pretty good at this hospital, but I don't think they like me very much," the patient replied.

"Why is that?" I asked.

"Because every time they bring me medication, I ask them exactly what it is and what it's for. I kind of give them the third degree."

"I wish every patient we have in the hospital would exercise that right," I replied.

"Well, I appreciate that," he said. "You see, I'm allergic to hydrocodone. Three years ago, I was at the hospital and I had on my arm bracelet—no one checked it. They gave me medicine without telling me what it was for. It turned out to have hydrocodone in it. Anyway, I had an allergic reaction. I about stopped breathing and ended up in the ICU.

"If I had been asking and had they been doing their jobs, I wouldn't have had that happen," he continued. "So now I ask them every time, 'What are you bringing me? What is it for? What is it going to do?' I get really nervous now. I don't ever want to be in that situation again."

—*Paul, Quality Assurance Nurse*

It turned out this "crabby" man wasn't crabby at all. He was nervous and scared. He needed better communication from hospital staff regarding the medication they were giving him. That's what all patients need from all hospital staff. When we provide it, we gain their understanding and their partnership in the care we are providing.

The Survey Questions

This aspect of the HCAHPS survey asks patients about their perception of Communication of Medications during their hospital stay. Answers are given in the frequency scale: *never, sometimes, usually,* or *always.* The percent of patients who respond *always* is publicly reported on www.hospitalcompare.hhs.gov.

Screening Question: During this hospital stay, were you given any medicine that you had not taken before?

1. **Before giving you any new medicine, how often did hospital staff tell you what the medicine was for?**

2. **Before giving you any new medicine, how often did hospital staff describe possible side effects in a way you could understand?**

In the chapter that follows, we will share some specific tactics that positively impact the likelihood that patients will answer *always* to the preceding two questions. (The first question is a screening question, and patients will not answer the following two questions if they answer "no" to the screening question.)

The following chapter does not include all possible relevant tactics. Rather, it conveys a few carefully targeted specific actions you can take to immediately impact patient perception of how well you communicated with them regarding medications.

These tactics do *not* replace medication reconciliation work with patients, education for nursing staff, or the need for multi-disciplinary teams to improve this process. However, we have found that they go a long way toward driving outcomes, especially in hospitals that are already working hard on The Joint Commission National Patient Safety Goals and multi-disciplinary medication reconciliation teams. They also assume that physicians, nurses, pharmacists, and case managers are all practicing safe medication ordering, fulfilling, and administering practices. These tactics are in addition to those standards.

Also, we have previously covered important communication strategies related to listening and explaining for nurses and physicians. It should be reinforced that those are foundational skills that are essential to success in this area—thus, they should be included in any plan to improve results in this domain.

The last tip before we get into the tactics is simple but important. Due to the complexity of the information being shared regarding medications, all information shared should be followed with written material. On the other hand, no written information should be shared without verbal explanation. This is all too often not the case; we routinely see patients with reams of papers and pamphlets and no earthly idea of what it all means.

The bottom line: Say it in words *and* in writing…this will greatly increase the likelihood that patients will understand and comply.

CHAPTER THIRTEEN:

EXPLANATION REGARDING MEDICATIONS AND SIDE EFFECTS

T HE HCAHPS QUESTION: Before giving you any new medicine, how often did hospital staff tell you what the medicine was for?

We know it has never been acceptable to walk into a patient's room, hand him a pill he has never taken before and a little cup of water, and ask him to swallow the medicine...yet it happens. A caregiver might skip the explanation because she feels she is too busy to take the time, or because the patient seems too drowsy to really be listening, or perhaps because she has just fallen into the bad habit of omitting the words.

Of course, none of these reasons are acceptable. In a time when patients expect to be partners in their own care, it's crucial that they understand exactly why they are taking any medication. Letting them know is a sign of courtesy and respect. What's more, it leads to better clinical outcomes.

Evidence (and common sense) tells us that when patients are involved in and understand their treatment plan, they are more likely to comply and their outcomes are more likely to be better. This doesn't mean stopping at what a medication is for (as the question is worded); it also means explaining why it is important that the patient take it as prescribed, and how long he or she will need to take it.

As healthcare professionals, we have a real opportunity to communicate these basic facts. A study published in the *Archives of Internal Medicine* found that 66 percent of patients surveyed did not know the duration of treatment of their medication.[1]

This HCAHPS question is a valuable opportunity to gauge whether we are always letting patients and family members know they are being given a new medication, what that medication is for, and what to expect from it. If we're not, we owe it to our patients to change the way we communicate with them.

THE HCAHPS QUESTION: Before giving you any new medicine, how often did hospital staff describe possible side effects in a way you could understand?

Being in the hospital causes anxiety. New medications cause anxiety. Worrying how a medication will impact you definitely causes anxiety. Consider the results of a recent study of newly discharged patients[2]:

- Only 41 percent were able to state their diagnoses

- Only 37 percent were able to state the purpose of their medications

- Only 14 percent knew the common side effects of all their medications

It is vital that patients understand what side effects are associated with the medications they have been prescribed. This is why it's so important that care providers:

- Explain the most common and most serious side effects to patients and ask in a variety of ways if they understand side effects

- Confirm that patients know what to do in the event of side effects

- Acknowledge patients' anxiety surrounding side effects

Validation of patient comprehension reduces anxiety. We don't want patients to worry and wonder with thoughts like, *My heart is racing; am I having a heart attack?* Or, *I am nauseated. What if I can't keep this medication down?*

One thing's for sure: The worry and anxiety caused by not knowing enough about the side effects of medication will not help the patient heal. In fact, studies show that having too little information can cause the patient to not cooperate with treatment and medication regimens and can lead to poor clinical outcomes.

...And the Tactics That Make "Always" Responses More Likely (for Both Questions)

Through research, we at Studer Group® have identified and put together the components of a proper explanation of medications. These components are centered on what patients and their family members need and want to know about the medications in order to put them at ease and help them become willing partners in their treatment. One of these components focuses on side effects.

We've found that we use the exact same tactics to help our partners be successful with communicating about patient medications in general and communicating about side effects in particular. Therefore, we've addressed these two HCAHPS questions in one chapter. When you implement these tactics and focus on sharing all the components of medication, patients will perceive their care to be better...and it will be.

Tactic 1: Use Key Words to Reinforce Information about Medications

Proper communication about medications means frequently sharing the right information with the patient. For all of us, awareness and learning require repetition. In fact, it's said that the average adult needs to be exposed to new information at least three times in order to commit it to memory. This is why we recommend the

DNS (Describe, Narrate, Summarize) technique that we describe in Chapter 6.

DNS: The Art of Good Explanations

1. **D**escribe what you are going to do before you do it.
2. **N**arrate the care again while you are doing it.
3. **S**ummarize what you have just done.

And in a hospital situation when patients and their families are often faced with pain and uncertainty, it is even more important to take the time to clearly explain medications and side effects in a meaningful way—over and over again.

Key Words at Key Times ensure that we have effectively communicated the *what* and the *why* to patients. This is especially critical when giving a patient a new medication that he will be required to manage himself when he goes home in a few days. Patients need to know *what* they are taking, and they need to know *why* they are taking it.

Hardwiring key words around medications ensures that all staff members are communicating in an effective and efficient manner. From the physician who orders a new prescription, to the nurse who administers a daily medication, to the respiratory therapist who uses medications in her respiratory treatments, to the case manager who educates a patient's family about home care—all staff can use key words to make sure that they have shared all the necessary information about all medications and their common side effects. When all staff members reinforce this critical element of safe, patient-centered care, we will truly impact patient outcomes in a positive manner.

This certainly includes readmissions to the hospital. One study funded by the Agency for Healthcare Research and Quality (AHRQ) showed that patients who have a clear understanding of their after-hospital care instructions, including how to take their medicines, are 30 percent less likely to be readmitted or visit the Emergency Department than those who lack this information. The study found that total costs were an average of $412 lower for the patients who received complete information than for those who did not.[3]

Here are some tips to help you implement Key Words at Key Times—and to emphasize communication of medicines and their side effects:

- **Hardwire an explanation of every medication with every dosage given.** When "accomplishing scheduled tasks of medication administration"—a key behavior of Hourly Rounding®—talk about medications with the patient. This communication should be documented and hardwired in the same way that you hardwire asking the patient about his pain level. (Tip: To help hardwire, add it to the Hourly Rounding Log.)

- **Encourage two-way communication.** Take the time to pause as you move through the medication explanation. Give the patient a chance to let the information soak in and also to ask you any questions. This should be more of a conversation than a lecture, so use patient-friendly terminology. Stick to sixth-grade language. If you use words, phrases, terms, and acronyms not understood by the patient, it might discourage two-way dialogue because the patient may be too embarrassed to say he doesn't know what you are talking about.

- **When explaining a medication, always share six critical components.** Following is all the information a patient needs to know in order to partner in his care—and to be more likely to comply with the medication instructions.

  o **Name of the medication:** Use the name of the medication as ordered. Doctors may order generic or brand name medication, so don't confuse patients by calling it something else. Confusion about medication names can be a big problem. We actually heard about one patient who was on three medications that all treated the same condition due to confusion between brand name and generic drugs prescribed by multiple care providers.

  o **Purpose of the medication:** When patients do not comprehend all aspects of their conditions or the importance of taking a specific medication, they are less likely to adhere to the treatment plan.[4] Share with the patient why *this medication* has been selected and how it will make him heal or be healthier.

○ **Duration of the medication:** Let the patient know how long he should anticipate taking the medication. Is it just for this hospital stay? Will he need to take it upon discharge? Is it a lifelong medication? Reinforce what the physician has told him about the medication and assess patient readiness to learn.

○ **When the medication will take effect:** If relevant, share the length of time the patient should expect to wait before feeling the effects. Some medications can make a patient very uncomfortable or sleepy. This will help him plan his day; for example, he can ask grandchildren to visit earlier in the day before the medicine takes effect.

○ **Dosage:** Let the patient know the amount of medication he will be taking. It can also reduce anxiety to let him know what to do if a dose is missed or how strict the timing requirements are. When we tell a patient to take a medication every six hours, do we really mean he is to set his clock and wake up in the middle of the night to take it? Validate the patient's understanding by asking him to tell you "how much and how often."

○ **Side effects:** Let the patient know of any potential side effects. Make sure to use the words "side effects." When we say, "Let me know if you have any nausea," the patient might not connect the dots that this is a common side effect of this medication. Sometimes medications have side effects that are irritating or can cause some discomfort but are manageable considering the alternative (i.e., the disease not being treated). Let the patient know that these common side effects are okay as long as he finds them manageable, and they can also be treated to make him more comfortable.

- **Ask for the patient's compliance.** Make sure he has the information he needs to agree to comply with the medication requirements. When a patient agrees, he is much more likely to comply with the treatment plan. You might say, *"I want to be sure I have communicated effectively. Could you repeat back to me the instructions for why and how you are going to take this medication?"* You might also ask, *"Is there anything that might prevent you from taking this medication when you go home?"*

Use AIDET® to Educate About Medications

A = Acknowledge. Verify you are speaking to the correct patient and greet him in a warm manner. *"Mr. Perdue, I have the new medication your doctor ordered for your blood pressure."*

I = Introduce. Reference your experience and credibility. *"As a registered nurse, I am specially trained to deliver*

*medications safely. Since this medication is new to you, I want
to take some time to tell you about it—why you are taking it and
some side effects to watch out for. Is now a good time?"*

D = Duration. *"You will take it just once a day. You will
need to remain on this medication through your follow-up appointment in two weeks."* Include how long it will take to
see results.

E = Explanation. *"You are taking (name of medication)
and it will help lower your blood pressure. Most people don't have
any trouble with this medication but some of the more common
side effects we have seen are dizziness, headache, and stomach
upset. I have printed out this information about your new medication for you to read and review. I am going to highlight two things
on this page for you to review because it is important you understand your medication when you go home. We will review it again
before you are discharged too. It is important you know what the
medication is, why you are taking it, and what the common side
effects are. Let's go over it one more time."* Have the patient
demonstrate understanding by asking him a variety of
questions and gauging his information recall.

T = Thank You. *"Thank you for paying such close attention and repeating the information back to me to ensure that you
have a clear understanding of your medications. As we discussed,
it is very important that you know how to take your medications
correctly when you get home. Please let me know if you have any
questions after you read through this document."*

Tactic 2: Reinforce Medication Education during the Bedside Shift Report

At shift change, the offgoing nurse and the patient should go through the explanation of the medication together with the oncoming nurse. Patient involvement helps her better understand and remember the medication. It also gives the oncoming nurse a better sense of the patient's concerns and ability to remember the important information.

It is okay—indeed, even better—to ask the patient to let her new nurse know what medications she is on and what the side effects are. (The more she repeats this information, the better she'll come to know it.)

Conveying the information this way has many benefits. The patient understands her care and her new medications. She is reassured because she plays an active role in the handoff of her care. She doesn't have to worry whether the new nurse knows what medications she is on or which side effects could occur.

The staff should have a standard report tool that highlights review of medications, purpose, and side effects. The patient should also have a document to review that essentially covers the same information. It may help to include graphics for clarity. For example, include a moon for an evening dose and a sun for a morning dose. Reinforcing these documents during each Bedside Shift Report will ensure all are on the same page.

The patient should play an active role in this discussion. Ask her to share any new medications that have been prescribed during that shift as well as side effects and other important information.

After the Bedside Shift Report is over you might want to place the patient's document in her Discharge and Medications folder (see Chapter 15). Tell her it's important, and that the nurse who calls her after she goes home will want to talk with her about it again and answer any questions she or her family might have about her medications. This will become a useful tool even when she leaves the hospital.

Tactic 3: Use M in the Box℠ for New Medications

Many of our partners use and recommend this communication strategy. Here's how it works:

1. When the patient has a new medication ordered, the nurse draws a box on the communication board and writes an "M" inside it. This signals to other caregivers that a new medication was ordered and is being taught to the patient.

2. Each nurse or caregiver who enters the room and sees the M in the Box℠ on the board asks the patient to articulate the purpose and potential side effects of the new medication.

3. Once the patient can easily teach back the information about the new medication, the M is erased.

Partners take great pride in their success with this simple strategy.

Hardwiring "Always" Makes a Big Difference with M in the Box^{SM}
17% Improvement vs 2% for "Usually"

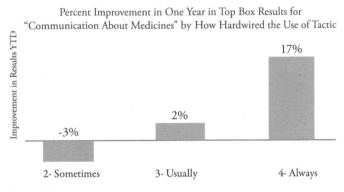

Figure 13.1

Tactic 4: Validate and Verify with Nurse Leader Rounding

Use Nurse Leader Rounding to ensure that patients are being educated about medications and their common side effects. The nurse leader can ask questions such as:

"Quality care is important and safe medication practices are part of that. What did you learn from your nurse regarding any new medications?"

"I see you are using your communication board and that there is an M in the Box. Share with me what that means to you."

When Nurse Leader Rounding is completed, use the information learned from the patients to reinforce staff behaviors. Giving their positive feedback to staff can be a powerful form of reward and recognition.

Tactic 5: Make Post-Visit Calls and Include Medication Information

It's a rare patient who is *not* in a hurry to be discharged from the hospital. As the patient is packing (or is already all packed) and just waiting to be told he can leave, the nurse takes him through everything he needs to do once he gets home. Unfortunately, much of this information is not retained…likely because the patient can think only about getting back to his familiar environment.

In cases where the patient is being discharged to other care facilities, the information is likely to be "lost in translation" between locations.

Post-visit phone calls offer us the opportunity to extend the care we provide outside the hospital. In the case of medications and side effects, we can ask some specific questions to ensure that patients have clear and accurate information.

Some potential post-visit call questions might be:

"Were you able to get your prescription filled?"

"Are there any obstacles preventing you from taking your medica-tion?"

"Now that you are home, what medications are you taking?"

"What are those medications for?"

"Do you have any concerns that you are having symptoms of side effects from any of your medications?"

We give medications in order to help patients improve their health status or in some cases to alleviate or minimize the symptoms of chronic or even terminal conditions. What we tell them about those medications—as well as how often we tell them and which words we use—is critical to ensuring that these intentions are met. The tactics you've just learned are about far more than achieving higher **HCAHPS** results. They're about restoring good health and saving lives—and nothing we do is more important than that.

Tools & Resources

Studer Group offers a variety of tools and resources that support the tactics discussed in this chapter. To access the most up-to-date offerings, to see what's new in healthcare, and to download a worksheet that will help you create a plan to improve patient perception of care in the "Communication of Medications" arena, please visit www.studergroup.com/HCAHPS.

SECTION SIX:

DISCHARGE INFORMATION

D ischarge from the hospital is a vulnerable time for patients. Nearly one in five patients experiences an adverse event during this transition, a third of which are preventable.[1, 2]

Generally speaking, and as will be discussed later on, most healthcare professionals consider "discharge" to encompass the 72 hours immediately following the moment the patient leaves the hospital. And you don't have to work in the industry to understand why this time period can be precarious.

If you've ever been a patient, you may remember what discharge was like. Chances are, you were so focused on leaving—picking up your meds from the pharmacy on the way home, sleeping in your own bed, seeing your pets again—that it was hard to process everything staff members were saying. That's how it is with most patients. And that's why sometimes they don't retain the vital information they need to stay safe and get well.

It goes without saying that a safe and successful discharge is almost always the end goal of a hospital stay. That's why the discharge process should *not* start an hour or two before patients are ready to leave. In fact, it really needs to start at admission and remain an integral part of the care plan throughout the entire stay.

Think of it like this: No parent would try to cram in 18 years of life wisdom the day before their child leaves for college. Hopefully, their instruction begins early in childhood and continues every day of the child's life. Likewise, healthcare professionals need to provide care and treatment details repeatedly and in a variety of ways throughout the patient's stay.

Many high-performing hospitals coached by Studer Group® have expanded the admission assessment to help prepare for potential discharge. They include tactics like performing a complete medication reconciliation, identifying who the primary caregiver will be upon discharge, ensuring that this person is present for educational sessions, identifying the primary language spoken at home, reaching out to the patient's family, and communicating with the primary care provider.

Why make such an effort? It's because we recognize that comprehensive discharge instructions are one of the most important elements of a smooth transition from hospital to home, as the responsibility for care shifts from providers to the patient and caregivers. Unfortunately, even when we *think* we've made those instructions known, we haven't: Patients often go home without understanding critical information about their hospital stay, such as their discharge diagnosis or medication changes, leaving them both dissatisfied with their discharge instructions and at serious risk for hospital readmission.[3, 4, 5]

Consider the data in the following figure. As you can see, there is a significant difference between the caregivers' perception of what is shared and understood by patients and what the patients themselves report that they know.

Communication Discrepancies

Patients Know
Their Diagnosis

Never Told of Adverse Effects
Regarding Medication
90%

77%

57%

19%

| Physicians Who Thought Patient Knew | Patients Who Correctly Identified | Physician Response | Patient Response |

Figure vi.1

Physicians believe patients know their diagnoses. They believe they told patients about the adverse effects of medication. Yet in many cases, there is a great divide between what physicians think patients know and what patients actually know.

Unfortunately, when patients don't know what we think they know, the consequences can be serious. They can make medication errors, miss follow-up appointments, or miss potential side effects of medications or warning signs of complications. As a result, they can end up right back in the hospital.

The Cost of Readmissions

Readmissions take a toll not only on the patients' health, but on hospitals' financial health as well. Preventable hospital readmissions cost the U.S. healthcare system an estimated \$25 billion each year.[6] The following figure shows the effect that good discharge practices have on heart failure patients, as just one example.

Providing Patients with Discharge Information Drives Procedural Outcomes

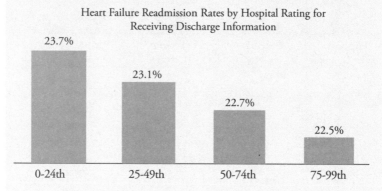

Heart Failure Readmission Rates by Hospital Rating for Receiving Discharge Information

23.7%
23.1%
22.7%
22.5%

0-24th   25-49th   50-74th   75-99th

Hospital Rating for Receiving Discharge Information

Figure vi.2

Among the populations studied, CHF 30-day readmission rates were particularly high at approximately the 20-24th percentile. Not only are these readmissions disruptive to the patient and family, but the hospital will no longer be reimbursed for them.

Also, in Chapter 1, you read about the impact of Medicare spending per beneficiary as a measure of efficiency for healthcare. The following data supports how important our work on providing excellent discharge information can be in reducing healthcare costs and creating efficiency.

Medicare Spending per Beneficiary VBP Efficiency

Domain Score by Hospital Ranking on "HCAHPS Discharge Information"

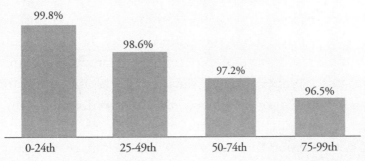

Hospital Rating for Providing Discharge Information

Figure vi.3

Providing discharge information throughout the hospital stay keeps the patient thinking about the next phase of her care—and that's exactly what discharge is. When the patient leaves the hospital, she isn't leaving our care; it's just that the responsibility for managing the details shifts to her and her home caregivers. This is a tremendous responsibility and one that is critical to excellent outcomes and our goal of reducing costly readmissions.

When you start sharing discharge information at admission, you allow time for the patient to begin discussing medications, diet, dressing/changing, or other instructions she'll need to know once she goes home. What's more, thinking about going home is a healthy psychological focus for the patient—it gives her something positive to work toward. It also includes her (and her family) in the care plan and helps manage expectations regarding length of stay.

Planning for discharge upon admission reminds us to share, repeat, and ensure retention of important information throughout the patient's stay. It allows us to provide a continuum of care by connecting the information staff members provide during the hospital stay to the patient's care at home. When you truly hardwire the processes for sharing this information with patients early on, the conversation that takes place on the day of discharge is essentially a recap and a clarification.

Of course, none of this is meant to downplay final discharge instructions. While education throughout the patient's stay may prepare her for managing her own care, her perception of the instructions she gets at the time of discharge will still make the greatest impact on how she feels when she leaves the hospital.

The Agency for Healthcare Research and Quality (AHRQ) recommends the following be provided and reviewed with patients prior to discharge to ensure they understand their discharge instructions.

- Details about the hospital stay

- Diagnosis

- Test results

- Treatment received in the hospital

- Follow-up appointments and tests

- Symptoms to be concerned about after discharge

- Lifestyle changes

- Medications

Each of these elements must be incorporated into a robust discharge process, including the written instructions as a tool to reinforce what has been shared with patients during their stay.

When we prepare the patient and her family for discharge from the moment she is admitted until the time she leaves the hospital, her confidence and compliance will increase.

The following story illustrates how important preparing for home care skills and resources can be.

Our unit had just implemented post-visit calls, and we were listening to Dwight, our nurse leader, make some calls. As he called patients, he had the discharge instructions, including the medication list, in front of him.

One woman the nurse leader called was to go home on Lovenox, an important medication that requires the patient or caregiver to give injections in the stomach. This particular patient had a history of stroke and had been admitted for a deep vein thrombosis. Dwight asked the patient if she was comfortable with the injections and she answered, "I don't know what you're talking about."

Of course, Dwight became concerned, as this medication was very important for the patient's health. He asked, "Okay, is there someone at home to help you?" The patient said, "Yes, my daughter will be helping me. She was here but she's gone right now."

The nurse leader asked if he could get in touch with the patient's daughter by cell phone. The patient provided a phone number, and the daughter verified that they did have the medication and were helping her mother with the injections—and following all the discharge instructions. She also explained that her mother refers to the injections as her "shots" and likely did not connect with what was being asked of her due to some cognitive deficits from her previous stroke.

The daughter was very appreciative that the nurse leader, who had also visited her during the inpatient stay, had taken time to track her down and check on her mother's progress.

—Keisha, RN

This story demonstrates the power of post-visit phone calls and how important good discharge preparation can be. It is obvious that if that patient had not had her daughter's support and that the daughter was well prepared to accomplish those injections that this patient would be high risk for an adverse event and possible re-admission.

The responses to the two HCAHPS questions in the Discharge Information composite allow a hospital to see how well it's helping patients make the transition between inpatient care and home care. And of course, responses to the new Care Transition Measure questions added on January 1, 2013—described in Section 8 of this book—will allow us to delve deeper into how well we are preparing patients for that transition.

When we believe wholeheartedly in our mission to provide the best possible patient care, we must take action to ensure that people continue to improve after they leave our campus. It's simply the right thing to do.

The Survey Questions

This aspect of the HCAHPS survey asks questions regarding how the hospital staff helped the patient prepare to leave the hospital. It is important to note that these questions are reported on a different scale from the previous questions; answers are given in *yes* or *no* scale. Results are reported as a percent of patients who responded *yes*, and that is what gets publicly reported at www.hospital-compare.hhs.gov.

Screening Question: After you left the hospital, did you go directly to your own home, to someone else's home, or to another healthcare facility?

1. **During this hospital stay, did doctors, nurses, or other hospital staff talk with you about whether you would have the help you needed when you left the hospital?**

2. **During this hospital stay, did you get information in writing about what symptoms or health problems to look out for after you left the hospital?**

The next two chapters will focus on behaviors and actions that evidence shows may positively impact the likelihood that patients will answer yes to these two questions.

The information that follows is not designed to be an all-encompassing list of relevant tactics. Rather, this section conveys a few carefully targeted specific actions you can take to immediately impact patient perception of how well your staff communicates regarding discharge instructions.

CHAPTER FOURTEEN:

STAFF DISCUSSION OF
POST-DISCHARGE HELP

T HE HCAHPS QUESTION: During this
hospital stay, did doctors, nurses, or other
hospital staff talk with you about whether you
would have the help you needed when you left
the hospital?

Nobody wants to go to the hospital, but if you are
sick, it is the best place to be. There is a whole team of
trained professionals to care for you, including doctors,
nurses, housekeepers, food and nutrition service staff, lab
staff, pharmacists, respiratory therapists, and so on. But
what happens when you are discharged from the hospital? These care providers certainly can't go with you.

The caregiving team must continually ask about the
help patients need when they leave the hospital and when
staff is no longer available to care for them 24/7. Many
times this help comes in the form of family members,
referrals for home care specialists, or even arrangements
for transfer to post-acute care facilities. The hospital

staff and providers will assess the specific resources each family has and determine the capacity and capability of the available resources and compare those with the specific needs of each patient to determine the most appropriate plan.

Discussion on this matter can begin right away. Often, a doctor can provide an estimate of how long a typical patient will stay in the hospital. This "potential" discharge date can be discussed early in the admission assessment. Mentioning an estimated date up front demonstrates respect for the family and caregivers. Plus, it helps prevent family members from having to scramble at the last minute to get time off work or get other arrangements in place, a situation that can cause the patient's discharge to be delayed.

Plenty of research shows that if complications are going to happen, they happen within the first 72 hours after a patient is discharged from the hospital. When the patient and his family have a discharge date in mind, they can plan for it and have preparations in place—which minimizes the likelihood of complications and ensures that someone is there to deal with them should they occur.

Unfortunately, too many organizations just don't do a good job in this area. One study found 44 percent of patients were not aware of their anticipated discharge dates.[1]

...And the Tactics That Make "Yes" Responses More Likely

Throughout the patient's stay, we need to take steps to make sure he not only knows his anticipated discharge date, but also that he has the help he needs at home and knows the appropriate information to take care of himself once he gets there. It's not enough to share this information once or even twice. We need to share it again and again, in as many ways as we can think of. Here are several tactics that will help:

Tactic 1: Use Key Words to Convey Discharge Information

Key words are all about "connecting the dots" with the patient. As he goes through his hospital stay, key words keep him thinking about his discharge date and help him connect information he receives daily to what he'll need when it's time to go home. Key words can also "trigger" the patient and his family or caregivers that this information is important for his discharge. (Family-centered care is important in all areas, but especially here since family plays a key role in the patient's healing process at home.)

Targeted questions help the patient clarify the help he will need and who will be helping him. They also convey empathy and compassion. A great time to use key words/questions is when reviewing the plan of care with the patient. Some suggestions might be:

"I want to make sure you and your family are prepared for your care after you go home. It looks like we are anticipating that will be Tuesday. Do you have someone who can arrange to come and get you that day?"

"We have been teaching your daughter how to do your wound care. Is she available every day, or do we need to train another family member as backup or make any arrangements for some home care support to assist her?"

"Do you have any concerns about your ability to care for yourself at home that we haven't addressed yet?"

Here are some tips and key words that help you reinforce the importance of going home:

- **Set the stage for discharge during the admission process.** Use statements like, *"We know being in the hospital is inconvenient. Based on your condition, we might expect that you would be here about three days. That means we can anticipate that you would go home Tuesday. I'll put that target date on your communication board and we will update it as we get more information about your plan of care."* This lets the patient know throughout his stay that you'll be sharing information he needs upon discharge.

- **During the admission assessment, ask the patient open-ended questions regarding her help at home to gather more in-depth information.**
  - *"Can you tell me about the person who will be helping you at home?"*

> ○ *"What is your biggest concern when thinking about going home?"*

As the care progresses, you can ask additional questions as part of the ongoing assessment of readiness. On the surface, some of the questions you ask may not seem like they are about who will be helping the patient. Yet they are relevant, because the home caregiver will need to think about these issues, too, in order to create a safe environment, provide the proper diet, and so forth.

- *"Since you are going home with a walker, do you have any concerns about how you will get around? How will you be accessing the bathroom / bedroom / kitchen?"*

- *"What do you know about the special diet your doctor wants you to follow when you go home?"*

- *"You will be going home on this medication, so can you tell me who will be helping you with it at home?"*

Tactic 2: Use Patient Communication Boards to Document and Reinforce Information That Will Help Prepare the Patient for Discharge

Some organizations now use a separate board dedicated to the discharge plan. These can be especially helpful in units or departments with more complex care needs such as rehab or bone marrow transplant. They facilitate dynamic updating and discussion not only with patients and families, but also with the entire care team. There is something highly valuable about having discharge information visibly in front of you throughout the stay.

Whether you have a dedicated "discharge info" board or use the standard whiteboard, keeping this information consistently in our dialogue is important. Some basic details to consider adding to the patient communication board are:

- Anticipated discharge date. Knowing this date from the beginning allows caregivers and patients to set up care needs and schedules ahead of time.

- Specific patient education needing validation prior to discharge: such as use of walker, diabetic diet education, adjusting insulin doses based on blood sugar results, etc.

- Case management resource name

- Name of the person who will be helping the patient at home (with the patient's permission, of course)

Finally, remember the phrase *Plan for Day; Plan for Stay*. The best-performing organizations have nurses discuss the plan for the day *and* the plan for the patient stay. Often, they find it helpful to write these easy-to-remember phrases on the patient's communication board as well. This will cue all parties to discuss goals, both short-term and long-term, with the discharge date in mind.

Tactic 3: Address "Help at Home" Issues during the Bedside Shift Report

First, it's important to incorporate key words about discharge into the Bedside Shift Report. The report is done with the patient involved, so key words can be used to ensure alignment with care providers and the patient and her family.

- *"Mrs. Jones and I reviewed some of her discharge instructions and the help she will have at home because it looks like she is leaving tomorrow. Sara, we need to ask the doctor about physical therapy orders, though. The therapy will help her be independent at home more quickly, and that's important because her daughter will be able to stay with her only one week. Will you please check on that when she rounds later today? Do you have any questions about discharge instructions at this time, Mrs. Jones?"*

- *"Dr. Hill said during his rounds today that if the chest x-ray looks clear tomorrow, you can go home. We want to be sure you have the help you need at home and I understand your daughter will be the best resource to help you. Is that still the plan? Sara, we will want to make sure you go over the medications again tonight when her daughter is visiting. Mrs. Jones, does that sound like a clear plan?"*

Following are a few more tips to ensure that discharge information is adequately addressed in the BSR:

- **Invite key caregivers or family members to attend the report.** Inviting participation of the caregivers in the report extends their knowledge and understanding of the care plan and progress of the patient. This opportunity to participate can be a key strategy in helping them feel included and well prepared to continue the care at home.

  - *"Two times every day, the nursing staff will be discussing the care plan for your dad when they change shifts. This will happen at your dad's bedside, and of course, your dad will be involved too. As a primary caregiver, your dad has given permission for you to participate. We highly encourage you to attend whenever you can. It will be very helpful for you to feel prepared to assist in his care."*

○ *"We want you to feel comfortable taking care of your dad when he is discharged. We know you will do a great job and we will answer any questions you have about his care."*

○ *"It can be pretty unsettling when we've been taking care of your dad for two weeks and now he's going home and it's going to be up to you. I want you to know that we're here to teach you how to move your dad from the wheelchair to the bed, and we'll be working with you to make sure you're comfortable doing this and both of you are safe."*

- **Ask for agreement on discharge instructions.** Sometimes a patient or her home-based primary caregiver will have an unarticulated fear, reservation, or uncertainty about a recommendation. If it's left unaddressed, they may leave the hospital and just not comply with the discharge instructions. Ask for their agreement with the instructions: *"Do you understand and agree with these instructions? I want to make sure that you are comfortable with these recommendations."* This should be asked again at the actual time of discharge.

- **Paraphrase key discharge instructions.** Ask the home-based primary caregiver and the patient to teach back information they learned through discharge instruction conversations. This powerful teaching modality can help identify potential gaps in understanding, fears, concerns, or opportunities to reeducate.

- o *"Can you share the diet requirements that you will follow when you are discharged home?"*

- o *"Can you tell me when you will be expecting the home care nurse to come by and what she will be working with you on?"*

- o *"Can you tell me what you learned about the importance of smoking cessation?"*

Document these responses in the patient education record.

Tactic 4: Implement Post-Visit Phone Calls

Nurses feel better knowing that their patients are prepared for discharge and have in place all the help they need to create the best healing environment. Unfortunately, research tells us that is often not the case. One study found that more than half of patients age 70 and over said they didn't recall anyone telling them how to care for themselves at home after discharge; among those who did receive instructions, two-thirds said they received only verbal instructions but no written material.[2] Post-visit phone calls help us identify and resolve such situations.

Post-visit calls have evolved from a satisfaction initiative where nurses called patients simply to ensure that they were home safe and sound to a tactic that is far more quality based. Evidence has proven that those patients who receive a post-discharge call are more satisfied with their overall experience with the hospital, but that is derived from the halo effect of making the call.

We want our post-visit calls to drive improvement in the patient's clinical outcome—not just check it off a checklist in order to get good HCAHPS results. That is why it's so important to make sure the calls are truly effective.

Post-Visit Calls: Clinical Quality

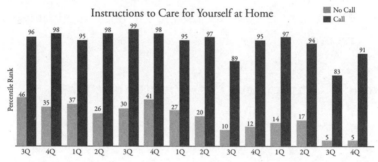

Figure 14.1

Here are a few tips that will impact the patient perception of staff asking about the help they'd need after discharge.

Before you call:

- **Set expectations for the call.** Share with patients that they will receive a phone call within 24-

48 hours of discharge. Many hospitals are asking the patient to confirm a convenient block of time for the call as well as the phone number where he can be reached (often this is not the home phone but rather a cell phone number).

- **Collect questions.** As you are preparing the patient for discharge, remind him that you'll be calling to check in on him. Ask him to write down questions he may have once he's home so that you can answer them when you call.

When you call:

- **Verify discharge instructions.** Always make sure the patient understands his discharge instructions. *"When you were discharged, Becky went over your discharge instructions with you. She asked you about the three priorities you were going to take care of when you got home. Can you share with me what you have done since you've been home with regard to your three priorities?"*

  - **Ask probing questions and dig deeper to gain insight.** *"When were you able to fill your prescription? When was the last time you changed your bandage? What time did home care contact you?"*

  - **Access patient records.** If possible, pull up the patient's records to refer to during the call. It's very helpful to have those discharge instructions in front of you.

- **Focus on care and follow-up.** Ensure that the discharge questions are about quality care and follow-up at home and are not intended to bias the patient or compete with any of the HCAHPS survey questions. Ask open-ended questions. Some examples to use include:

  - *"How would you rate your comfort level right now? How is your pain now, compared to when you were in the hospital?"*

  - *"What questions do you have about your medications?"*

  - *"When is your follow-up appointment with your doctor or clinic?"*

  - *"May I ask how your nursing care was?"*

  - *"We like to recognize our employees, volunteers, and physicians who provide exceptional care. Is there anyone you would like to recognize?"*

- **Focus on clinical.** The post-visit call is the perfect time to speak about clinical indicators:

  - Ask if the patient understands his self-care instructions, medication uses, doses, and side effects.

  - If appropriate, probe for indicators of infection, such as swelling, redness, fever, and so forth.

  - Confirm compliance and understanding of discharge instructions.

  - Remind the patient to schedule a follow-up

appointment with his physician and to call with any questions.

- **Validate!** If appropriate, pick one focus area in which to validate staff actions on post-visit phone calls. This will help evaluate the patient perception of hardwired processes such as hand washing, ID checks, and so forth.

  - *"Did you see staff washing their hands before they touched you?"* or *"How often did you see...?"*

  - *"Did the staff check your ID band before giving you medication?"* or *"How often did the staff...?"*

- **Set some goals.** You may wish to set some goals for discharge call completion rates. A sample goal might be 100 percent attempted, 70-80 percent reached for inpatients, and 50-60 percent reached for Emergency Department patients. We suggest you make up to three attempts within the first 48 hours. We have found that calls after 72 hours are considered more of a nuisance than a help for patients.

- **Set cyclical calls.** For complex patients at high risk for readmission, such as heart failure patients, we may want to talk with these patients every week for 30 days. This will help ensure that they are staying true to their discharge plan and that they aren't at risk for complications or readmission.

Good communication, Bedside Shift Reports, and post-visit phone calls allow you to communicate with the patient, family, or caregiver about what they need to know about the transition to home—and then follow up to ensure that things are progressing as expected. Together, these tactics help you make this transition as smooth, as comfortable, and most important of all, *as safe* as possible.

Tools & Resources

Studer Group offers a variety of tools and resources that support the tactics discussed in this chapter. To access the most up-to-date offerings, as well as to see what's new in healthcare, please visit www.studergroup.com/HCAHPS.

CHAPTER FIFTEEN:

WRITTEN SYMPTOM/ HEALTH PROBLEM INFORMATION

T HE HCAHPS QUESTION: During this hospital stay, did you get information in writing about what symptoms or health problems to look out for after you left the hospital?

When patients leave the hospital, they should not leave empty-handed. It's important that they have the material and information needed for their care at home. No matter how excellent a job staff members have done to prepare the patient, she will still need hard copies to reference. It's similar to keeping a favorite recipe filed away: You're pretty sure you could make it without the written recipe, but it's certainly reassuring to have it on hand...just in case.

Also, increasingly, we send patients and families home to perform very complex treatments such as injections, dressing changes, and even indwelling catheter maintenance. Without appropriate written instructions and resources, this can be a recipe for disaster. Providing written information at discharge is a way to reassure the patient and to make sure she doesn't miss a vital step.

Most organizations enclose this written symptom and health information in a discharge folder that contains all kinds of documents and brochures about the hospital or services. Typically, this folder is placed at the patient's bedside...and rarely looked at again except for when she wants to know what the TV channels are or how to place a long distance phone call.

It's our goal to make sure patients reference and follow these important instructions after they get home.

...And the Tactics That Make "Yes" Responses More Likely

Our job is to provide patients and their families this critical information in a way that ensures they can easily find the most important points. The discharge folder is a good storage spot for all the patient information...but how can we make it more effective? The answer follows.

Tactic 1: Provide Patient-Friendly Educational Materials

All too often, we hear about patients going home with a full packet of instructions—yet, when a care provider calls to ask, they say, "I never got any instructions." If you've ever had a baby, you can probably relate. You were almost certainly discharged from the hospital with a folder filled with information. Now ask yourself, *Where is the folder? Did the folder ever get opened? And if it did, was there just too much information?* See our point?

Here are tactics to make the patient education materials more effective.

- **Introduce information folders at admission.** When patients receive these folders early on, they will get the message that this education material is important. Don't just "hand them out." Tell the patient that they should carefully read the information and ask any questions they may need answered. From admission on, all caregivers who distribute other relevant patient information should utilize the discharge folder. Consider healthcare literacy when creating materials. Written materials should be written at the 5th-6th grade reading level, have no medical jargon, and be available in languages of the patient populations you serve with high frequency.

- **Design the folder for action. Use bright colors and clearly marked labels.** This folder is about the patient and not the hospital. It is not a marketing brochure. Create brightly colored discharge instruction folders, clearly labeled "Discharge Instructions." Consistently use one color for the folder, so all staff members can easily reference and find "the purple folder." We find that high-performing organizations also add "Including Current Medications" to the front of the folder or on the inside pocket.

Assign a color to each information sheet: For example, all medication information is printed on pink paper, hygiene/self-care is printed on blue paper, and so forth. Some of our partners add a label to the front with a space to write, "Top three things to do when I get home…" If you do this, be sure to use that space: As you and the patient talk about discharge, ask the patient (if possible) or the patient's at-home caregiver to write down the three most important to-dos.

- **Treat the folder like it's important and the patient will as well.** Let the patient know that this folder will hold important documents that she may need to reference while she's in the hospital—but will certainly need to reference upon discharge. Refer to it frequently throughout the patient's stay.

- **Don't just leave the folder on the bedside table.** It will get lost in the shuffle of magazines, newspapers, and other personal items. Draw the patient's attention to it as you add information to it throughout the patient's stay. Each time new information is added to the folder, a conversation and explanation needs to occur with the patient and her family. If the team ensures that the folder is kept as an important part of the care plan, the patient will pay attention to it as well.

- **Align the materials that go into the folder with quality initiatives.** Of course you'll want to include all essential materials, like information on activity level, diet, medication side effects, follow-up appointments, and symptoms to look out for after discharge. But also be sure to identify patients' potential risk for readmission. This will ensure that all care plans and processes include diagnosis-specific information that's shared and tracked appropriately. An example of this would be heart failure patients who need written instructions around medications, diet, activity, follow-up appointments, weight gain, and what to do if symptoms worsen.

- **Include written medication schedules.** In addition to sharing the patient's medication schedule with her each day, you should also provide her with a final schedule upon discharge, after appropriate medication reconciliation. These schedules help prevent patient medication errors, elevate compliance rates, and create a living document to share with primary physicians and care givers.

  Daily medication schedules usually have grids to help the patient identify dosage and timing of medications. Yours might include a space for the patient to record what time she took the medication and to log how she feels before/after each dose. It might also include medications she was taking at home and any others that she was previously taking that have been discontinued. Figure 15.1 is a sample Medication Schedule.

Medication Schedule

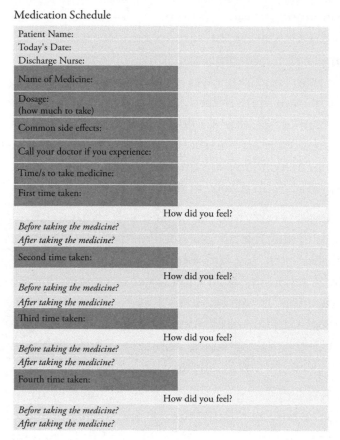

Figure 15.1

- **Highlight key points.** When you provide discharge information or medication sheets to the patient or the at-home caregiver, have her physically highlight key information. This will serve as an easy reference for the future regarding points that were important to her.

- **Don't let paper replace human interaction.** Discharge instructions are becoming very detailed, but we can't let a piece of paper talk for us. Nothing takes the place of explaining instructions to the patient person-to-person. Ideally you've covered the information in the discharge folder at various points during the patient's stay—but review the entire folder with her again at the actual time of discharge.

- **Train those who escort the patient at discharge to notice the folder.** The person might say: *"Here is your purple discharge folder—I want you to carry it out so you will have it handy. It has lots of important information, so make sure and put it in a safe and convenient place when you get home. Please keep your discharge folder by your phone. You'll want to have it handy when I call you tomorrow to see how you are doing at home."*

Having a thorough, well-organized, reader-friendly written record of what patients should do once they get home makes compliance far more likely. Having that document be something that reflects the same information that has been explained dynamically and thoroughly throughout the patient's stay makes the document relevant and important. Thus, these materials go a long way toward improving clinical outcomes and reducing avoidable readmissions—both of which are even more important than improving HCAHPS results.

Tactic 2: Validate Effectiveness of the Written Materials during a Post-Visit Call

While we discussed post-visit calls in the last chapter, we can't fail to mention the value of this tactic here as well. It's a good method for ensuring that the patient and families don't have further questions or need clarification and reinforcement of their written discharge instructions. As a matter of fact, the follow-up phone call is primarily for just this purpose, as the two greatest risks for adverse events or readmissions are patients taking their medications incorrectly and otherwise inaccurately following their discharge plan.

Simple questions can help assess if patients need more guidance. The more complex the medical instructions, the more detailed the questions should be. That means callers should have the discharge instructions available so they can query specifically how the patient is progressing on certain aspects of the discharge plan.

Post-Visit /Stay Clinical Phone Call Sample

Empathy and Concern	Hello, [Patient Name], this is [Caller Name] from [Hospital Name], and Dr. [Name] asked that I call and check on you after your recent visit to the hospital. Is this a good time?
Clinical Outcomes	• Were your discharge instructions clear and understandable? (Yes/No) Please tell me in your own words how you are to care for yourself at home. • Are you having any unusual symptoms or problems? (Specific to problem- i.e., dressing, pain, bruising or swelling, N/V) • Have you filled your new prescriptions yet? Do you have any questions about those medications? • Were you able to make a follow-up appointment with the physician?
Reward and Recognition	Are there any physicians, nurses, or hospital staff you would like us to recognize for doing a very good job?
Process Improvement	We want to make sure you were satisfied with your care. How were we, Mrs. Smith?
Appreciation	Thank you for taking the time to share with me about your care and recovery. Do you have any suggestions for us?

Figure 15.2

The more we can help patients achieve a safe transition home, the more we can further our mission to provide excellent care. Our patients deserve the kind of guidance and instructions that will allow them to continue this excellent care at home. Let's do all we can to provide it to them.

Tools & Resources

Studer Group offers a variety of tools and resources that support the tactics discussed in this chapter. To access the most up-to-date offerings, to see what's new in healthcare, and to download a worksheet that will help you create a plan to improve patient perception of care in the "Discharge Information" arena, please visit www.studergroup.com/HCAHPS.

THE HOSPITAL ENVIRONMENT (CLEAN & QUIET)

"Noise is the cruelest absence of care." —Florence Nightingale

It's hard to argue with Florence Nightingale. The environment of care was a priority even in her day.

As healthcare professionals, we'll go to great lengths to help patients get the best outcomes: We'll make sure they have the right medications, get the appropriate tests, and know we care. We'll respond quickly and efficiently to their requests. We'll make sure they know what to do after they're discharged. But what about the physical environment? Are we doing everything possible to ensure that it's conducive to the healing process?

A clean, quiet hospital is vitally important. Obviously, the "clean" part can have life-or-death implications for patients, but both cleanliness and quietness have psychological effects as well—which, in turn, impact clinical outcomes.

First, let's briefly talk about cleanliness. While this book is *not* intended to address the vitally important processes for reducing infections and protocols for actually cleaning and sterilizing a room, we *do* want to discuss steps we can take to improve patients' *perceptions* of cleanliness.

A qualitative study was undertaken to understand public perceptions of hospital cleanliness and how this might be improved. Results demonstrated that for both patients and visitors, perceptions of cleanliness are shaped by the things they see, hear, smell, and taste. According to the study, key factors that led to perceptions of cleanliness included[1]:

- Ensuring hospital floors, walls, doors, and toilets are kept clean, tidy, and free of stains.

- Patients have the opportunity to shower/bathe regularly.

- Staff have clean hands and uniforms.

- Eye-catching materials posted visually for patients and family to see why cleanliness is important as well as what people need to do to follow guidelines.

Through transparency and public reporting, patients now more than ever are making a conscious choice of where to seek treatment. Hospital cleanliness is likely to influence their decision.

Noise, too, is a deeply important issue for patients. And there is a good reason for that—it seems hospitals are noisier than they once were.

In fact, since 1960, average daytime hospital noise levels have risen from 57 decibels to 72; nighttime levels have gone from 42 decibels to 60.[2] (A vacuum cleaner is about 70 decibels.)[3]

Yet noise is an environmental stressor that is known to have physiological and psychological effects. The body responds to noise in the same way it responds to stress, meaning that too much noise over time can impair health. Research clearly shows that hospital noise levels exceed noise level recommendations and this has the potential to increase complications in patients.[4]

And it's not only patients who suffer. Employees who work in noisy environments for long periods—as nurses do—also experience stress symptoms that can affect health. In addition to blood pressure changes, burnout, depression, and irritability are possible.[5]

So, what can we do to provide a healing environment? For starters, we can focus on the patients' perception of how often we have *always* kept their rooms and bathrooms clean and kept their rooms quiet at night. The Hospital Environment composite of the HCAHPS survey allows us to measure just how well we are doing in the eyes of patients.

Patients, particularly those spending days or weeks primarily in a single room, are deeply aware of the hospital environment. They notice when we're doing a good job of keeping things clean—and when we're not. They're also acutely sensitive to the hospital environment and how quiet and restful the hospital is (or is not). When we hardwire tactics to keep our hospital clean and quiet, we can positively impact patients' perception of their healing environment.

The chapters that follow will share tactics that have helped the organizations Studer Group® works with achieve outcomes well above those of the nation in HCAHPS results connected to the clean and quiet questions.

The Survey Questions

These two questions are on the HCAHPS survey for the patient perception of the "Hospital Environment" arena. Answers are given in the frequency scale: *never, sometimes, usually*, or *always*. The percent of patients who responded *always* is publicly reported at www.hospital-compare.hhs.gov.

1. **During this hospital stay, how often were your room and bathroom kept clean?**

2. **During this hospital stay, how often was the area around your room quiet at night?**

In the chapters that follow, we will share a few specific tactics for each question that positively impact the likelihood that patients will answer *always* to these two questions.

While there are surely other tactics that could be implemented, we find that the ones presented here tend to immediately impact patient perception of the cleanliness and quietness of your hospital.

NOTE: While we understand these two questions are reported separately, we believe they both contribute to a healing physical environment. That's why, though we recognize they're not presented together in reports, we've opted to address them together in this book.

CHAPTER SIXTEEN:

ROOM AND BATHROOM CLEANLINESS

THE HCAHPS QUESTION: During this hospital stay, how often were your room and bathroom kept clean?

Most of us would do just about anything to avoid using most gas station restrooms. Why? Plain and simple: We think they are dirty. Sometimes, it is dirt we can see. Other times, we can visualize the microscopic germs on every single surface. What we're really afraid of is getting some infection or disease.

Now imagine how patients feel about such germs— real or imagined—in a hospital setting. Cleanliness matters. It especially matters at a hospital when germs can cause infections that can have a profound impact on our patients' recovery and overall well-being. And of course, since patients can choose where they wish to be treated, hospital cleanliness may influence their decision-making process.

This HCAHPS question may focus just on patients' rooms and bathrooms, but their perception of their experience is possibly impacted by other areas of the hospital. Public restrooms, reception areas, and the cafeteria are all areas where cleanliness, or the lack thereof, can create impressions that carry over to patients' response to this question. All areas of the hospital need to be immaculately clean.

What's more, cleanliness isn't just about Housekeeping or Environmental Services. All staff must be focused on this HCAHPS question and can impact it by reducing clutter, picking up trash, and so forth. They can demonstrate courtesy and respect at the same time by treating the patient's room like it is their guest bedroom and the patient like she is their guest.

This is demonstrated by the following story:

I was called to Mr. Anderson's room because the staff had shared with me that he was quite upset and was refusing to let the current nurse care for him this day. I was surprised because he didn't seem to be the kind of patient we might typically consider "difficult."

I went to his room and shared that the staff said he wanted to talk with me. He started out sharing that Karen, his nurse, was the same nurse he had for the last three days and that she was incompetent and he wanted someone else to assume his care.

As I started to question him about what contributed to this impression of Karen, he pointed to a cotton ball under the bed. "That cotton ball has been under that bed for two days and she hasn't done anything about it." At first, I was stunned to think that he was having such a severe reaction to something so trivial but then he went on to explain that he was readmitted to the hospital this time after a

25-day stay only three weeks ago for a severe hospital-acquired infection. He was terrified that the cotton ball on the floor and therefore the perception of poor cleanliness would lead to another infection. Once I knew his concerns, his reaction was quite rational based on his experience.

After I spoke with both Karen, his nurse, and the EVS staff and supervisor, we made extra efforts to ensure that he felt his room was clean to his satisfaction. I often wonder now how many patients feel the same way but never say anything.

—Shannon, Nurse Manager, Medical Unit

...And the Tactics That Make "Always" Responses More Likely

How can we demonstrate to our patients the importance we place on keeping their rooms and bathrooms clean? Following are tactics that will make a difference in the patients' perception of cleanliness. (Please be aware that clean doesn't mean new. Some organizations with the oldest facilities perform best on this HCAHPS question.)

Tactic 1: Create a Partnership between Environmental Services and Nursing

Make no mistake: Even if your Environmental Services staff performs as if they were working at the Ritz-Carlton, they can do only so much. With the limited EVS staffing resources most hospitals have, each patient room gets around 20 minutes of dedicated housekeeping time over a 24-hour period. The tactics here will ensure not only that those 20 minutes consist of premier levels of "cleanliness" care, but that the 23 hours and 40 minutes that EVS staff are not present do as well. (It's this portion of the day that actually has the most impact on HCAHPS results.)

The good news is that the clinical staff, nursing, and patient care technicians have the framework to ensure that this happens. It is called Hourly Rounding,® and Behavior #5, conduct an environmental assessment of the room, includes making sure that the room and bathroom are clean and neat. Every hour, someone is in the patient's room assessing the environment for safety, so this should include looking at trash, spills, or anything that makes the room appear unclean.

In one large, Midwest teaching facility, the nursing and EVS staff partnered in a campaign they called TLT: trash, linen, and trays. They decided to do this after learning that these were the three items that most often made patient rooms seem cluttered, giving patients and families the perception that the area was not clean. In other words, the EVS staff and the nursing staff joined forces to watch for opportunities to empty trash when the can was 75 percent full, remove excess linens even if clean, and see that patient trays were picked up in a timely manner. In the units that executed this very well, cleanliness scores improved six top box points in just one quarter.

As with many tactics, we need a partnership to be sure that ongoing attention gets paid to the things that matter to patients. Cleanliness is one of them. So yes…it takes a village to keep a hospital room clean.

Tactic 2: Practice Environmental Leader Rounding

There is no better way to find out if you are truly serving your customers than by asking them directly. Environmental leader rounding allows you to check in with nursing leaders and patients to gain insight into what is working well and what can be improved. It is a chance for the EVS leader to verify that the room and bathroom are clean, to recognize staff members who do a good job, and to coach those who need improvement. It also lets patients know that providing them with a clean, safe, and healing environment is a priority for you.

We've found that, for any patient who has an issue regarding cleanliness, EVS leader rounding increases the opportunity to change her perception to excellent by addressing any issues in real time. Just checking back in to be sure the issue was resolved helps patients and their families know they are cared about.

Here are some rounding tips for Environmental Services leaders:

- **First, work with the unit manager to establish a rounding plan.** This should address frequency of patient rounding and a follow-up process to be used if a problem is identified.

- **Make it manageable.** Many EVS leaders or supervisors incorporate physical validation of the cleanliness of the rooms into their daily plan. If not, however, it's a good idea for them to round randomly for spot checks. Start with the lower-performing units and those with the largest number of admissions and discharges. The unit nurse leader will be rounding on every patient every day, so partner with that leader to get insight from her rounds and ensure that you are not over-rounding and bothering patients.

- **Prepare for rounding by checking with the supervisor of the unit first.** This will help ensure that you are rounding at an appropriate time. It will also help you learn about any service recovery opportunities and make sure you are not asking patients the same questions.

- **As you round:**
    - Question the patient about the cleanliness of her room. (See the following key words.)
    - Check for cleanliness: Look into the bathroom before you leave, using the key

words, *"May I check your bathroom to ensure that it is clean and safe?"* After checking, say, *"(Name of housekeeper) did a very good job of cleaning and sanitizing it for your safety."* (If the bathroom is not clean, address it right away, without criticizing other staff: *"Looks like housekeeping hasn't gotten to this yet—I'll make sure someone comes in to clean the bathroom shortly."*)

- ○ Build in recognition: Ask if there's any staff member who should be recognized. Immediately follow up with any staff member mentioned to reward or coach to higher performance.

- ○ Leave contact information: Give the patient or family member your card and indicate that you are available if at any time the patient feels the room and bathroom are not consistently clean. Say that you will check in again tomorrow to follow up.

- ○ Follow up on any concerns: If a patient concern is identified, follow up with the patient as well as the nursing staff member who was assigned to that room.

- **Try to see the room and bathroom through their eyes.** As you round, adopt the perspective of patients and their families. Keep in mind that patients are lying in a bed, so don't forget to look at the ceiling or, if it's a room with multiple patients, the floor under the other bed. (Remember the cotton ball story!)

- **Use key words that speak to cleanliness.**
When rounding on the patient, build in words like "clean" and "sanitized." Here is a sample of key words for an EVS leader rounding on a patient:

> *"Hi, my name is Benjamin. I am the director of Environmental Services here at I-Care Hospital.* (Greet the family.) *May I have a few minutes of your time to ask you a few questions? Is this a good time?"* (If not, say, *"I am sorry to have disturbed you. I will try again at a better time."*) *"At I-Care Hospital, it is important to us that we do a very good job of cleaning your room and bathroom."*

> *"Vanessa is your housekeeper. She is one of our best and always does a very good job of not only cleaning but also sanitizing the room for your safety. Did Vanessa introduce herself when she came into your room?"* (If you find she does this consistently, then change the question when you round the next time to validate duration—i.e., *"Did she tell you how long it would take for her to clean your room?"*) If the housekeeper gets a compliment, tell the patient, *"I will be sure to let Vanessa know—I am sure she will be very pleased!"*

> Ask family members: *"What is your impression of the cleanliness of the hospital?"*

> *"Would you mind if I checked your bathroom to make sure everything is in order and we did a very good job of cleaning it?"* (If everything is okay, say, *"Vanessa did a very good job."* If not, say, *"I would like Vanessa to stop back by to be sure it is very clean."*)

"Is there anything we missed? Is there anything else we can do to improve your stay?"

"Let me leave you my business card. This is the number you may call if you have any issues with our Environmental Services Department. Call if at any time we are not consistently doing a very good job with cleaning your room and bathroom." Or, if a number is already available, review it with the patient: *"I see Vanessa's name and number are on the whiteboard as well."*

"Thank you for your time."

- **Regularly round on the key nursing units and document outcomes.** EVS leaders and supervisors can round on nurse leaders, charge nurses, and nursing unit or department staff to harvest information regarding the effectiveness of the EVS staff. They will typically spend at least an hour a week rounding on their high volume nursing units and gathering important feedback. In an hour a leader can easily visit four to six units and gather good feedback. The following examples reflect approaches used by EVS directors to get feedback, share desired actions, and communicate outcomes on HCAHPS results with leaders:

  "What is working well with EVS?" (Sometimes a simple question can help you glean valuable insights into potential problems or can help identify best practices to harvest and move to other areas.)

  "I noticed your 'patient perception of cleanliness' rating is above our hospital's goal. We perform far better

than most other hospitals across the nation in terms of patients feeling that their rooms were always kept clean, and I want you to know that your team is a big part of that."

"Our paper toilet seat covers will be installed in all rooms on September 1. In your opinion, is there anything specific I can do to help improve the patient perception of cleanliness on your unit?"

"Do you have any suggestions on how we can improve our cleanliness on your unit or in your department?"

- **Use specific survey results to reward and recognize employees.** To make this even more impactful, EVS leaders can ask other nurse leaders to join in the effort. For example:

  "The HCAHPS result on the question regarding cleanliness has improved from 72 percent saying we always kept the room and bathroom clean to 86 percent. This puts our performance above the 95th percentile nationally. Jane, your unit housekeeper, has a big role in these overall results, so I wanted to call this to your attention, and I thought we could partner in acknowledging her for this important contribution to your unit and the team."

Tactic 3: Teach EVS Staff to Use Key Words at Key Times

We want our patients to get a consistent message: *"We care about you and want to provide a healing environment for you."* Key words are the best tool for standardizing communication to consistently demonstrate care and concern for the patient.

Our top-performing hospitals have invested the time and resources to train all environmental staff to have actual conversations with patients. In many cases, this takes staff members out of their comfort zones. Key words can also reduce anxiety for those staff members who are not accustomed to speaking with patients.

Key words also help connect staff with the *why*— i.e., why you want them talking to a patient in the first place. First and foremost, communicating with patients and families when we have entered their personal space (their room) is a matter of courtesy and respect. Any staff member entering for any reason should be prepared to speak genuinely and kindly with the patient.

Another reason (though it comes in a distant second after courtesy and respect) is that speaking to patients makes the EVS staff more visible, which impacts perception of cleanliness.

AIDET® is the foundation for opening this communication and it is followed with general conversation. Specific key word phrases such as *"Mr. Jones, I have finished sanitizing your room and bathroom. Is there anything I have missed?"* can be very effective in making sure the patients have a role in the quality control of the outcome of this service.

It's important to let staff know that it's good to talk to patients. What's more, they need a minimum level of communication skills to be in a patient room.

This may challenge some organizations to reconsider the skills that EVS staff need when assigned to areas that will require interaction with patients and families. Language barriers must be considered and addressed. The EVS staff doing dailies in patients' rooms should have the basic abilities required to speak and connect with patients, so it's important to provide any training or tools they need to do so.

A few tips:

- **Establish a consistent cleaning routine.** Housekeepers should have a consistent list and order for cleaning their rooms. This will build good habits and ensure that steps aren't missed. They can also build in key words to reinforce the action with the patient and build a relationship. Here are some examples of steps and key words to go with them:

  ○ Remove soiled linens and trash. *"Let me get you some fresh linens and empty your wastebaskets. Do you have anything you'd like me to take?"*

  ○ Sanitize and wipe down surfaces. *"Mr. Murphy, I want to make sure your room is sanitized so I am wiping down all surfaces. Do you see anything I missed?"*

  ○ Clean bathroom. *"I have cleaned and sanitized your bathroom. Please let me know if there is anything I missed."*

- Devote special attention to the toilet as it typically causes the most patient dissatisfaction. *"I paid extra attention to the toilet area. You should be all set."*

- Dust and mop floor. *"I'm almost done. Is there anything you see that needs further attention? Is there anything I can do for you before I leave?"*

- **Train staff to ask permission to clean.** They should knock prior to entering and say, *"Hello, Mr. Jones. I am Oscar and I will be cleaning your room and bathroom. It will take about ten minutes. Is now a good time for me to come in? Thank you. Before I begin, I just want to wash my hands."*

This is another way to ensure the patient and family know that cleanliness and handwashing is expected of all staff, not just nursing.

- **Teach key words around cleanliness.** For example:

  "We want to make sure your room and bathroom are always clean and sanitized—is there anything I've missed?"

  "I've cleaned your bathroom and noticed an area that needs to be repaired in the shower, so I'll contact the Engineering staff and let them know."

  "Let me go ahead and empty your trash can because I see it is getting full and we want your room to be clean."

- **Expect EVS team to talk to and connect with patients.** Set the expectation that they will treat patients with courtesy and respect. They can and should proactively ask how patients are feeling, address the family members, and offer to perform small acts of kindness for patients or their families if appropriate. These can be simple things like watering flowers, making folded towel animals, bringing a coloring book for a child who is visiting, etc.

- **Empower the EVS team to resolve problems.** For example, if when cleaning a room, the housekeeper notices a leaking faucet, have him request it be repaired. Also, have him communicate to the patient that the repair will occur:

  > *"Mr. Rodriguez, I noticed the faucet on your sink is dripping. I hope it hasn't been disturbing you. I will contact Engineering and ask that they repair it as soon as possible. I will check back to ensure it has been taken care of."*

- **Give the patient some control in determining time for cleaning.**

  - Have EVS staff member ask, *"Is now a good time for me to clean your room?"*

  - If the patient is eating, have staff member say, *"I see you are eating dinner. May I start in your bathroom?"*

- **Ask EVS staff to engage the family.** *"Your mom's room looks clean. Do you see anything that needs more attention?"* Make eye contact with the patient and any visitors in the room.

- **If the patient isn't in the room, make sure he knows housekeeping has been there.**

  o Leave a card: Create tent cards as noticeable proof that the room has been cleaned. Use key words that align with the hospital's concern for cleanliness. Do *not* let tent cards become "clutter" or a replacement for actually connecting personally with the patient.

  o Check back in later: Have the housekeeper stop back in the room and say, *"I cleaned your room while you were gone. I wanted to check back and see if there was anything additional I could do."*

- **Reinforce your cleaning philosophy in a video.** Some high-performing organizations have created a short video for patients that explains the room cleaning process and how it contributes to a safe, healing environment. You can put it on your closed-caption TV channel if you have one and ask patients and families to watch it upon admission.

Cleanliness and the Importance of Feedback

The ability to get feedback regarding the effectiveness of the EVS staff and the level of service being provided is essential to improvement. This is done is several ways:

- Listen to the "voice of the customer" data received directly from patients via the HCAHPS survey. This is valuable feedback for both clinical and EVS leaders.

- Use EVS leader rounding to elicit feedback from both patients and staff.

- Use a Support Service Survey. This establishes a mechanism for clinical leaders to provide regular quantitative data to evaluate the level of service being provided.

The Support Service Survey is a Studer Group®-recommended tool that is designed to a) get feedback from clinical staff on a variety of key performance standards and b) offer the ability to identify opportunities for improvement or areas that are performing well. (While we're discussing this in the context of EVS for this domain, other key support departments are typically included in the process, including lab, radiology, pharmacy, transport, etc. Any area that is not performing well, and therefore might take key clinical resources away from direct patient care to fix those problems, would benefit from being included.)

Sample Support Service Survey

Please evaluate the following department on communication, attitude, responsiveness, and accuracy based on your interactions in the last 90 days.

Definitions of these terms are as follows:

Communication	My team communicates with you effectively.
Attitude	My team treats you with courtesy and respect.
Responsiveness	My team meets your needs with the appropriate sense of urgency based on the priority of your request.
Accuracy	My team provides consistent and reliable services with appropriate follow-up.

Department description:

- Environmental Services (EVS): Provides a clean environment for patient care areas and non-patient care areas.

	N/A	Never	Sometimes	Usually	Always
Communication					
Attitude					
Responsiveness					
Accuracy					

What can this department do to improve (please make sure to answer for categories not rated "always")?

Figure 16.1

The survey, which is typically quite simple in its design and approach, can be distributed monthly or quarterly. It can be disseminated via email using an electronic survey site like Key Survey or SurveyMonkey, and might simply ask the nurse leaders to evaluate each department on a 1-5 scale on attitude, timeliness, accuracy, accessibility, and other areas.

Being able to assess and report this data over time, coupled with the qualitative information received during rounding can assist EVS with information that will improve the service they and their team are providing both staff and patients.

One More Tip

Here is another tip to consider as you are hardwiring the previous tactics.

Tip: A Few Cleanliness "Extras" to Consider

Create a clean team. This group might consist of EVS, nursing, and ancillary leaders. They would look for opportunities organization-wide to focus on cleanliness. For instance:

- Ask for help: Ask administration to empty their own trash, so housekeepers get more time on the units.

- Audit trash can locations: Review and make sure trash cans are in the best possible locations and that there are enough of them in public areas.

- Make sure everyone's on trash duty: Train all staff to pick up trash on the floor in the hallways and incorporate these expectations in the standards of behavior.

Consider assigning housekeepers to units. Organizations do better on this composite if the housekeepers are part of the nursing unit team.

Connect the dots with the housekeeping staff. Be sure they understand they aren't simply cleaning rooms. Many times they are the first line of defense in stopping infections. Teach EVS workers about MRSA and other organisms and their role in stopping them from spreading and keeping patients healthy. This will improve the consistency of cleaning something even when it looks clean. One organization gave their EVS staff unofficial job titles of Infection Prevention Specialists. This really connected with that staff and made them feel great purpose in their work.

Don't forget the importance of cleaning "other items" like the telephone, remote control, and call button. These can harbor germs just like any other surface.

Schedule multiple patient/housekeeping encounters. One hospital that we work with altered the housekeepers' assignment, so that patients had more frequent encounters with housekeeping each day. Here's how it works:

- When the housekeeper arrives on the unit at the start of her shift, she empties patient room trash. She takes this opportunity to introduce herself and let the patient know she will return later in the day to clean and sanitize the room and bathroom.

- The housekeeper returns for full room cleaning. She uses prescribed key words and behaviors.

- At the end of her shift, the housekeeper checks with the patient on room cleanliness, empties trash, and refreshes towels if needed.

- The housekeeping leader rounds on the patient using key words described earlier (although this encounter would not necessarily be every day).

Seeing housekeeping staff so many times keeps their efforts top of mind for patients, shoring up their perception of hospital cleanliness.

Patients are all too aware of the health risks associated with germs in the healthcare environment. After all, they hear the news reports and many may know people who've gotten hospital-acquired infections. They will truly appreciate your efforts to keep rooms and bathrooms clean and sanitized—and your efforts to let them know you're doing so.

As health reform laws tighten up and hospital-acquired infections become an even more critical issue, a laser-focus on cleanliness will be paramount. But the true impetus for providing a clean environment goes far deeper than finances: We do it because we want to provide the very best place for our patients to receive care. We keep our hospitals clean and quiet because it's the right thing to do. By paying attention to the details of our physical environment, we help patients heal. There can be no more important reason to strive for *always*.

Tools & Resources

Studer Group offers a variety of tools and resources that support the tactics discussed in this chapter. To access the most up-to-date offerings, as well as to see what's new in healthcare, please visit www.studergroup.com/HCAHPS.

Chapter Seventeen:

Nighttime Quietness

THE HCAHPS QUESTION: During this hospital stay, how often was the area around your room quiet at night?

The average hospital is a busy place. It certainly isn't the kind of business that can close the doors and shut off the lights at 9 p.m. Patients need assistance 24 hours a day, 7 days a week. There are late admissions and discharges, medications to be given, dressings to be changed, and so forth. There are family members and friends of patients coming and going at all hours. And, of course, the floors need to be cleaned, light bulbs changed, and equipment transferred.

This all adds up to *noise*. Hospital staff members are accustomed to it and probably barely notice it. They're not the ones trying to sleep, and besides, it's *their* noise. But patients perceive this "background noise" differently. Have you ever been awakened at 3 a.m. by a neighbor's barking dog? It's far more disruptive and frustrating than, say, the cry of your own baby from down the hall. We're far more tolerant of conditions we create than those imposed on us by another party.

The HCAHPS "quiet" question specifies nighttime, but the fact is that if the hospital is noisy and chaotic during the day, patients will not perceive it to be a healing environment. What's worse, they literally may *not* heal as quickly as they would in a serene setting—there is plenty of evidence that stress impedes healing.

In view of all these realities, *can* hospitals create a quiet environment for patients at all hours—but particularly at night? The answer is yes, we can—or at least we can create a *quieter* environment. For many patients, rest is an important part of their recovery...and we owe it to them to ensure that they get as much as they possibly can.

...And the Tactic and Tips That Make "Always" Responses More Likely

In almost all cases, achieving a quiet environment means reducing activity. Yet in a hospital environment, that is very hard to do. But there are many other things we can do to reduce the noise in the areas around patient rooms.

At Studer Group, we have found that of the organizations we coach, the highest performers have instilled a level of sensitivity and accountability around noise management into their own staff. Staff members in these organizations are completely willing to confront loud behaviors, whether they are coming from fellow caregivers, other staff, or patients and families.

That said, we have found that there is one major tactic that impacts this question. In general, the perception of greater quietness results from the words you say along with a combination of little things you can do (many of which are listed in the following tips). Also, while the HCAHPS question is about noise at night, these strategies can also help with noise at any time of day, as healing takes place around the clock.

Tactic 1: Use Key Words at Key Times to Proactively Address Noise

We all know a certain amount of noise inside hospitals is inevitable. By using key words to acknowledge the challenges it causes and to narrate the things we are doing to alleviate the problem, we can set realistic expectations with patients that we care about their well-being. Here are a few opportunities to use key words:

During leader rounds and Bedside Shift Reports. For example, a leader or staff member might say: *"While it is not possible to stop all noise at night, since we need to actively care for patients, it is our priority to keep noise levels as low as possible. Can you tell me if you got some good rest last night?"* or *"We want you to heal quickly. How well did you rest last night?"*

If the patient says she slept okay: *"That's great. Rest is so important to healing; we'll make sure to do the same routine tonight."*

If the patient indicates that she didn't rest well: *"I'm so sorry. Let's discuss some options that might help you get better rest tonight."* (Then, offer up choices like earplugs, headphones, and so forth. See tips later on in the chapter.)

It's important to use these and similar key words both morning and evening. (In the evening you might just reiterate what you discussed earlier in the day in regard to noise.) By repeating these words at the end of each day, all caregivers know what's being done to manage noise levels, and the patient hears that this issue is a priority.

When you anticipate nighttime lab draws. Often patients are woken up in the middle of the night for a lab draw. If this needs to happen, share the *why* with the patient (ahead of time, if possible): *"I'm going to need to wake you in the night for a lab draw. I hate to wake you, but it is important that the test be done because your doctor wants to be sure that he has your results before he comes to see you in the morning."*

On particularly noisy occasions. These will help staff members deal with problems related to noisy roommates, family issues, or even construction. For instance: *"We want to provide the best healing environment for all our patients. Would you please lower your noise level to help our other patients get the rest they need?"*

As you read through the tips in the rest of this chapter, you will see a few more examples of key words. Feel free to use them or create your own.

Key words can be extremely powerful. Even when they can't change the reality of a situation, they can surely reduce the negative feeling patients may have about it. What's more, when we use key words to "connect the dots" on why we're doing what we're doing, we show our empathy and compassion for patients. This can shift their perception of their entire stay.

A Few Tips to Help Your Hospital "Quiet Down"

Provide "noise reduction" tools such as headphones and earplugs. While they don't address the root cause of noise, earplugs are inexpensive and a good "Band-Aid," as well as a goodwill-builder. Headphones can often be plugged into the pillow speakers for background noise. Soothing music is a research-based complementary strategy for reducing pain and stress or anxiety.

If you encourage patients to bring their own music for distraction, be careful about keeping tabs on these items. Treat any iPods, MP3 players, etc. as valuables. Consider providing patients with reloadable MP3 players, which are inexpensive (and can be sanitized) and can be used with "throw-away" earphones, to reduce noise. Soothing "white noise" can be loaded onto the players as well.

Close the doors as often as possible. Of course, safety comes first, but when possible, at least partially close doors to protect privacy and hold out noise as well. This has been shown to be the best strategy for reducing noise and enhancing patient perception of hospital quietness. Formal "close the doors" campaigns have proven to raise HCAHPS results dramatically in the first quarter.

So, if you pick one thing to implement for this question, implement "close the doors."

- Make standard at exit: Train all staff to close the door upon leaving a room.

- Use key words when closing the door: *"I am going to close the door for your privacy and so you can rest better."*

- Use key words with patients who express the desire to keep their doors open: *"I am happy to leave the door open, but it may be noisier. Are you sure?"*

- Address exceptions: For clinical situations where the door may need to stay open—fall risk, clinically unstable, etc.—develop a system to notify staff of this. One organization places a star on the doorframe of patients whose doors need to remain open. Another has a reversible sign for the doorframe that reads, "I prefer my door open" OR, "I prefer my door closed."

Give patients a "quiet kit" at admission. One of our partner hospitals in Missouri provides quiet kits for patients at the time of admission. The kit (a small, clear plastic bag with a drawstring) holds a disposable pair of earplugs and a disposable eye mask. If you adopt the idea, you might also include in each bag a card that reads, "For our commitment to your healing" or, "Rest is the best medicine." The presentation of kits at admission is a proactive attempt to acknowledge that while hospitals can be a noisy place, the staff is dedicated to dampening the noise to promote healing.

Cluster nighttime tasks together. This helps ensure that patients are not woken up during the night more often than absolutely necessary. Also, explain nighttime Hourly Rounding® to patients and make sure staff are sensitive to quiet rounds.

Establish a "Quiet Hour" or "Quiet Time." During the day, designate one hour (or perhaps a lesser amount) of each shift to maintaining quiet. At this time, to the extent that it's reasonable and doesn't compromise care, refrain from interrupting or disturbing patients. Cease as much hospital commotion as possible (including food service, housekeeping, rounding, etc.). Dim lights, play calming music over the intercom, and pull shades. The idea is to remind staff and patients that this time is dedicated to quiet healing.

Perform a noise audit. Assign leaders or staff to conduct "secret shopping" with the intent of "listening" for improvement opportunities as they relate to noise at night. Have them pay special attention to staff voices and noisy equipment that needs immediate attention. Things that may seem like "normal business" to staff—squeaky wheels on carts, chart assembly with binders opening and closing, linen closet door hinges clanging, ringing telephones, unit doors latching and unlatching, overhead pages even for emergencies, the jovial conversations of staff, and the disruption of care by roommates in dual occupancy rooms—can be incredibly irritating to patients.

Ask a leader to be a "patient for a night." You'll be surprised at the noise the volunteer reports back. We've found that patients hear a lot of conversations between nurses and other hospital staff. Just going through this exercise can make the problem "real" to leaders, creating more urgency around finding solutions.

Address construction noise. Don't pretend the pounding of hammers and roar of heavy machinery don't exist. Be up front about it. Proactive communication about construction noise tells patients that while the noise is inevitable, you are concerned for their well-being and their ability to rest and heal. Prepare for this disruption by taking proactive steps with items such as earplugs, small fans for ambient noise, music therapy, etc.

Develop some "key words" to address construction noise: *"Sorry it is not as restful as we would like due to our construction. We have taken some steps to offer things that might help reduce the noise. Here are some earplugs, and if those aren't helpful we also have a small fan that might reduce the noise of the construction."*

Use bed management teams to protect privacy. When census allows, keep rooms private until absolutely necessary. Also identify the "loudest" rooms, like those closest to the nursing station or those by elevators, main thoroughfares, or staff lounges, and fill them last.

Adapt patient-centered visiting guidelines. While we are strong proponents of family-centered care and open visitation regarding hours, this does not mean that patients can have ten visitors at the bedside at all times. Patient-centered visitation should not come at the expense of other patients' ability to rest. Train all staff on dealing with the (usually minor) problems relating to excess visitation.

Dim the lights. Just lowering the lighting can naturally get staff to talk more softly. Even better news: You'll save on electricity.

Post "shhh" signs in appropriate locales. These do a great job of reminding patients, family, and staff about the focus on creating a healing environment. Engage physicians and staff and change the posters regularly, so they are new and noticeable. For example:

- In hallways, post signs that read, "Doctors' Orders: Our Patients Are Resting" or "Use Your Inside Voice" or "Quiet: Healing in Process."

- Place similar signs by loud areas like elevators and nursing stations.

- Consider using doorknob hangers (similar to hotel rooms) that inform visitors and staff: "Quiet, please. I am resting."

- Place yellow caution signs at entrances to units, alerting visitors that they are visiting a "Small Voice Zone." (We've seen one sign that has an eye-catching graphic of a tiny mouse encouraging a lion to "hush.")

Meet with EVS, food service, and materials management to address squeaky wheels and other maintenance noise. Changing to soft wheels on noisy dollies and linen carts is usually one of the first items on an action plan and definitely worth the investment.

Eliminate overhead paging and paging into patient rooms from the desk unless absolutely

necessary. Sometimes, of course, overhead paging is necessary. However, you can adjust the volume to make it less jarring.

If you use electronic noise monitors, make sure they're not a substitute for human monitoring of noisy staff behaviors. Ensure that staff members are trained that these electronic devices are just visual representations of our efforts to raise awareness of noise levels. Engage night supervisors to monitor the devices for appropriate placement, volume monitor, and compliance when it goes off—these "awareness raisers" are only as good as the people who pay attention and change their behaviors based on the information. The best unit to see value from the noise monitor is the NICU, where a quiet environment is essential.

Connect the dots on *why* we care about noise. It is not enough to implement strategies like noise monitors, headphones, and so forth without telling the patients about the goal to create a quiet environment.

- *"We want to keep your room quiet at night so you can rest—would you like us to close your door? We'll be in to check on you approximately every two hours during the night."*

- *"We do our best to keep it quiet for you, especially at night, but sometimes it is noisy as we care for our patients. Would you like some earplugs to help you rest better?"*

- *"Sometimes our voices seem louder at night, so please let us know if we are bothering you or if you cannot sleep."*

- *"I am checking this pump now, so hopefully the alarm won't go off while you're sleeping."*

A quiet environment is a healing environment. By taking steps to lower your nighttime noise level, you help patients reduce stress, get plenty of restful sleep, and ultimately enjoy better clinical outcomes.

Tools & Resources

Studer Group offers a variety of tools and resources that support the tactics discussed in this chapter. To access the most up-to-date offerings, to see what's new in healthcare, and to download a worksheet that will help you create a plan to improve patient perception of care in the "Clean & Quiet" arena, please visit www.studergroup.com/HCAHPS.

SECTION EIGHT:

CARE TRANSITION

Duromering the patient's stay, caregivers tend to focus on her immediate needs—what is happening in the hospital and what steps are necessary at the moment to promote healing. That's understandable. It's natural to pay more attention to what's happening right in front of us today than to focus on what may or may not happen tomorrow.

Yet we need to start thinking about the long-term implications of everything we do. Why? Because an equally important part of the patient's care takes place *after* he leaves our hallways.

The three-question Care Transition Measure composite (CTM) became mandatory for all HCAHPS users in January 2013 and publicly reported for the first time in October of 2014. It measures the aspect of our care that "goes home" with each patient along with his new medications, discharge folder, and care instructions. That means the results for this composite will eventually be factored into the formula that impacts VBP reimbursement—but that's only part of the story.

The new Medicare Spending Per Beneficiary (MSPB) efficiency measure tracks the costs accrued for three days prior to admission and 30 days post-discharge. Because of this, strategies for managing the transition of care to home are an integral and mandatory requirement for hospitals and providers.

Unplanned readmissions and hospital-acquired conditions can also negatively impact reimbursement. They, like MSPB, have ramped up the healthcare industry's sense of urgency to assume ownership of the quality of care across a broad continuum. More than ever before, it's imperative to improve performance in the tactics that make it more likely patients will comply with their plans of care after they leave the hospital.

Of course, the implications of excellent care transitions go far beyond the financial ones we've just discussed. Our patients are still our patients even after they are discharged. As professionals and as human beings, we want to be confident they are receiving the best possible care and continuing to heal outside the hospital walls.

When we improve continuum of care, we improve clinical outcomes, reduce preventable readmissions, maximize reimbursement, *and* enjoy better HCAHPS results.

Helping you do all this is, of course, what the next three chapters of *The HCAHPS Handbook* are all about. While we'll cover each question individually as we have others in the book, please be aware that the first step is to establish a process to build cohesive care transition plans for each patient.

According to the National Transitions of Care Coalition (NTOCC), the elements of a good transition plan are as follows[1]:

- **It's based on a comprehensive *care plan*.** This plan is created via a collaboration of nursing staff and physicians using a multidisciplinary approach.

- **It's based on availability of well-trained practitioners** who have current information about the patient's treatment goals, preferences, and health or clinical status.

- **It includes logistical arrangements and education** of patient and family, as well as coordination among the health professionals involved in the transition.

As you work on implementing the tactics associated with each individual question, please make sure they are incorporated into your care transition plans.

Before we get into the three new CTM questions, please note that two new "about you" questions were also added to the survey in January of 2013. It is important to understand these questions and why they were added:

1. **During this hospital stay, were you admitted to this hospital through the Emergency Room?** (*yes* or *no*)

The ER admission question will be used as a patient-mix adjustment for HCAHPS scores, not unlike the adjustments that are currently made for case mix and mode adjustments based on the survey type (phone, paper, electronic, etc.). Until June 2010 this information was collected from hospitals as an administrative code. Then, CMS presented evidence that this variable is meaningful and that adding the question to the HCAHPS survey would allow CMS to again use Emergency Room admission as a patient-mix adjustment variable.

2. In general, how would you rate your overall mental or emotional health? (*excellent, very good, good, fair, poor*)

The mental health question was added due to requests from hospitals and researchers. CMS also noted recent studies suggest that up to 20 percent of hospitalized patients suffer from severe depression.

Research has shown that there is a *significant decline in HCAHPS results* in patients identified as severely depressed in standardized mental illness assessment questionnaires in the pre- and post-operative ambulatory setting. Collecting this data via the HCAHPS survey will allow more analysis of the impact depression and other mental illnesses are having on perceptions of care and accuracy of survey results.

Now, let's explore the three HCAHPS questions that capture the patient's perception of how engaged and effective you were in helping her transition to home or to the next phase of the care continuum.

The Survey Questions

The CTM-3 questions were added due to a tremendous body of evidence showing that many patients leave the hospital not knowing how to approach their next phase of care. For example, patients may make medication errors, which in turn may lead to adverse events and re-hospitalization.

By adding these questions to the survey, CMS hopes to focus care providers' attention on improving performance on the issues that make positive responses to this aspect of the care continuum more likely.

The questions are as follows:

1. **The hospital staff took my preferences and those of my family or caregiver into account in deciding what my healthcare needs would be when I left the hospital.**

2. **When I left the hospital, I had a good understanding of the things I was responsible for in managing my health.**

3. **When I left the hospital, I clearly understood the purpose for taking each of my medications.**

For these three questions, results will be calculated using the Likert scale. Remember: In HCAHPS, the Likert scale allows patients to report the degree of their agreement with the statement, using *strongly agree, agree, disagree,* and *strongly disagree* or *don't know / don't remember / not applicable.* Results are then reported on a 0-100 basis using those responses.

In the following chapters, we share some specific tactics that increase the likelihood that patients will answer *strongly agree* to all three questions in the Care Transition Measure. As with other composite sections, we have not provided an all-inclusive list of tactics but have zeroed in on the most impactful ones.

You'll find specific actions you can take to immediately impact patient perception of how well you plan, communicate, and execute the transition from hospital to home or rehabilitation facility.

CHAPTER EIGHTEEN:

Recognizing Patient Preferences for Care Continuum

T**HE HCAHPS QUESTION: The hospital staff took my preferences and those of my family or caregiver into account in deciding what my healthcare needs would be when I left the hospital.**

This question really addresses how successful we are at listening to a patient and her family members and incorporating their needs and desires into her post-hospital care plan.

When a patient is ready to leave the hospital, a whole spectrum of emotions typically surrounds her departure: anxiety, joy, fear, and anticipation. To send her home with a care plan whose details she can remember (and comply with) in the face of this emotional time is no small feat.

To help ensure a successful transition home, we need to discover patient and family preferences early in the process and integrate them into a plan with which the patient is comfortable. It just makes sense: When the patient plays a vital role in planning her own care, she understands it better and is more invested in carrying out all the details.

Before we go into the tactics geared to help us impact results on this particular question, let's talk for a moment about the bigger HCAHPS picture.

This entire composite (Care Transition) is obviously rooted in communication. Therefore, your results on the Nurse Communication composite, and specifically the "listened carefully" question, are an indicator of how well positioned you might be to get favorable results on this new question.

As you strive to truly listen for the preferences of the patient and her caregiver, keep in mind the Nurse Communication tactics explored earlier in this book. They are invaluable here, as they are in other areas of HCAHPS. It wouldn't hurt to pause and review them right now.

There is a small but growing body of evidence that shows when the preferences of the patient are sought and considered their outcomes improve. For example, one study tested gaining elderly patients' preferences for self-care capability and providing this information to nurses and care providers.

Titled "Improving patient outcomes by including patient preferences in nursing care" and authored by C.M. Ruland, the study showed that "information about patient preferences changed nurses' care priorities to be more consistent with patient preferences and improved patient outcomes of preference achievement and physical functioning. These results emphasize the importance of continuing to refine strategies for eliciting and integrating patient preferences into patient care as a means to improve patient outcomes."[1]

Results like these are truly encouraging. They create a real sense of urgency for determining patient preferences and holding discussions around them—not just with hospital nurses but also with those caregivers who will help care for the patient after discharge. It stands to reason that compliance with discharge instructions would likely increase, and patient outcomes would likely improve.

... And the Tactics That Make a "Strongly Agree" Response More Likely

We've seen it again and again: Sending a patient home with a plan *she helped create and that incorporates the preferences of those who will help care for her* increases the probability that she will follow instructions and, in turn, improve clinical outcomes and reduce the likelihood of readmission.

If the patient and her family/caregiver clearly understand what they are responsible for in the managing of her health, and the potential risks when she doesn't, she can greatly reduce her risk of an adverse event after discharge.

The following tactics will help you make sure all of this gets accomplished: patient and family are included in the creation of the plan, all parties feel their preferences were considered (and respected) along the way, and everyone knows their role in helping the patient get better.

Tactic 1: Include Family in Creating the Care Transition Plan

First, please be aware that this tactic also addresses the next HCAHPS question on patient responsibilities, which is the focus of Chapter 19. To avoid too much redundancy, we won't repeat the tactic there, but please be aware that it strongly impacts the results of both questions.

As we are seeking to include the family, our strategy must include *active listening*. As you may recall, this is one of the Nine Factors of Engagement (see Chapter 3: The Fundamentals) and involves not just shutting out all distractions but also repeating statements back to the person you're talking to.

What's more, we must go into conversations understanding that sometimes the patients' and families' preferences can be in conflict with the plan we are recommending. More than ever, we will be challenged to explain and defend the *why* behind our recommendations as well as the cost and risk/benefits of the care and treatment plans we are suggesting.

This question forces us to expand our skills to ensure that we have effectively included the family. That is not a nice *to-do* anymore. It is a *must-do*. Here are some strategies to assist with this:

1. Identify the family member or members who will be assisting the patient with his care post-discharge. As soon as possible after admission, begin a dialogue with them and the patient about what will happen once he goes home.

2. Identify case management resources immediately. Or coordinate with insurance plans or others to know what resources will be available to the patient and his family.

3. Follow all recommendations for excellent discharge preparation per the action plans on the Discharge Information composite discussed earlier. Doing well with the tactics identified in that composite are prerequisites to doing well with the tactics in this one.

4. Develop a tool that will fully assess the capacity and capability of the patient and family to perform the necessary care post-discharge. The assessment needs to include the physical, psycho-social, emotional, and financial needs of the patient. It should also ensure that the patient, family, and caregivers have reached a mutual decision about that plan. Some suggested questions to include are:

   - *"Do you have a family member who is your healthcare decision maker/designee and who the hospital team should include in making decisions about your follow-up care? Can you sign a release allowing us to discuss your healthcare information with this designee?"*

- *"Do you and your family have specific preferences that we should consider when making follow-up and home-care arrangements?"*

- *"Is Dr. _____ still your primary care provider? If not, would you like us to connect you with our resources to help you identify one?"*

- *"Do you have a pharmacy that you use regularly so that you feel you have good counsel about the purpose, dosages, and side effects of each of your medications? If not, would you like us to connect you with our network of resources to be sure you and your family have pharmacy support?"*

- *"Does your insurance company provide case management or medication reconciliation support?"*

By implementing this tactic, you are advocating for the well-being of the patient after he leaves the hospital and improving patient perception that his preferences were heard and incorporated into the plan.

Tactic 2: Use Bedside Shift Report to Confirm Patient Preferences

By involving patients and family members in critical conversations regarding medications and post-discharge care plans, we go a long way toward making sure everyone understands the details of a safe transition. Many of these conversations will take place during the Bedside Shift Report (BSR).

Every nurse has seen families go to great lengths to be there when the physician makes rounds each day. Yet after the physician leaves, the nurse will often need to explain what the physician's decisions mean and translate things the family didn't understand. Bedside Shift Report is an opportunity for nursing to take center stage as an equally important player in the eyes of patients and families with regard to getting important information on their plan of care, voicing concerns, and getting questions answered.

Bedside Shift Report is also the perfect time to gain alignment regarding the anticipated discharge date, "going home" preparations, and preferences of the patient and family.

One of the authors of this book had a young son who was hospitalized after an accident. During his stay, he befriended another little boy named Charlie. When Charlie was sent home, he and his family felt unprepared. To them, discharge seemed to happen too soon. Had the nurses spoken of Charlie's discharge and his and his family's feelings around it, they would have been able to voice their concerns early on—and the care team and family could have worked together to prepare them for the transition.

To connect this classic tactic to the new HCAHPS criteria, care providers might include in the BSR a discussion centered on the patient's care transition plan that highlights how her preferences and those of her family will be taken into account. Be sure your standardized BSR form includes triggers for staff to cover discharge plan information so that is not missed.

The conversation might include something like the following:

"As we continue to prepare for your transition home, here is where we are currently with your plan: Post-discharge, your care provider will continue to be Dr. Smith, your primary care physician, as you have requested. We will ensure that he has records of what occurred during your hospitalization.

"We also have heard your request and documented that you pre-fer not to have physical therapy after you return home but rather will manage this process yourself through your own personal resources. However, we will continue to do physical therapy through your stay to keep you progressing. Today, you will have PT two times. We will also be calling you within 72 hours after you go home to be sure you are progressing well, and we can make any adjustments we need to at that time if you aren't feeling comfortable.

"Finally, as we assist you in managing your health status, I am so glad you and your wife agreed to continue to work with us during the rest of the hospitalization in preparing you for smoking cessation so that you can continue those efforts at home. That means no smoke breaks today."

We've shared how you can use the Bedside Shift Report to help identify and discuss patient preferences. It is also important to introduce and "manage up" BSR to patients and families in a way that helps you gain patient participation as these conversations occur. For example, a nurse might say:

"Mr. Jones, twice each day the nurses will conference with you to go over your plan of care, including discharge, and review your progress. This will happen when the nurses are changing shifts to ensure a seamless exchange. It is also a great opportunity for you and

your family to take advantage of this time for questions. You will have two great nurses and their collective experience to take advantage of. Would you like to take part in that?"

This HCAHPS question on care continuum preferences reminds us that caring for patients and helping them get well is not something we do "to" or "for" them but instead is a dynamic and organic process. It's far more than following procedures, prescribing pills, and handing out "homework" assignments. It's a matter of working collaboratively for the patient to have the best outcome.

Great healthcare means approaching each person as an individual (not as a diagnosis or a category) and asking them sincerely, *"How do you prefer to tackle this illness (or injury or surgical recovery) once you get back home? What makes the most sense for your life and your family? You are still our patient after you leave our front door…so we want to make sure you're doing things in a way that you can get behind and embrace."*

The more we can approach the care transition in this matter, the better off the patient will be—and the more we'll live up to our mission.

Tools & Resources

Studer Group offers a variety of tools and resources that support the tactics discussed in this chapter. To access the most up-to-date offerings, as well as to see what's new in healthcare, please visit www.studergroup.com/HCAHPS.

CHAPTER NINETEEN:

HELPING PATIENTS UNDERSTAND POST-DISCHARGE RESPONSIBILITY

THE HCAHPS QUESTION: When I left the hospital, I had a good understanding of the things I was responsible for in managing my health.

While patients are in the hospital, they are under our supervision. We put them in a bed. We bring them their meals. We provide their medications and care for their injuries and keep an eye on the machinery to which they're connected. In other words, we're in charge of their lives. They have a certain amount of autonomy, but for the most part, they've trusted their well-being to us.

Once they go home, it's a different story. Suddenly, they are making all the decisions again. Yet we still have an interest in their well-being. That means before they leave we need to make certain that they know what they need to do and why they need to do it—and of course, what happens if they don't.

During the discharge instruction process, it's important to reinforce specific details that will increase a patient's willingness to take responsibility for managing their health. A big part of this is making sure he understands the potential risks or consequences if he doesn't adhere to the plan—if he doesn't take the medication as prescribed, follow up with the primary care physician, do the physical therapy.

Also, we know that many patients have underlying issues that dramatically impact their overall health status. Smoking, for instance. Excess weight. Poor nutrition. Most of these are long-term concerns that are very hard (if not impossible) to change in the period of time we have them in the hospital. Thus, we need to strongly advocate that the patient work on them post-discharge as well.

Of course, there's no guarantee that patients will follow their care plans or work to turn around their harmful lifestyle habits. Still, we must do everything we can to make sure they understand a) what they need to do and b) why they need to do it. Effective communication before, during, and after care transitions will go a long way toward helping ensure safe care transitions and better patient outcomes.

We have always *wanted* to ensure quality outcome experiences for patients across the continuum of care. But now, with CMS programs pushing us to become ever more efficient and more effective in doing this, the urgency has been ramped up. It is becoming clearer that all providers of healthcare need to work seamlessly and with the patients and their families as full partners in the process. Our ability to get patients involved in managing their health and better prepare them to do so is now going to be assessed and reported.

Consider a cardiac patient who is admitted after having his first heart attack. The patient is morbidly obese, has a history of smoking 1.5 packs of cigarettes a day, and has a completely sedentary lifestyle. His primary care physician has for years advised him of lifestyle changes he needs to make to avoid his current condition, but he has ignored them.

In fact, even in the wake of this major health event, the patient is complaining about the 1,800-calorie low-salt, low-fat diet that the physician has prescribed while he is in the hospital. As a result, his wife is bringing in fast food for him. The staff has discouraged this "cheating" behavior, but the patient and his wife have not complied. The nurses have no confidence that the patient will incorporate any of the lifestyle changes he's been asked to make after he goes home. But what can they do about it?

In times past the nurses might have just laughed about the wife sneaking in the burgers and fries. They may have even gently admonished the patient, but it likely would have been in a joking tone. Chances are, they wouldn't have pushed it any further. Their attitude might have been, *Well, I can't control what the patient does outside the hospital!*

Now that HCAHPS is in place with these care transition questions, the story might play out differently. The hospital now has a vested interest in making sure the patient changes his lifestyle. If the nurses are to successfully impact this patient long term, they will need to ensure that he knows and can articulate the plan for smoking cessation, changing his diet, and exercising—and the consequences if he fails to follow through.

All hospitals must deal with this issue. We need to create methods of validation and teach back so we know patients and their families truly understand what they need to do and the implications if they don't. We can't "make" them follow their care plan or change their habits, but we can do as much as possible to influence them to do so.

... And the Tactics That Make "Strongly Agree" Responses More Likely

So how can we make sure patients know how to manage their recovery, avoid potential risks, and practice healthy lifestyle habits once they go home from the hospital? Basically, we do it by sharing the information with them many times in many different ways.

Tactic 1: Make Interdisciplinary Rounds

Here's how this tactic works: A team comprised of case management staff, pharmacy staff, and care providers gets together and rounds on the patient and family each day. The rounds done by this team will ultimately focus on the care transition plan. This way, the group is able to all be on the same page with the patient.

Interdisciplinary rounding is a time when the patient can hear and validate what responsibilities he'll have once he goes home. The goal is to ensure daily that the patient and family are progressing well on the plan and that no barriers or challenges have arisen that will prevent a seamless transition to home.

When any barriers and challenges arise, this team will collectively gather the resources to ensure that the patient can stay on track. This team typically problem solves issues like lack of financial means to follow through with medication or care and equipment needs. They may help find access to care facilities or determine if further education is needed to prepare a family member to become a caregiver (and provide them access to that education).

Identify "Three Cs"—Communication, Coordination, Collaboration

When you have these "care transition" conversations with the patient and family members, it creates a feeling of open communication, effective coordination of the entire care team (including the patient), and collaboration by all, aimed at achieving the best outcomes. The patient and family should feel that they are part of a cohesive team that's focused on supporting them. Here are some tips to keep in mind:

- With the patient and her family, brainstorm the top three concerns she has about leaving the hospital. Working together, locate appropriate materials and resources to address these concerns, and after discussing, put materials into discharge folders.

- Create a list of three individuals (other than the primary caregiver) the patient can contact if she has a question or needs assistance. Encourage the patient to include her primary physician as a contact.

- Ask the patient and her family to identify three constrictions or obstacles that might prevent her transition home from being a success. Help brainstorm ways to work around these challenges.

- Discuss what warning signs and symptoms to look for and whom to contact if one of them happens. Place this information on the front of the discharge folder or on an easy-to-see piece of paper inside. It is important that this information be easily accessible to all members of the care team, so the process needs to be standardized.

- Develop a checklist of what needs to occur for the patient to be discharged. This includes training and validating any care needs, fulfilling PT and OT expectations, and so forth. Maintain the checklist in the discharge folder and update it as expectations are met.

- Collaborate with the patient and caregivers, including teaching and practicing care routines and skills that will be needed post-discharge. If possible, set up an opportunity for the patient

and/or caregiver to perform these routines under the supervision of a nurse. This will validate
knowledge and build confidence.

Hint: Ask each individual involved in the planning
session to answer each of these prompts individually
and then compare the responses. This will encourage
honest answers and bring out different perspectives.

Please be aware that all of these tips align with the
Joint Commission's focus on multidisciplinary communication, collaboration, and coordination from admission to transition. For more information, visit www.
jointcommission.org/assets/1/18/hot_topics_transi-
tions_of_care.pdf.

Tactic 2: Use Key Words at Key Times to Help Patients Understand Their Responsibilities

We have recommended the use of key words to move
results on many of the previous HCAHPS questions.
The tactic is especially pertinent here as we seek to help
patients understand what they can do to help themselves
heal. Carefully chosen words will go a long way toward
helping the patient better understand her care as well as
her responsibilities. They can also reduce anxiety and
build trust.

For example, a nurse might say, *"It is important for your safety that you understand the purpose of each of your medications. The number one reason for patients' having complications and being readmitted is taking medications incorrectly. Let's review them so that we can ensure that you know the purpose of each one and the possible side effects. I will want you to be able to repeat this back to me so that I know you understand. It will be important that you remember this information at home when you have responsibility for your own medication."*

Using key words when addressing the following areas gives your patient a better understanding of what it means for her (and her family) to be responsible for her care. Address "going home" patient preferences and incorporate these actions into the care plan that identifies patient (and family) responsibilities, including:

- **Personal care:** Bathing, eating, dressing, toileting. Do both the patient and caregiver feel confident in this area? Are there special dietary needs or restrictions?

- **Household care:** Cooking, cleaning, laundry, shopping. Does the family need contact information of others who can help in this area?

- **Healthcare:** Medication management, physician appointments, follow-up appointments or tests, physical therapy, wound treatment, injections, medical equipment, and techniques. Encourage her to repeat back her responsibilities regarding therapy and future treatment. Troubleshoot obstacles that could hinder the healing process.

- **Emotional care:** Companionship, meaningful activities, and conversation. Can the family arrange visits from friends, relatives, and pets to help keep the patient from getting bored and depressed? Will the patient have access to favorite books? Can family members join her when her favorite TV shows come on so they can watch together and maybe share a few laughs?

- **Referrals:** Home care agency and/or appropriate support organizations in the community. Discuss how the referrals work and what responsibilities the patient has in managing them.

Here are some ways you can use key words to make sure the patient and family understand their responsibilities:

- **Ask for agreement on discharge/responsibility of care instructions.** If a patient is not fully aware of what her care responsibilities are once away from the hospital, she may not comply with the discharge instructions. Asking for her agreement will uncover such gaps in her understanding:

  "Do you understand and agree with what your home care responsibilities are once you leave the hospital? We want to be sure you have the resources you need for your personal and household care when you leave here. Can we help you identify who will be responsible for your chores, medications, and personal care?"

- **Paraphrase key discharge instructions.** Ask the patient and the primary caregiver to repeat back information they gained during discharge education sessions:

"Can you share with me the first three things you will do when you are discharged home?"

"Can you tell me the three essential parts to your care plan?"

"I want to be sure we have communicated clearly. Can you please repeat back to me who will be taking you to your doctor appointments, who will be cooking your meals, and who will be helping with your physical therapy?"

Tactic 3: Implement Post-Visit Patient Calls

As explained in the Fundamentals section in Chapter 3, post-visit patient phone calls are a process in which staff members connect with patients after they've been discharged from the hospital. They are sometimes referred to as care transition calls. Done properly and executed consistently across the organization, these calls reduce readmissions and save lives.

Post-acute, diagnosis-specific calls also create better clinical outcomes, decrease anxiety, and in general provide a better experience for patients. Evidence shows this tool reduces adverse outcomes, reinforces compliance with discharge instructions, and improves overall patient perception of quality as measured by HCAHPS.

Readmission Reduction
Post-Visit Calls

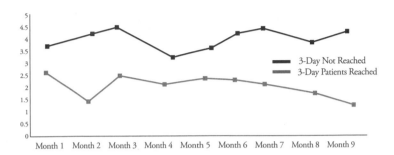

Figure 19.1

Post-visit phone calls offer the opportunity to check in on patients and make sure they are okay and have the help they need. They're also a good tactic for reinforcing patient responsibilities.

During these calls, it's important to ask questions aimed at making sure patients understand their post-discharge instructions, the purpose of their medications, and their responsibilities with each medication.

A few hints when making a post-visit call:

Verify discharge instructions. Always make sure the patient understands her discharge instructions. *"When you were discharged, Becky went over your discharge instructions with you. What questions do you have regarding the instructions you went home with?"*

Ask probing questions and dig deeper to gain insight. These questions need to be aimed at making sure the patient is doing what she is supposed to be doing. For example:

- *"Tell me how many times you've taken your medicine so far."*

- *"Can you repeat back to me what the doctor said about building strength in your leg?"*

- *"Please tell me what you've had to eat today."*

Access patient records. If possible, pull up the patient's records to refer to during the call. It's very helpful to have those discharge instructions in front of you.

Focus on care and follow-up. Ensure that the discharge questions are about quality care and follow-up at home, and are not intended to bias the patient or compete with any of the HCAHPS survey questions. Ask open-ended questions—they will yield the kinds of answers that indicate the extent to which the patients understand their responsibilities. Some examples include:

- *"Are you as comfortable as you can be right now? How is your pain now, compared to when you were in the hospital?"*

- *"What questions do you have about your medications?"*

- *"Tell me what has happened concerning your follow-up appointment with your doctor or clinic."*

- *"Tell me about the diet you were prescribed. How successful have you been in following it?"*

- *"Your home care instructions included some dressing changes. How often did you change your dressing yesterday and can you describe for me what your wound looked like at that time?"*

Focus on clinical. The post-visit call is the perfect time to speak about clinical indicators. Some ways you can do this include:

- Asking if the patient understands her self-care instructions, medication uses, doses, and side effects.

- If applicable, probing for indicators of infection, such as swelling, redness, fever, and so forth.

- Confirming compliance and understanding of discharge instructions.

- Reminding the patient to schedule a follow-up appointment with her physician and to call with any questions.

As we've said before, being in the hospital is stressful for patients, and going home is stressful in another way. A post-visit call, received after the patient is settled in at home, may be the communication link she needs to feel absolutely confident that she is progressing as expected.

The affirmation that a patient understands her medications, discharge instructions, and how to otherwise care for herself at home is a vital part of the experience we provide. Care transition calls are one of our most important tools for making patients an integral part of the collaborative care team. They help us live up to our responsibility to extend care outside the hospital walls.

It is a great privilege to work in healthcare. We get to touch patients' lives at times when they most need guidance. Sometimes we are even able to inspire them to make needed lifestyle changes that have a tremendous impact on their long-term health and happiness. In a very real way, part of us goes home with our patients.

We must never forget the responsibility we have to send them out the door with the knowledge they need. We must never let our staff members forget, either. When we help them connect back to the great trust patients place in them, they will make sure to provide the best care transition education possible. For most healthcare professionals, it's a matter of values.

Tools & Resources

Studer Group offers a variety of tools and resources that support the tactics discussed in this chapter. To access the most up-to-date offerings, as well as to see what's new in healthcare, please visit www.studergroup.com/HCAHPS.

CHAPTER TWENTY:

PURPOSE OF MEDICATIONS

THE HCAHPS QUESTION: When I left the hospital, I clearly understood the purpose for taking each of my medications.

Have you ever sat in the office of a busy family practice and watched patients trying to make sense of all the medications they've been instructed to bring in? In fact, have you ever *been* that patient? Have you ever accompanied that patient—perhaps he was your parent, your grandparent, your child, your sibling, or your friend—as he struggled to write down the list of medications, how often he took them, what dosage, how long ago each was prescribed, and so forth?

If so, you know how overwhelming this experience can be. Taking multiple medications is deeply confusing for anyone. If you're not very careful, you can miss doses, take the medication at the wrong time, take Pill A when you were actually supposed to take Pill B (or C or D), and so forth.

All of this is why it's so very important that we send patients home with a clear understanding of their medications and the possible side effects of each. Doing so will increase the probability that they will follow the plans and, in turn, improve clinical outcomes and reduce preventable readmissions.

That, of course, is why this question is so important. It addresses how successful we are at communicating to a patient the purpose of each of his medications and how it fits into his continuing care plan. Obviously, the more successful we are, the more likely patients are to get better and thrive.

Please understand there is a very clear difference between this care transition question and the question discussed in Chapter 13 on *new* medications and their side effects. The focus of this question is on understanding the *purpose of ALL* the patient's medications. It therefore can become quite a challenge.

We must take into account the medications that were prescribed during the hospital stay PLUS those they were taking before they arrived. Suppose one of the new medicines has an adverse effect when combined with an old one? To keep patients safe after they've transitioned home and returned to their daily routine, we must consider these possibilities. Even if a patient isn't taking other prescription medications, does he still need the over-the-counter baby aspirin or vitamin supplements he was taking? The point is we must consider all the pills he is taking as we create a new daily plan for home.

Currently, medication errors harm 1.5 million people each year in the United States, according to the Institute of Medicine, at an annual cost of at least $3.5 billion.[1]

What's more, in a recent survey of discharged patients:

- Only 41 percent were able to state their diagnoses.

- Only 37 percent were able to state the purpose of their medications.

- Only 14 percent knew the common side effects of all their medications.[2]

Statistics like these make it clear that healthcare professionals need to do a better job of ensuring that patients not only understand the "whats" (not to mention the "whens" and "hows") of their medications but also the "whys." Knowing *why* drives compliance, and compliance saves lives.

...And the Tactics That Make "Strongly Agree" Responses More Likely

IMPORTANT NOTE: Before we get into the tactics in this section, we'd like to emphasize the fact that they *do not* replace medication reconciliation work with patients. The research is clear that the best resource to do medication reconciliation most accurately is a pharmacist. While many times this role is taken on by nursing, it will be incumbent on the healthcare teams to assess the resources being applied to this important strategy and to determine plans to improve the frequency, timing, and effectiveness of our processes of medication reconciliation.

Tactic 1: Use Key Words at Key Times to Ensure Meaningful Communication about Medications

Communicating about medications with patients means sharing the right information frequently and in written form. Many patients have long lists of medications, and without good systems to keep this information organized, accurate, and available, doing so can become a nightmare. For all of us, awareness and learning require repetition and this truth certainly applies here.

The Key Words at Key Times (KWKT) tactic affords us an opportunity to ensure that all caregivers are proactively and consistently assessing a patient's knowledge about his medications, looking for gaps in his knowledge about side effects or drug interactions, and identifying any barriers to his compliance with his medication treatment plan.

Here are a few hints to help you when utilizing KWKT to convey critical information about medication throughout the patient's stay as well as at discharge:

Frame information in a way that invites questions. Don't use vague phrasing like, *"Do you understand?"* Instead, try more specific wording that shows you welcome their questions, such as, *"Okay now, what questions do you have for me?"*

Ask for the patient's compliance. Make sure he has the information he needs to agree to comply with the medication requirements. When a patient agrees, he is much more likely to comply with the treatment plan.

- *"Is there anything that might prevent you from taking this medication when you go home?"*

- *"What preferences do you have in regard to your medications? Who will help you obtain your prescriptions and help you keep track of taking the medication properly?"*

- *"Will you repeat back to me your intentions for taking this medication after you've gone home from the hospital?"* or *"Can you share with me how you will incorporate these medications into your daily routine?"*

Tactic 2: Use M in the House^{SM} to Improve Patient Understanding of All Medicines

Remember M in the Box^{SM}? It is a simple strategy designed to ensure that staff members place the appropriate focus on medications in their communications with patients. While the tactic is mostly focused on new medications and their side effects as introduced in Chapter 3 (and again explored further in Chapter 6), it is also an opportunity to open the door for reinforcement and discussion about the purpose for *all* medications.

M in the House^{SM} is an extension of M in the Box. It ensures that the patient/family knows what medicines they should take once they leave the hospital, the purpose of these medicines, and their responsibility for managing their health at home (as it pertains to the medicines). As you'll see shortly, the last step of M in the House involves nurse assessment regarding the capacity and capability of the patient/family to perform the necessary care post-discharge and fosters a discussion with the patient and/or their family to reach a mutual decision about their care at home.

This tactic also addresses the HCAHPS composite of Communication about Medications and may also positively impact the Nurse Communication and Overall Rating composites.

M in the House helps to engage the patient/family in interactive care and improves clinical outcomes. It not only ensures that nurses discuss vital information about the patient's home care with the patient/family, it also provides an opportunity to check understanding of discharge instructions and answer any questions that the patient/family may have. The visual of the house also really focuses attention of all staff on the home environment and how medications will be incorporated there.

Here is how it works:

Step 1: Nurse draws a house with two windows.

"Mrs. Smith, in preparation for your discharge from the hospital, I would like to discuss your care at home. First, let's talk about the medicines you have been prescribed."

Step 2: Nurse writes an "M" in the first window of the house and reviews the patient's list of medicines, discussing each as follows:

"Your [first] medicine is called [insert name here], and you will need to take it [tell how the medicine will be administered and how often]. There are a few side effects of the medicine that you may experience that are normal. They are [detail normal side effects]. However, if you experience [detail abnormal or potentially dangerous side effects], please call your doctor immediately, okay?"

"Will you please let me know if you will be taking any other medications that were not prescribed during your hospital stay? What about any over-the-counter medications or vitamin supplements?"

Step 3: The nurse will then write an "H" in the second window of the house and discuss the patient/family's responsibility for managing their health at home, answering any questions that the patient/family may have, and helping them to finalize and document a plan for home care. (She might even take it to the next level and discuss non-medication issues like dietary changes, exercise, smoking cessation, and so forth.)

"We've discussed the dosage and time that each medication should be taken at home. Can you repeat back to me what we just discussed? I will also write the information down so you can easily reference the information once you are home."

Step 4: After the plan is finalized and understood by all, the nurse draws a heart around the house.

"Now that we all understand what you will be doing at home to manage your health, we will continue to prepare the paperwork needed for your discharge."

Step 1

The nurse *draws*:
A house with two windows
and a door

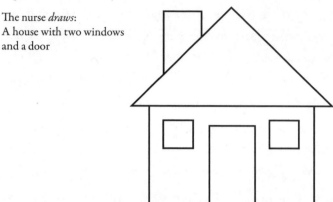

Figure 20.1

Step 2

The nurse *writes*:
An "**M**" in the window of the
house

The nurse *discusses*:
The purpose for taking each
medication with the
patient/family (CTM3)

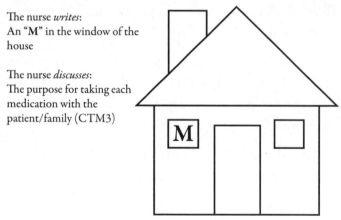

Figure 20.2

Step 3

The nurse *writes*:
An "**H**" in the window of the house when the plan is finalized, documented, and understood by the patient and family

The nurse *discusses*:
The patient's individual responsibility for managing their health at home (CTM2)

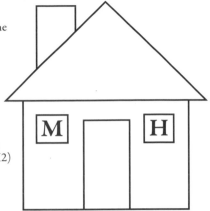

Figure 20.3

Step 4

The nurse *assesses*:
The capacity and capability of the patient/family to perform the necessary care post-discharge

The nurse *discusses*:
With patient/family to reach mutual decision about their wishes (CTM 1)

The nurse *draws*:
A heart around house

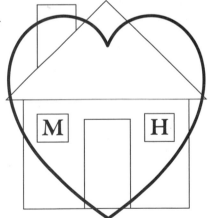

Figure 20.4

Organizations that have piloted this practice have seen a positive effect on their CTM question responses. Those coached by Studer Group® have also had reports from patients on how valuable the information was and how helpful the communication board was because it kept the topic on their minds. The nurses also liked having the visual tool. Some patients even reported great pride when they were able to successfully report all the items completed and got to see the heart on their board.

Tips for Implementing M in the House Effectively:

- Include staff training regarding the tool and its purpose.
  - ○ Review the positive impact of M in the House in a department meeting and/or huddle.
  - ○ Role model the discharge conversation that involves M in the House.
  - ○ Round with nurses and role model the key features of the tool.
- Validate staff competency in use of tool.
  - ○ Round with nurses and validate understanding and use of M in the House.
  - ○ Verify use of tool during Nurse Leader Rounding by asking patients about discharge instructions and care at home.

Staff Knowledge of Medications

Many experienced nurses remember the days when they were in nursing school and had to complete medication cards. They literally had to look up each medication and know the dose, route, purpose, interactions, and side effects of each one they would be administering to the patients, and they would be quizzed by their nursing instructors to demonstrate what they knew before they could administer to patients. Of course, today's nursing students have apps for that, but still are required to have and demonstrate the knowledge.

It is also true that once nurses graduate and start to practice, no one is quizzing them anymore. Many nurses stop looking up their medications and begin a slow downward trend of knowledge and awareness of this information for the common medications they administer. In addition, the number of medications available and being ordered is ever increasing so nursing staff rely heavily on the physicians and pharmacists to be the screening mechanisms to be sure the best medications are used and ordered appropriately. However, this is not the best approach, nor is it the safest.

Nursing leadership must ensure that nurses keep up their skills in this area—via skills labs, department training, and hearing information reiterated in huddles—and validate their competency in adhering to safe medication administration practices.

A successful transition to home with no complications and good preparation and resources only serves to further solidify the healthcare team as a valued part of patients' lives. While no one wants to be hospitalized, when they are, we want them to experience a care team that is compassionate, competent, and connected to them and their family. The work you have read about in this chapter and in this book will assist you in giving them just that.

Tools & Resources

Studer Group offers a variety of tools and resources that support the tactics discussed in this chapter. To access the most up-to-date offerings, to see what's new in healthcare, and to download a worksheet that will help you create a plan to improve patient perception of care in the "Care Transition" arena, please visit www.studergroup.com/HCAHPS.

Overall Rating of Hospital and Willingness to Recommend

All things considered, what kind of experience do your patients have? What "grade" might they give your hospital? Will they give you the ultimate compliment and recommend you to someone else? And do they feel loyalty to your hospital—an important predictor of future utilization and revenue?

These are the kinds of questions whose answers make up a patient's overall impression of your organization. An impression, by its very nature, may seem pretty subjective. From the patient's perspective, though, it's cut and dry. When we fail to give a patient an overall positive experience, in her mind it's because we haven't learned what is important to her.

A patient who gives us a less-than-perfect rating or fails to recommend us may have had positive experiences in every area covered by HCAHPS except, perhaps, for one. Maybe a stressed-out staff member spoke sharply to her or one dose of her pain medicine was late or maybe the patient next door had lots of noisy visitors who interfered with her sleep. One small incident can color her entire experience in a negative way.

Healthcare organizations must do everything possible to ensure that every patient perceives every aspect of her care to be the best. That translates to patient-centered, quality care, which yields the insight needed to keep care providers from ever being in a position where they have to say, "If only we had known."

Hospitals that are highly rated by patients are fundamentally different from other hospitals in the outcomes they achieve. When you group hospitals into quartiles by their "patient experience of care" results, the hospitals in the highest quartile have statistically significantly better outcomes across a variety of measures.

If you'll recall from Chapter 1, patients in hospitals that have higher HCAHPS performance tend to have fewer infections, pressure ulcers, and manifestations of poor glycemic control. Those hospitals experience fewer "never events," shorter ED wait times, and better efficiency ratios. Part of the reason is that they have been able to effectively implement quality improvement initiatives like Lean, Six Sigma, and Baldrige, which help them create cultures that drive higher reliability and better outcomes.

Studer Group® coaches have demonstrated their ability to help hospitals make the changes they need to make in order to move into that top quartile of hospitals. In fact, several organizations we've coached have gone on to receive the Malcolm Baldrige National Quality Award.

Studer Group itself is a 2010 Baldrige recipient, so we have been able to take what we know about execution and help others apply it to their own systems and processes.

The following graphics show that hospitals in the top quartile for overall rating have better clinical process of care outcomes. They are more likely to receive bonuses rather than penalties for value-based purchasing (VBP) and excess readmissions, have fewer hospital-acquired infections, lower readmissions, better efficiency ratios, shorter ED wait times, fewer patients leaving without being seen, lower Medicare spending per beneficiary (MSPB) after discharge, and are increasing admissions during a time when other hospitals are seeing theirs decline.

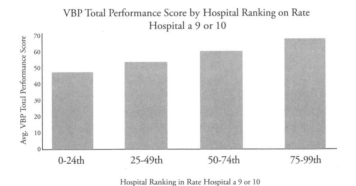

Figure ix.1

The graph in Figure ix.1 shows the average FY2013 VBP Total Performance Score for hospitals segmented by their patient experience of care. The TPS in 2013 was the sum of the clinical process of care domain weighted at 70 percent and the patient experience domain weighted at 30 percent.

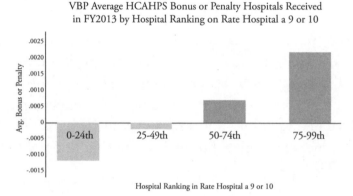

Figure ix.2

The graph in Figure ix.2 shows the average percent of penalty or bonus calculated by CMS for each of our four hospital groupings, which are segmented by the patient experience of care. This bonus or penalty affects Medicare payments for each discharge in the relevant fiscal year (October 1 – September 30). As this graph shows, hospitals with higher quality patient experience of care results received bonuses, while those with lower quality patient experience of care results received penalties.

The Survey Questions

In this chapter we will progress from the HCAHPS composites that focus on specific issues like pain management to those that ask overarching "summary" questions. By the time the patient gets to this portion of the survey, she is being asked to step back and take a broad view of her experience. It's the proverbial "at the end of the day" impression: *How good was the hospital, really? Would you want to come back here—or send someone you love here?*

This section of the HCAHPS survey asks patients about their overall perception of their stay. For the first question, which asks patients to rate the hospital, answers are given on a 0 to 10 scale. The percent of patients who give answers of 9 or 10 is publicly reported on www.hospitalcompare.hhs.gov.

1. **Using any number from 0 to 10, where 0 is the worst hospital possible and 10 is the best hospital possible, what number would you use to rate this hospital during your stay?**

The second question asks patients whether they would recommend the hospital to friends and family. Answers are given in *definitely no* to *definitely yes* scale. The percent of patients who give the answer *definitely yes* is publicly reported on www.hospitalcompare.hhs.gov. (Please note that while this question is asked and reported publicly, it is not included in the VBP calculation for your organization. This is because there's some bias associated with the question that couldn't be filtered out with the standard mode adjustments being used for some other of the calculations. For example, large tertiary centers with more services tended to be biased toward more positive "would recommend" responses than small, rural facilities with limited services.)

2. Would you recommend this hospital to your friends and family?

In the chapter that follows, we will discuss an overarching approach and a few tips that, together, positively impact the likelihood that patients will respond with a *9* or *10* and a *definitely yes*, respectively.

CHAPTER TWENTY-ONE:

GLOBAL RATING/WILLINGNESS TO RECOMMEND

The HCAHPS QUESTION: Using any number from 0 to 10, where 0 is the worst hospital possible and 10 is the best hospital possible, what number would you use to rate this hospital during your stay?

Every experience your patient has during his stay factors into his overall evaluative perspective of your hospital. It all counts: how well nurses (and everyone else) communicated with him…how physicians treated him…how responsive staff members were when he asked for something…how well his pain was managed…how clearly his medication was explained…how discharge instructions and transition of care were handled…and how clean and quiet the hospital itself was.

Ultimately, did he get quality care from people he felt cared for him? If he strongly feels the answer is yes, he will give your hospital a high rating—hopefully, the highest rating possible.

The HCAHPS QUESTION: Would you recommend this hospital to your friends and family?

Patients are just like you. They want their family members and friends to have the best possible care. For a patient to be willing to recommend your hospital to a friend or family member, you need to provide the kind of care that you'd want your own mother or father or child to receive.

It's an honor to have patients be willing to entrust the very life of someone they love to your hospital. It's important to work hard to be worthy of that honor.

...And the Approach and Tips That Make "10" and "Definitely Yes" Responses More Likely

These two questions are incredibly important. They are the culmination of every encounter patients have had with your hospital, from pre-admission to inpatient care to post-discharge follow-up. They are the "final grades" you get in the school of public (patient) opinion.

We are addressing them together in one chapter because they are highly correlated. In other words, if someone doesn't give your hospital a high rating on the 0 to 10 scale, he probably isn't going to recommend you to friends and family. In general, the things you do to get a favorable result on one question tend to lead to a favorable result on the other.

The three HCAHPS composites that are the most highly correlated statistically with these questions are Nurse Communication, Pain Management, and Responsiveness of Staff. So yes, you need to make absolutely certain your organization is well versed in the tactics that impact these composites. We'll discuss this a bit further shortly. For now, though, let's focus on what your culture needs to look like in order to get *10* and *definitely yes* responses.

A Culture of *Always*

A culture of *always* is about taking your focus on providing excellent care from the bedside to the organization. It's about hardwiring excellence into your culture. Hardwiring is a measure of frequency. When you've hardwired a tactic into every department, every process, and the mind of every staff member, that means high performance is a given. That means "always."

A culture of *always* is also about making sure your Emergency Department—one of the major points of entry into many hospitals—is the absolute best it can be. Remember, a bad ED experience is tough to overcome. And Studer Group® research shows that as ED perception of care results improve, so do inpatient results.

In terms of HCAHPS, a culture of *always* means that everyone in the hospital is doing everything possible to make sure patients are so well served that they answer *always* to every appropriate survey question.

In larger, more holistic terms it means that everyone—
from the CEO to the doctors and nurses to the ancillary
service and support service people—lives the hospital's
mission to create the best place for patients to receive
care...*always*. The entire organization holds themselves
accountable to the standards of behavior that create the
best environment and outcomes for the patient.

A culture of *always* has three major elements:

Alignment. This means all levels of your organization must have the same sense of urgency regarding the
patient experience and quality.

We recommend that leaders at all levels regularly
share the importance of the patient experience and other
issues regarding health reform with the people they su-
pervise. They should connect the dots so that every staff
member understands *why* these issues are important.
Every employee needs to understand that executing the
tactics that lead to great clinical quality is critical to the
hospital's financial future.

Consistency. A culture of *always* is synonymous with
consistency. Every patient must have a consistently good
experience no matter what department she's in, whether
it's Monday morning or Saturday night, and no matter
which leaders and staff members are working that day.

Of course, this is not an easy task to accomplish. It
necessitates that proven best practices (many of which
are included in this book) be hardwired into the organization. That begins with leadership. All leaders and staff
must speak in the same voice, follow the same processes
and procedures, and work toward the same results. And

all leaders and staff members need to understand why they're being asked to do what they're being asked to do—and to be held accountable for doing it.

Consistency is often where hospitals have the greatest opportunity for improvement. Some people may do certain things right all the time, and some people may get it right some of the time but not all of the time. "Sometimes" and "usually" will not create a quality outcome.

An inconsistent culture hurts you in many ways. It hinders your relationship with physicians, for instance. At Studer Group we hear about it all the time—physicians saying, "I want my patients on this unit, not that one," or, "Don't admit my patients on the weekend." Inconsistency also hurts your relationship with other staff members. For example, great nurses don't want to work with not-so-great nurses who don't seem to care. Organizational cultures in which this kind of inconsistency is allowed to exist can't provide the kind of care that leads to favorable HCAHPS responses.

We have found that when partners do well across the board, it's because they've moved from a culture of optionality to supporting tactics with a culture of *always.*

Accountability. It's not enough to set performance goals. Hospitals must make sure people are actually achieving them. That may mean embracing new systems and processes that hold people at all levels accountable for executing well.

We have found that it's not unusual for healthcare organizations to overstate the performance of leaders and staff. This is often due to poor evaluation tools. The leader evaluation tool is the most critical to drive organizational improvements. It's important that your leader evaluation tools are based on objective, measurable goals and that they allow you to weight the goals in order to create priorities and in some cases communicate a real sense of urgency in achieving important outcomes.

Another common problem is an organization-wide failure to deal with low performers. Our study of over 10,000 leaders in healthcare found that 40-60 percent of employees identified by their managers as "not meeting expectations" are not in any performance counseling. Leaders must have a system for moving low performers up or out, developing and retaining middle performers, and re-recruiting high performers.

So, how do you achieve this level of alignment, consistency, and accountability...*always*? Simply, you make sure the right foundation is in place.

It All Comes Back to Evidence-Based Leadership^{SM}

The one overarching approach that drives *always* is Evidence-Based Leadership^{SM}. It is your framework to get to *always* and stay there. You might recall back in Chapter 1 that we mentioned Studer Group's Evidence-Based Leadership (EBL) framework as a good foundation for creating a performance culture. We'd like to come back to this again.

Evidence-Based Leadership℠ Framework

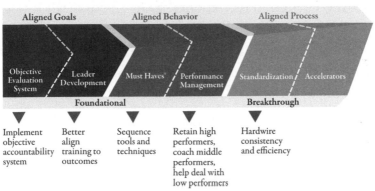

Figure 21.1

If you have the EBL framework in place, you are well situated to create a culture of *always*, which in turn allows you to improve patient experience results. That's because all three major components, Aligned Goals, Aligned Behaviors, and Aligned Processes, work together in a cohesive, systematic way.

Where to Start

In this book, we've given you plenty of tactics you can start implementing right away to improve your HCAHPS results in specific composites. And as we've discussed, they all work together with your culture to impact the two questions this chapter focuses on.

If you have read the entire book, you may feel a bit like you are drinking from the fire hose. Perhaps you're looking for one or two changes you can make right now to accelerate your culture change and immediately impact the likelihood of patients giving you overall ratings of 9 or 10 and "definitely" being willing to recommend you. Here are two tips that give you plenty of bang for your buck:

Tip 1: Focus on Nurse Communication

Remember, the Nurse Communication composite is most highly correlated with both Overall Rating and Willingness to Recommend. That's why it makes sense to focus on it first. Best of all, when you improve Nurse Communication, your efforts will have a collateral effect on the other composites. For immediate impact:

- **Select units that provide the greatest opportunity for impact.** Focus on the units that have the highest number of discharges. These units will also have the highest number of surveys. Get it right here and you've already impacted a critical mass of patients.

  Then focus on the units that are performing at a mid-level (overall rank of 6, 7, or 8 and willingness to recommend of *probably yes*). Why? Just as it is easier to move a B grade to an A than a C grade to an A, it is easier to move middle results than poor results. Plus, getting a quick win here will boost the morale of everyone else.

- **Align nursing and ancillary goals.** Organizations tend to assume HCAHPS success rides on nursing and much of it does. That encompasses lots of staff members! We have found that other departments are also key to getting from *usually* to *always* and *probably yes* to *definitely yes*. When the ancillary and support departments partner with nursing to remove barriers or add resources to the nursing staff, it can make a great difference in the eyes of patients and their families.

As you focus on the Nurse Communication composite, remember those ancillary and support service teams that will partner with nurses to provide *always* care. For example, do the physical therapy leader and the nurse leader on Unit A both know that their goal is to bring up the results on the Nurse Communication composite? The physical therapy staff members who assist Unit A patients with ambulation can and do impact Nurse Communication. Aligned goals create a united front as both leaders work toward the same outcome.

Tip 2: Focus on the Emergency Department

The Emergency Department experience is such an important part of patient perception of care that CMS has added the following "yes or no" question to the HCAHPS survey:

During this hospital stay, were you admitted to this hospital through the Emergency Room?

Taking into account that an average of at least 50 percent of inpatients come in through the ED, and that results in the ED correlate to inpatient results, we advise you to recall what we said in Chapter 1: Don't underestimate the importance of the Emergency Department. We've found through intensive ED coaching that providing an excellent experience in this critical department has an immediate impact on patients' perception of inpatient care. It also improves attending physicians' perception of quality as well as ED throughput.

Following are four key tactics that support improvement in both the ED and inpatient experience. To learn more about them, you may wish to consult some of the books in Studer Group's Fire Starter Publishing Library—specifically, *Advance Your Emergency Department: Leading in a New Era* by Stephanie Baker, RN, CEN, MBA; Regina Shupe, RN, MSN, CEN; and Dan Smith, MD, FACEP; *Excellence in the Emergency Department: How to Get Results* by Stephanie Baker, RN, CEN, MBA; *Hardwiring Flow: Systems and Processes for Seamless Patient Care* by Thom Mayer, MD, FACEP, FAAP; and Kirk Jensen, MD, MBA, FACEP; and *The Patient Flow Advantage: How Hardwiring Hospital-Wide Flow Drives Competitive Performance* by Thom Mayer, MD, FACEP, FAAP; and Kirk Jensen, MD, MBA, FACEP; due for release in the winter of 2014/2015. (Please visit www.firestarterpublishing.com to access these and other helpful titles.)

- **Round on ED staff and patients.** There are various types of rounding that happen in the Emergency Department: rounding on patients, rounding in the waiting room, rounding on staff members, and Hourly Rounding®. While some of these types of rounding are described in this book, they are meant for an inpatient setting and are slightly different when they happen in the ED.

  Rounding leads to more satisfied patients, staff, and physicians. It has also been proven to reduce patients leaving without treatment.

- **Implement bedside reporting.** This tactic, which in best-practice organizations is consistent with how it's done in the inpatient units, prevents medical errors and also builds employee teamwork, ownership, trust, and accountability. We recommend that it be implemented only after hardwiring leader rounding on staff and patients to ensure that there is a strong feedback loop for staff.

- **Conduct post-visit phone calls.** These calls improve clinical outcomes, increase patient satisfaction and market share, reduce formal complaints, help decrease costly and unnecessary readmissions, and save lives. In high-performing EDs, staff and physicians make calls daily with a goal to reach out to 100 percent of eligible discharged patients and actually make contact with 60 percent of these patients within 72 hours after discharge. Organizations that use this best practice typically see results in 60 to 90 days, particularly in their ability to reduce readmissions.

- **Manage throughput in a way that reduces time patients have to wait.** Wait times and the time it takes patients to see the doctor are key indicators of quality and experience in the ED. Ensuring that you have done a thorough analysis of your opportunities to improve this and are taking measures to improve both front end and back end flow can go a long way in helping improve the experience for your patients.

Getting better and better is important for many reasons, health reform uppermost among them. As the rate of change in healthcare increases—due to pressure from the government, from insurers, from patients themselves—no hospital can afford to stand still.

Ultimately, healthcare organizations exist to serve humanity. The people drawn to this field are driven by a fierce desire to help others. By creating the kinds of organizations that patients sincerely rate as "the best hospital possible"—the kind that they trust enough to recommend to the people they love—we are helping the men and women who work for us serve their highest sense of purpose. That is a true gift to all the healthcare professionals we work with, to the patients we serve, and to ourselves.

Tools & Resources

Studer Group offers a variety of tools and resources that support the tactics discussed in this chapter. To access the most up-to-date offerings, to see what's new in healthcare, and to download a worksheet that will help you create a plan to improve patient perception of care in the "Overall Rating" and "Willingness to Recommend" composites, please visit www.studergroup.com/HCAHPS.

CHAPTER TWENTY-TWO:

THE IMPORTANCE OF VALIDATION: A CLOSING THOUGHT

Throughout this book, we've talked about creating a culture of *always*. It's not enough to *sometimes* do the right thing. We must *always* do it—every department, every employee, every patient interaction. Otherwise, as we've discussed already, we may get the occasional spike in results, but we won't be able to consistently sustain a high level of performance—the level patients deserve.

As we at Studer Group® visit hospitals across the country, people sometimes tell us, "We cannot seem to get consistent results and hold them. We're doing Hourly Rounding®. We're doing AIDET®. But our HCAHPS results still aren't moving."

Our response is always: "But are you *really* doing them, fully focused on the outcomes, or are you just going through the motions in order to check off the boxes? Are you doing them consistently? Are you doing them correctly? Are the tactics truly hardwired?"

If you hardwire the tactics we've covered in this book, and if you execute them as we've described them, you will see upward progress on your HCAHPS results. And best of all, you'll be able to maintain it over time.

We are not suggesting any of this is easy. It's not. Yes, most of these tactics may seem like common sense, but we all know that common sense is uncommonly practiced. Life gets in the way, and change—even change everyone knows should happen—falls by the wayside.

This difficulty is one reason Studer Group exists. We partner with organizations to help them overcome the many barriers to hardwiring the crucial behaviors that lead to healthcare excellence. One of the tools we use is validation.

If you're not seeing that upward progress—or if you're getting performance spikes that quickly subside—it's time to look at frequency, consistency, and quality. That's what validating is all about.

Driving Performance

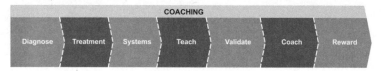

Figure 22.1

The process shown in this graphic, which we call driving performance, begins with diagnosis. Maybe overall you're strong in some composites and weak in others. Maybe certain departments are getting great results, and others are not. It sounds obvious, but great outcomes start with knowing exactly where you need the most focus and knowing your data well enough to be sure you are working on the right problem.

Knowing your data allows you to drill down, department by department, and analyze who is doing what well (and who isn't). Compare HCAHPS scores on composites and questions across different departments. You may be able to harvest best practices within your organization and move them throughout the entire facility. Measure improvement; share your success stories.

As with a medical condition or illness, once the diagnosis is complete, you can then determine the evidence-based practices that will make up the treatment plan and put in the systems and tools that will ensure improvements. This is followed by teaching and validating.

You might discover that even though a tactic was officially "rolled out," it isn't being implemented with consistency. Maybe people were gung-ho on it for a little while, but then had an exceptionally busy week, stopped doing the tactic, and just never started again.

Look at it this way: Few of us would ever compliment a doctor because he *usually* gets the pain medication right or *usually* performs the proper surgery or *usually* goes through all the steps in the surgery or *usually* visits his patients when he's on duty at the hospital. And very few doctors would ever accept that standard in themselves. So why should we let other staff members live in a "usually" world?

Usually isn't good enough for patients. They live in an "always" world. They expect us to *always* do what we should do to provide the best care for them. By focusing on HCAHPS and implementing the tactics in this book, we're creating the kind of environment they expect and deserve—an *always* environment.

Once you've figured out that these tactics are not yet hardwired, you've won a big part of the battle. Then you can develop an improvement game plan. For instance:

- Set up skills labs with senior leadership to ensure that their individual leaders are meeting frequency and quality standards.

- Implement a process improvement initiative. Often, ineffective or broken processes create barriers to success. Remember, outcomes are dependent upon two things: processes and people. If there's a lack of process structure or inconsistency in how people are carrying out the behaviors, variances will occur and the *always* factor will be minimized.

- Conduct observations of staff to make sure tactics like Hourly Rounding and AIDET are being done properly on every patient, every day, and use coaching skills to provide feedback to staff after each observation.

- Do HCAHPS training. Make sure each and every employee knows that HCAHPS is how patients rate their experience and how that experience relates to quality. Be sure, also, that each staff member is able to state his or her role in improving results.

- Ask staff members to fill out an HCAHPS survey to see how they rate their areas. Then work with them to create an improvement plan.

- Start with the *why* and end with the *why*. When employees know *why* they are learning new tactics, they are more likely to pay attention to the *what* and the *how*. Use the *why* to set the stage when training and to help employees reconnect to their sense of purpose when validating.

Some leaders worry that validating seems like "checking up" on people—as if the implication is that we don't trust them. But validation isn't a matter of trust. It's a matter of process and a matter of quality. Training without validating is just words. Training *with* validation is action. It's making sure that we're not just going through the motions but are truly performing tactics in a way that gets results. And it's applying the key learnings that result to your future process efforts.

Most people in healthcare want to do their best possible work. They appreciate it when leaders help them improve. Not only does validating achieve that goal, it's a good way of rewarding and recognizing high performers. It's a way of ensuring that the departments driving your HCAHPS results set a performance standard for the rest of the organization.

Validation and coaching are critical parts of creating a culture of *always*.

In the end, validating leads to better outcomes. In fact, when you really connect the dots, you'll see that it saves lives. Isn't that why we're all here? Isn't it why we came to healthcare in the first place...and why we stayed?

ACKNOWLEDGMENTS

S o many different people have left their fingerprints on this book. Without the experience and the insights of countless industry professionals, both inside and outside Studer Group®, *The HCAHPS Handbook,* and now this expanded version, could never have come to be. To all of them, we offer a collective and heartfelt thank-you.

Specifically, we would like to extend our gratitude to:

The leaders of organizations coached by Studer Group across the nation…

Thank you for your commitment to using Evidence-Based Leadership℠ to create a culture of always, so your patients consistently get the best care. By sharing your results and best practices with Studer Group, you've enabled us to build a national Learning Lab of hundreds and hundreds of hospitals. Thanks to this coalition of top industry minds, we can all learn from each other.

Thank you specifically to the partners below for providing assistance with the material in these pages.

- Kaiser Permanente, Portland, OR
- Central West Texas Division of HCA, Austin, TX
- Advocate Sherman Hospital, Elgin, IL
- St. Alexius Medical Center, Hoffman Estates, IL
- Community Health Systems, Franklin, TN
- OSF St. Luke's (previously Kewanee Hospital), Kewanee, IL
- Community Health Network, Indianapolis, IN
- UAB Health System, Birmingham, AL
- Intermountain Healthcare, Inc., Salt Lake City, UT

The Studer Group experts who coach these organizations...

Your tireless work on the frontlines is making a difference in hospitals and organizations everywhere. An extra helping of gratitude goes to those coaches who directly provided their insight and expertise during the writing of *The HCAHPS Handbook*.

...And the other individuals who made it all come together.

Dottie DeHart and team—Thank you for taking the down-and-dirty tactics and content provided by three very different personalities and turning them into a cohesive, didactic tool. You did a fabulous job, as always, and we appreciate your talent and professionalism.

Julie Chyna and Laura Koontz—Thank you for the many hours spent in piecing together the research and musings of the three authors to really bring to life the work we do and impact we have on hospitals across the nation.

Guy Livingston—Thank you for combing through data and building comparisons and correlations to demonstrate the impact of our work.

Sara Harris—Thank you for creating so many graphs, charts, and tools to lend to the visual learning impact of this resource.

Jamie Stewart—Thank you for bringing structure to *The HCAHPS Handbook* and coordinating countless versions of chapters in various stages of editing as they moved back and forth between authors and reviewers.

If we've left anyone out of this list, we offer our deepest apologies. A book like this is truly magical. It's tangible evidence that human beings can come together and create something greater than the sum of its parts—something that changes the way hospitals operate, touches the lives of patients, and leaves the world a bit better off than it was before.

ENDNOTES

Chapter 1:

1. Conway, Patrick. Star Ratings Coming Soon to Compare Sites on Medicare.gov. June 18, 2014. http://blog.cms.gov/2014/06/18/star-quality-ratings-coming-soon-to-compare-sites-on-medicare-gov/.

2. Meade, C.M. et al. "Effects of nursing rounds on patients' call light use, satisfaction, and safety." *Am J Nurs* 106, no. 9 (2006): 58-70.

3. Halbesleben, Jonathon R.B., Grant T. Savage, Douglas S. Wakefield, and Bonnie J. Wakefield. "Rework and workarounds in nurse medication administration process: implications for work processes and patient safety." *Health Care Management Review* 35, no. 2 (2010): 124-33.

Chapter 3:

1. "CMS Targets Readmission Through Payment, Audits; 'Coaching' Model Reduces Rates." *Report on Medicare Compliance* 17, no. 24 (2008): 1-2.

Chapter 5:

1. McCabe, C. "Nurse-patient communication: an exploration of patients' experiences." *J Clin Nurs* 13 (2004): 41-49.

Section 2 Introduction:

1. Duffy, F.D. et al. "Assessing competence in communication and interpersonal skills: the Kalamazoo II report." *Acad Med* 79, no. 6 (2004): 495-507.

2. Accreditation Council for Graduate Medical Education. Toolbox for the evaluation of competence.

3. Stewart, M.A. "Effective physician-patient communication and health outcomes: a review." *CMAJ* 15, no. 9 (1995): 1423-33.

4. Bull, S.A. et al. "Discontinuation of use and switching of antidepressants: influence of patient-physician communication." *JAMA* 288, no. 11 (2002):1403-09.

5. Ciechanowski, P.S. et al. "The patient-provider relationship: attachment theory and adherence to

treatment in diabetes." *Am J Psychiatry* 158, no. 1 (2001): 29-35.

6. Bogardus, S.T. Jr. et al. "Perils, pitfalls, and possibilities in talking about medical risk." *JAMA* 281, no. 11 (1999):1037-41.

Chapter 7:

1. Chang, J.T. et al. "Patients' global ratings of their care are not associated with the technical quality of their care." *Ann Inter Med* 144, no. 9 (2006): 665-72.

2. Arora, V. et al. "Ability of hospitalized patients to identify their in-hospital physicians." *Arch Intern Med* 169, no. 2 (2009): 199-201.

3. Makoul, G. et al. "An evidence-based perspective on greetings in medical encounters." *Arch Intern Med* 167, no. 11 (2007): 1172-76.

4. Joint Commission, "Sentinel Event Data: Root Causes by Type, 2004-2013."

5. Johnson, R.L. et al. "To sit or not to sit?" *Ann Emerg Med* 51, no. 2 (2008): 188-93.

6. Bruera, E. et al. "A randomized, controlled trial of physician postures when breaking bad news to cancer patients." *Palliat Med* 21, no. 6 (2007): 501-05.

Chapter 8:

1. Bright, B. "Doctors' Interpersonal Skills Are Valued More Than Training." *Wall Street Journal*, September 28, 2004.

2. Ambady, Nalini et al. "Surgeons' Tone of Voice: A Clue to Malpractice History." *Surgery* 132, no. 1 (2002): 5-9.

3. Morse, D.S. et al. "Missed opportunities for interval empathy in lung cancer communication." *Arch Intern Med* 168, no. 17 (2008): 1853-58.

Chapter 9:

1. O'Leary, K.J. et al. "Hospitalized patients' understanding of their plan of care." *Mayo Clin Proc* 85, no. 1 (2010): 47-52.

2. Martin, Leslie R., Summer L. Williams, Kelly B. Haskard, and Robin DiMatteo. "The Challenge of Patient Adherence." *Therapeutics and Clinical Risk Management* 1, no. 3 (2005): 189-99.

3. Ibid.

4. Ibid.

5. Ibid.

6. Ibid.

Section 3 Introduction:

1. Deitrick, L. et al. "Dance of the call bells: Using ethnography to evaluate patient satisfaction with quality of care." *J Nurs Care Qual* 12, no. 4 (2006): 316-32.

2. Tzeng, H.M. "Perspectives of staff nurses of the reasons for and the nature of patient-initiated call lights: an exploratory survey study in four USA hospitals." *Health Services Research* (2010): 2.

3. Tzeng, H.M., and C.Y. Yin. "Do call light use and response time contribute to inpatient falls and inpatient dissatisfaction?" *J Nurs Care Qual* (2009).

4. Tzeng, H.M., and C.Y. Yin. "Relationship between call light use and response time and inpatient falls in acute care settings." *J Clin Nurs* 18, no. 23 (2009): 3333-41.

5. Tzeng, H.M., and C.Y. Yin. "The extrinsic risk factors for inpatient falls in hospital patient rooms." *J Nurs Care Qual* 23, no. 3 (2008): 233-41.

6. Tzeng. "Perspectives of staff nurses..." 2.

7. Ibid.

8. Tzeng, H.M., and C.Y. Yin. "Predicting patient satisfaction with nurses' call light responsiveness in 4 US hospitals." *Nurs Care Qual* 25, no. 3 (2010): 261-65.

Chapter 10:

1. Spanke, M.T., and T. Thomas. "Nursing assistant walking report at change of shift." *J Nurs Care Qual* 25, no. 4 (2010): 366-72.

Section 4 Introduction:

1. Institute of Medicine. "Relieving Pain in America, A Blueprint for Transforming Prevention, Care, Education, and Research." June 2011.
2. Blizzard, Rick. "How Hospitals Can Effectively Manage Patients' Pain." *Gallup Business Journal*, January 2013.

Chapter 12:

1. Gittell, J.H. et al. "Impact of relational coordination on quality of care, postoperative pain and functioning, and length of stay: A nine-hospital study of surgical patients." *Med Care* 38, no. 8 (2002): 807-19.
2. Horsley, J. et al. *Pain: Deliberative Nursing Interventions.* New York: Grune & Stratton, 1982.
3. McCaffery, M. "What is the role of nondrug methods in the nursing care of patients with acute pain?" *Pain Manag Nurs* 3, no. 3 (2002): 77-80.
4. Wells, N. et al. "Improving the quality of care through pain assessment and management." AHRQ Agency

for Healthcare Research and Quality. http://www.
ahrq.gov/professionals/clinicians-providers/resourc-
es/nursing/resources/nurseshdbk/WellsN_SMTEP.
pdf.

Section 5 Introduction:

1. Forster, A.J., H.J. Murff, J.F. Peterson, T.K. Gandhi,
   and D.W. Bates. "The incidence and severity of adverse events affecting patients after discharge from the
   hospital." *Ann Intern Med* 138, no. 3 (2003): 161–67.

2. Hayes, Ron D. et al. "Physician Communication
   When Prescribing New Medications." *Archives of Internal Medicine* 166, no. 17 (2006): 1855-62.

3. National Priorities Partnership and National Quality
   Forum. *Preventing Medication Errors: A $21 Billion Op-
   portunity*. Washington, DC, December 2010. http://
   psnet.ahrq.gov/resource.aspx?resourceID=20529.

4. AHRQ Patient Safety Network. "Patient Safety Primers, Medication Errors." http://psnet.ahrq.gov/
   primer.aspx?primerID=23.

5. National Action Plan for Adverse Drug Even Prevention. http://www.health.gov.hai.ade.asp.

6. National Priorities Partnership and National Quality
   Forum. *Preventing Medication Errors*.

7. Massachusetts Technology Collaborative (MTC) and
   NEHI. *Saving Lives, Saving Money: The Imperative for
   CPOE in Massachusetts*. Cambridge, MA, 2008.

8. Center of Information Technology Leadership (CITL). *The Value of Computerized Provider Order Entry in Ambulatory Settings.* 2007.

9. AHRQ Patient Safety Network. "Patient Safety Primers."

10. Starmer, A.J. et al. "Rates of Medical Errors and Preventable Adverse Events Among Hospitalized Children Following Implementation of a Resident Handoff Bundle." *JAMA* 310, no. 21 (2013): 2262-70.

11. Schnipper, J.L. et al. "Role of pharmacist counseling in preventing adverse drug events after hospitalization." *Arch Intern Med* 166, no. 5 (2006): 565-71.

12. Kripalani, S. et al. "Deficits in communication and information transfer between hospital-based and primary care physicians: implications for patient safety and continuity of care." *JAMA* 297, no. 8 (2007): 831-41.

13. Kucukarslan, S.N. et al. "Pharmacists on rounding teams reduce preventable adverse drug events in hospital general medicine units." *Arch Intern Med* 163, no. 17 (2003): 2014-18.

14. Sullivan, C. et al. "Medication reconciliation in the acute care setting: opportunity and challenge for nursing." *J Nurs Care Qual* 20, no. 2 (2005): 95-98.

15. Hsiao, C.J. et al. *Preliminary Estimates of Electronic Medical Records Use by Office-Based Physicians.* National Center for Health Statistics. 2008. www.cdc.gov/nchs/data/hestat/physicians08/physicians08.pdf.

16. Kaushal R., L.M. Kern, Y. Barrón, et al. "Electronic prescribing improves medication safety in community-based office practices." *J Gen Intern Med* 25, no. 6 (2010): 530-36.

17. Weingart, S.N., B. Simchowitz, H. Padolsky, et al. "An empirical model to estimate the potential impact of medication safety alerts on patient safety, health care utilization, and cost in ambulatory care." *Arch Intern Med* 169, no. 16 (2009): 1465-73.

18. Poon, E.G., C.A. Keohane, C.S. Yoon, et al. "Effect of bar-code technology on the safety of medication administration." *N Engl J Med* 362, no. 18 (2010): 1698-707.

19. Bates, D.W., J.M. Teich, J. Lee, et al. "The impact of computerized physician order entry on medication error prevention." *J Am Med Inform Assoc* 6, no. 4 (1999): 313-21.

20. Budnitz, D.S., N. Shehab, S.R. Kegler, and C.L. Richards. "Medication Use Leading to Emergency Department Visits for Adverse Drug Events in Older Adults." *Ann Intern Med* 147, no. 11 (2007): 755-65.

Chapter 13:

1. Smith, A.K. et al. "Resident approaches to advance care planning on the day of hospital admission." *Arch Intern Med* 166, no. 15 (2006): 1597-602.

2. Coleman, E.A. et al. "Assessing the quality of preparation for posthospital care from the patient's per-

spective: The care transitions measure (CTM)." *Medical Care* 43, no. 3 (2004): 246–55.

3. Jack, B.W. et al. "A reengineered hospital discharge program to decrease rehospitalization: a randomized trial." *Ann Intern Med* 150, no. 3 (2009): 178-87.

4. Harmon, G. et al. "Overcoming barriers: the role of providers in improving patient adherence to antihypertensive medications." *Curr Opin Cardiology* 21 (2006): 310-15.

Section 6 Introduction:

1. Forster A.J., H.J. Murff, J.F. Peterson, T.K. Gandhi, and D.W. Bates. "The incidence and severity of adverse events affecting patients after discharge from the hospital." *Ann Intern Med* 138, no. 3 (2003): 161–67.

2. Forster, A.J., H.D. Clark, A. Menard, et al. "Adverse events among medical patients after discharge from hospital." *Can Med Assoc J* 170, no. 3 (2004): 345–49.

3. Makaryus, A.N., and E.A. Friedman. "Patients' understanding of their treatment plans and diagnosis at discharge." *Mayo Clin Proc* 80, no. 8 (2005): 991–94.

4. Maniaci, M.J., M.G. Heckman, and N.L. Dawson. "Functional health literacy and understanding of medications at discharge." *Mayo Clin Proc* 83, no. 5 (2008): 554–58.

5. Jha, A.K., E.J. Orav, J. Zheng, and A.M. Epstein. "Patients' perception of hospital care in the United States." *N Engl J Med* 359, no. 18 (2008): 1921–31.

6. Price Waterhouse Coopers' Health Research Institute. "The Price of Excess: Identifying Waste in Healthcare." 2008.

Chapter 14:

1. O'Leary, K.J. et al. "Hospitalized patients' understanding of their plan of care." *Mayo Clinic Proc* 85, no. 1 (2010): 47-52.

2. Flacker, J. et al. "Hospital discharge information and older patients: do they get what they need?" *J Hosp Med* 2, no. 5 (2007): 291-96.

Section 7 Introduction:

1. Whatley, Vanessa, Louise Jackson, Jane Taylor, et al. "Improving public perceptions around cleanliness and health care associated infections in hospitals." *Journal of Infection Prevention* 13, no. 6 (2012): 192-99.

2. Busch-Vishniac, I.F. et al. "Noise levels in Johns Hopkins Hospital." *J Acoust Soc Am* 118, no. 6 (2005): 3629-45.

3. "Noise Sources and Their Effects." https:///www.chem.purdue.edu/chemsafety/Training/PPETrain/dblevels.htm.

4. Choiniere, D.B. "The Effects of Hospital Noise." *J Neurosci Nurs* 42, no. 4 (2010): 217-24.

5. Penney, P.J., and C.E. Earl. "Occupational noise and effects on blood pressure exploring the relationship of hypertension and noise exposure in workers." *AAOHN J* 52, no. 11 (2004): 476-80.

Section 8 Introduction:

1. National Transitions of Care Coalition. *Improving Transitions of Care: Findings and Considerations of the "Vision of the National Transitions of Care Coalition".* September 2010.

Chapter 18:

1. Ruland, C.M. *Improving Patient Outcomes by Including Patient Preference in Nursing Care. Proc AMIA Symp* (1998): 448-52.

Chapter 20:

1. Harris, G. "Report Finds a Heavy Toll from Medication Errors." *New York Times,* July 21, 2006.

2. Maniaci, M.J. et al. "Functional health literacy and understanding of medications at discharge." *Mayo Clinic Proc* 83, no. 5 (2008): 554-58.

ADDITIONAL RESOURCES

About Studer Group:

Learn more about Studer Group by scanning the QR code with your mobile device or by visiting www.studergroup.com/about_studergroup/index.dot.

Studer Group® helps bring structure and focus to organizations through the creation of cultures of accountability. Studer Group works with hundreds of healthcare organizations worldwide teaching them how to achieve, sustain, and accelerate exceptional clinical, operational, and financial outcomes. We work to bring structure and focus to organizations through the creation of cultures in which people hold themselves accountable and help set them up to be able to execute quickly. By installing an execution framework called Evidence-Based Leadership^{SM}, organizations are able to align goals, actions, and processes. This framework creates the foundation that enables transformation in this era of continuous change. We also help them foster better integration with physicians and other service providers in order to create a smooth continuum of patient-centered care.

Studer Group Coaching:

Learn more about Studer Group coaching by scanning the QR code with your mobile device or by visiting www.studergroup.com/coaching.

Healthcare Organization Coaching

As value-based purchasing changes the healthcare landscape forever, organizations need to execute quickly and consistently, achieve better outcomes across the board, and sustain improvements year after year. Studer Group's team of performance experts has hands-on experience in all aspects of achieving breakthrough results. They provide the strategic thinking, the Evidence-Based Leadership framework, the practical tactics, and the ongoing support to help our partners excel in this high-pressure environment. Our performance experts work with a variety of organizations, from academic medical centers to large healthcare systems to small rural hospitals.

Emergency Department Coaching

With public reporting of data coming in the future, healthcare organizations can no longer accept crowded Emergency Departments and long patient wait times. Our team of ED coach experts will partner with you to implement best practices, proven tools, and tactics using our Evidence-Based Leadership approach to improve results in the Emergency Department that stretch or impact across the entire organization. Key deliverables include improving flow, decreasing staff turnover, increasing employee, physician, and patient satisfaction, decreasing door-to-doctor times, reducing left without being seen rates, increasing upfront cash collections, and increasing patient volumes and revenue.

Physician Integration & Partnership Coaching

Physician integration is critical to an organization's ability to run smoothly and efficiently. Studer Group coaches diagnose how aligned physicians are with your mission and goals, train you on how to effectively provide performance feedback, and help physicians develop the skills they need to prevent burnout. The goal is to help physicians become engaged, enthusiastic partners in the truest sense of the word—which optimizes HCAHPS results and creates a better continuum of high-quality patient care.

Books: categorized by audience

Explore the Fire Starter Publishing website by scanning the QR code with your mobile device or by visiting www.firestarterpublishing.com.

Senior Leaders & Physicians

Straight A Leadership: Alignment, Action, Accountability—A guide that will help you identify gaps in Alignment, Action, and Accountability, create a plan to fill them, and become a more resourceful, agile, high-performing organization, written by Quint Studer.

Engaging Physicians: A Manual to Physician Partnership—A tactical and passionate roadmap for physician collaboration to generate organizational high performance, written by Stephen C. Beeson, MD.

Excellence with an Edge: Practicing Medicine in a Competitive Environment—An insightful book that provides practical tools and techniques you need to know to have a solid grasp of the business side of making a living in healthcare, written by Michael T. Harris, MD.

Leadership and Medicine—A book that makes sense of the complex challenges of healthcare and offers a wealth of practical advice to future generations, written by Floyd D. Loop, MD, former chief executive of the Cleveland Clinic (1989-2004).

Physicians

Practicing Excellence: A Physician's Manual to Exceptional Health Care—This book, written by Stephen C. Beeson, MD, is a brilliant guide to implementing physician leadership and behaviors that will create a high-performance workplace.

All Leaders

A Culture of High Performance: Achieving Higher Quality at a Lower Cost—A must-have for any leader struggling to shore up margins while sustaining an organization that's a great place for employees to work, physicians to practice medicine, and patients to receive care.

The Great Employee Handbook: Making Work and Life Better—This book is a valuable resource for employees at all levels who want to learn how to handle tough workplace situations—skills that normally come only from a lifetime of experience. Wall Street Journal bestselling author Quint Studer has pulled together the best insights gained from working with thousands of employees during his career.

Hey Cupcake! We Are ALL Leaders—Author Liz Jazwiec explains that we'll all eventually be called on to lead someone, whether it's a department, a shift, a project team, or a new employee. In her trademark slightly sarcastic (and hilarious) voice, she provides learned-the-hardway insights that will benefit leaders in every industry and at every level.

The HCAHPS Handbook: Hardwire Your Hospital for Pay-for-Performance Success—A practical resource filled with actionable tips proven to help hospitals improve patient perception of care. Written by Quint Studer, Brian C. Robinson, and Karen Cook, RN.

Hardwiring Excellence—A BusinessWeek bestseller, this book is a road map to creating and sustaining a "Culture of Service and Operational Excellence" that drives bottom-line results. Written by Quint Studer.

Results That Last—A Wall Street Journal bestseller by Quint Studer that teaches leaders in every industry how to apply his tactics and strategies to their own organizations to build a corporate culture that consistently reaches and exceeds its goals.

Hardwiring Flow: Systems and Processes for Seamless Patient Care—Drs. Thom Mayer and Kirk Jensen delve into one of the most critical issues facing healthcare leaders today: patient flow.

Eat That Cookie!: Make Workplace Positivity Pay Off...For Individuals, Teams, and Organizations—Written by Liz Jazwiec, RN, this book is funny, inspiring, relatable, and is packed with realistic, down-to-earth tactics to infuse positivity into your culture.

"I'm Sorry to Hear That..." Real-Life Responses to Patients' 101 Most Common Complaints About Health Care—When you respond to a patient's complaint, you are responding to the patient's sense of helplessness and anxiety. The service recovery scripts offered in this book can help you recover a patient's confidence in you and your organization. Authored by Susan Keane Baker and Leslie Bank.

101 Answers to Questions Leaders Ask—By Quint Studer and Studer Group coaches, offers practical, prescriptive solutions to some of the many questions he's received from healthcare leaders around the country.

Over Our Heads: An Analogy on Healthcare, Good Intentions, and Unforeseen Consequences—This book, written by Rulon F. Stacey, PhD, FACHE, uses a grocery store analogy to illustrate how government intervention leads to economic crisis and eventually, collapse.

Oh No...Not More of That Fluffy Stuff! The Power of Engagement—Written by Rich Bluni, RN, this funny, heartfelt book explores what it takes to overcome obstacles and tap into the passion that fuels our best work. Its practical exercises help employees at all levels get happier, more excited, and more connected to the meaning in our daily lives.

Nurse Leaders and Nurses

The Nurse Leader Handbook: The Art and Science of Nurse Leadership—By Studer Group senior nursing and physician leaders from across the country, is filled with knowledge that provides nurse leaders with a solid foundation for success. It also serves as a reference they can revisit again and again when they have questions or need a quick refresher course in a particular area of the job.

Inspired Nurse and Inspired Journal—By Rich Bluni, RN, helps maintain and recapture the inspiration nurses felt at the start of their journey with action-oriented "spiritual stretches" and stories that illuminate those sacred moments we all experience.

Emergency Department Team

Advance Your Emergency Department: Leading in a New Era—As this critical book asserts, world-class Emergency Departments don't follow. They lead. Stephanie J. Baker, RN, CEN, MBA, Regina Shupe, RN, MSN, CEN, and Dan Smith, MD, FACEP, share high-impact strategies and tactics to help your ED get results more efficiently, effectively, and collaboratively. Master them and you'll improve quality, exceed patient expectations, and ultimately help the entire organization maintain and grow its profit margin.

Excellence in the Emergency Department—A book by Stephanie Baker, RN, CEN, MBA, is filled with proven, easy-to-implement, step-by-step instructions that will help you move your Emergency Department forward.

Studer Conferences:

Studer Conferences is a three-day interactive learning event designed to provide healthcare leaders with an authentic, practical learning experience.

Learn from innovative and inspiring keynotes with hands-on workshops and nuts-and-bolts sessions. The faculty at Studer Conferences go beyond PowerPoint slides and lectures to show you "what right looks like" with live-on-stage role playing and "how-to" sessions.

In 2015, Studer Group reformatted our conferences to bring you multiple conferences in one place to maximize your learning, reduce travel costs, and better utilize time away from your job.

Find out more and register for Studer Conferences at www.studergroup.com.

LYN KETELSEN, RN, MBA

Lyn Ketelsen, RN, MBA, is Studer Group's VP of national partnerships as well as a coach and speaker. She has experienced healthcare in a variety of settings for nearly 30 years. Her clinical nursing background is pediatrics and neonatal intensive care. Lyn has also worked with acute care, managed care, clinics, ambulatory and ERs.

Since joining Studer Group over 12 years ago, Lyn has worked with hundreds of organizations to put prescriptive elements in place that drive results. Several of Lyn's partners have won the coveted Healthcare Organization of the Month Award and have presented at What's Right in Health Care because they have achieved and sustained results. Lyn herself received the Flame Award in 2008, which is Studer Group's highest honor for employees.

Lyn coauthored the largest study ever conducted on reducing call lights, which was published in *AJN* in September 2006, and in conjunction with that study became the birth mother of hourly rounds. She was also a coauthor of *The Nurse Leader Handbook: The Art and Science of Nurse Leadership* in 2010.

Lyn was an integral participant in the preparation of Studer Group's successful Baldrige journey that culminated in a Baldrige Award in 2010. She is a senior leader within the Studer Group organization and currently oversees coaching in its largest and most complex segment of business—national multi-state and multi-market systems.

KAREN COOK, RN

Karen Cook, RN, has been a registered nurse for more than 30 years and a senior coach with Studer Group for more than 13 years. She was one of the first coaches to join Quint Studer, the founder of Studer Group, in Pensacola, Florida. A former leader of Studer Group's Knowledge Management Division, she has coached some of the largest healthcare systems in the country, as well as individual hospitals in all geographic regions.

Demonstrating her passion for quality patient-centered care, Karen participated in early focus groups with leaders from the Agency for Healthcare Research and Quality and was the primary author of the Studer Group HCAHPS toolkit in 2007. This work became the springboard for the popular and practical *The HCAHPS Handbook*, published in 2010.

A strong advocate of building safe cultures, Karen is a national speaker known for her passionate, enthusiastic style and her ability to "get to the heart of the matter."

The Studer Group partners she works with have received numerous awards and accolades including Magnet facility, Top 50 Hospitals, and Top 100 Places to Work designations. They've also earned patient satisfaction achievements like Client Success Story and the Summit Award.

BEKKI KENNEDY

Bekki Kennedy is a senior executive at Studer Group. During her 14 years with Studer Group, she has led branding and content development while greatly expanding its learning institutes and speakers' bureau. She spearheaded the launch of Fire Starter Publishing, which has contributed over one million books to the marketplace, greatly advancing Studer Group's mission to make a difference in healthcare.

In addition, Bekki played a key role in developing the Learning Lab, a collection of videos, training tools, articles, and other resources and networking opportunities reserved only for Studer Group partners. She was also a crucial part of creating the firm's initial software offerings. In 2007 Bekki received the Flame Award—Studer Group's highest honor for employees—due to her impact on the firm's thought leadership brand via speaking and institutes, as well as for her pivotal establishment of Fire Starter Publishing.

She plays a vital role in Studer Group's knowledge management efforts, helping the firm keep a pulse on the industry and monitor what's working well. She collaborates with coaches and other experts to collect mountains of research and evidence, distill it all down to the "best of the best," and connect it to the high-impact tactics that help organizations thrive in the pay-for-performance era.

Bekki develops and maintains premium intellectual capital across all mediums. She strives always to simplify complex information and provide relevant, clear, actionable advice. Her materials help healthcare professionals at all levels make sense of and respond to industry changes, reinforcing Studer Group's coaching efforts and shoring up its role as a trusted advisor to senior leadership.

Bekki is grateful for the opportunity to help Studer Group evolve and grow as it seeks always to advance its mission to create great places for employees to work, physicians to practice medicine, and patients to receive care.